CAMBRIDGE TEXTS IN THE
HISTORY OF POLITICAL THOUGHT

———

JOHN OF SALISBURY
Policraticus

CAMBRIDGE TEXTS IN THE HISTORY OF POLITICAL THOUGHT

Series editors

RAYMOND GEUSS *Columbia University*
QUENTIN SKINNER *Christ's College, Cambridge*
RICHARD TUCK *Jesus College, Cambridge*

The series is intended to make available for students the most important texts required for an understanding of the history of political thought. The scholarship of the present generation has greatly expanded our sense of the range of authors indispensable for such an understanding, and the series will reflect those developments. It will also include a number of less well-known works, in particular those needed to establish the intellectual contexts that in turn help to make sense of the major texts. The principal aim, however, will be to produce new versions of the major texts themselves, based on the most up-to-date scholarship. The preference will always be for complete texts, and a special feature of the series will be to complement individual texts, within the compass of a single volume, with subsidiary contextual material. Each volume will contain an introduction on the historical identity and contemporary significance of the work or works concerned, as well as a chronology, notes on further reading and (where appropriate) brief biographical sketches of significant individuals mentioned in each text.

For a list of titles published in the series, please see end of book.

JOHN OF SALISBURY

Policraticus

Of the Frivolities of Courtiers
and the Footprints
of Philosophers

EDITED AND TRANSLATED BY

CARY J. NEDERMAN

Department of Political Science
University of Canterbury
Christchurch, New Zealand

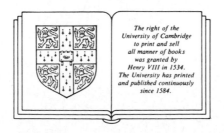

The right of the
University of Cambridge
to print and sell
all manner of books
was granted by
Henry VIII in 1534.
The University has printed
and published continuously
since 1584.

CAMBRIDGE UNIVERSITY PRESS
CAMBRIDGE
NEW YORK   PORT CHESTER
MELBOURNE   SYDNEY

KH

Published by the Press Syndicate of the University of Cambridge
The Pitt Building, Trumpington Street, Cambridge CB2 1RP
40 West 20th Street, New York, NY 10011, USA
10 Stamford Road, Oakleigh, Melbourne 3166, Australia

© Cambridge University Press 1990

First published 1990

Printed in Great Britain at the Bath Press, Avon

British Library cataloguing in publication data
John, of Salisbury, *Bishop of Chartres*
[Policraticus]. Policraticus: of the frivolities of
courtiers and the footprints of philosophers.
(Cambridge texts in the history of political thought)
1. Monarchy
I. [Policraticus] II. Title III. Nederman, Cary J. 321.6

Library of Congress cataloguing in publication data
John, of Salisbury, Bishop of Chartres. d. 1180.
[Policraticus. English]
Policraticus: of the frivolities of courtiers and the footprints of philosophers
edited and translated by Cary J. Nederman.
p. cm. – (Cambridge texts in the history of political
thought)
Includes bibliographical references.
ISBN 0-521-36399-3. – ISBN 0-521-36701-8 (pbk.)
1. Political science – Early works to 1800. 2. Education of
princes. I. Nederman, Cary J. II. Title. III. Series.
JC121.J5813 1990
320'.01 —dc20 89-22327 CIP

ISBN 0 521 36399 3 hard covers
ISBN 0 521 36701 8 paperback

WV

12/23/05

Contents

Contents

BOOK IV

Contents

BOOK V

Contents

BOOK VI

Contents

BOOK VII

Contents

BOOK VIII

Acknowledgements

Many people have given generously of their time and knowledge to improve and refine this translation. My greatest debt is to my research assistant, Ms Sarah Crichton, who read every word of the English text and suggested significant changes to and reformulations of my renderings of John's words; the value of her intelligence and good humour can never be adequately calculated or repaid. Friends and colleagues throughout the world lent practical aid and moral support at crucial moments, including Professor Kate Forhan, Ms Allison Holcroft, Dr Katherine Keats-Rohan (whose forthcoming critical edition of the *Policraticus* is eagerly awaited), Dr David Denemark, and Professor Quentin Skinner. While all of these people have in some way made this a better translation, none are to be held responsible for any of its flaws. Thanks are also due to Ms Susan van de Ven, who copy-edited the text, and Miss Catherine E. J. Campbell, who prepared the index. Finally, I owe a considerable debt to my colleagues in the Political Science Department at the University of Canterbury for their exemplary patience and support and to the University itself, which defrayed expenses associated with this work out of its Minor Research Grant programme.

This book is dedicated to two teachers, friends and, for a brief time, colleagues who in all these capacities fuelled my interest in medieval political thought: Neal Wood and the late John Brückmann. The present volume is but small thanks for their efforts to challenge and extend the horizons of my learning.

Editor's introduction

John of Salisbury's *Policraticus: Of the Frivolities of Courtiers and the Footprints of Philosophers* is commonly acclaimed as the first extended work of political theory written during the Latin Middle Ages. At approximately 250,000 words in length, the *Policraticus* is however far more than a theoretical treatise on politics. It is equally a work of moral theology, satire, speculative philosophy, legal procedure, self-consolation, biblical commentary and deeply personal meditation. In sum, the *Policraticus* is the philosophical memoir of one of the most learned courtier-bureaucrats of twelfth-century Europe. The title *Policraticus*, a pseudo-Greek neologism, itself seems to have been invented by John in order to convey the implication of classical learning and erudition as well as to capture the political content of the work.

Because of the diversity of John's interests, the reader must take care to approach the *Policraticus* without reference to current disciplinary boundaries. It is anachronistic to ignore or exclude from consideration those sections of the *Policraticus* which do not meet strict contemporary criteria for political theory. Indeed, even John's conception of what constitutes the realm of the political was different from a modern one, a fact which is reflected in the substance of his writing. Yet if we acknowledge the distance of his fundamental assumptions from our own, we can learn much about the political attitudes and beliefs of medieval Europe as well as about the origins of many of our own cherished political and social values.

Biography

John was born at Old Sarum (the former site of Salisbury) in England between 1115 and 1120. Specific knowledge of his family background and early life is scant; we know in detail only about a brother, Richard, and a half-brother, Robert, both of whom held offices within the English church. The first date we can safely associate with John is 1136, when he travelled to Paris to study at Mont-Saint-Geneviève. The list of his teachers during the ensuing dozen years includes many of the great minds of the mid-twelfth century. He received instruction at one time or another from Peter Abelard, Robert of Melun, William of Conches, Thierry of Chartres, Adam de Petit Pont, Gilbert of Poitiers, Robert Pullan and others; his studies encompassed speculative philosophy, rhetoric, linguistic theory, literature and theology.

Like so many other educated churchmen of his era, John chose an active career in the corridors of power rather than life in the cloister or the school. He joined the household of Archbishop Theobald of Canterbury, a vocal and energetic advocate of the rights of the English church, in 1147. In his capacity as secretary to Theobald, John was an omnicompetent bureaucrat: he composed the Archbishop's letters, advised him on legal and political affairs, travelled to the Continent as an archiepiscopal envoy, and altogether lived in the manner of a trusted intimate.

Because Theobald's court attracted many clerics with training and experience similar to John's own, he could continue to indulge his intellectual pursuits in a sympathetic environment at Canterbury during the 1140s and 1150s. John seems to have been a member of a small circle of learned bureaucrats whose members included Thomas Becket, the future martyr, a trusted servant of Theobald's before he was appointed as King Henry II's Chancellor in 1155. It was this circle of like-minded men that constituted the immediate audience for much of John's writing. The *Policraticus*, for instance, is not only dedicated to Becket but often addresses him personally about current events or personalities.

John's activities on behalf of the Archbishop brought him into contact with some of the most powerful and prominent men of twelfth-century Europe. He was present at the Roman curia for many crucial occurrences during the pontificate of Eugenius III (1145–

1153), four years of which he would later chronicle in his *Historia Pontificalis*. He enjoyed a warm friendship with his fellow countryman Nicholas Breakspear, who ascended the papal throne as Adrian IV in 1154. The *Policraticus* often relates stories and sayings derived from its author's interviews with Adrian, with whom John was sufficiently intimate to raise criticisms of the conduct of the papal curia.

John was also well acquainted with important figures in twelfth-century secular life, especially the young Henry II (1153–1189). He had supported Henry's side in the struggle against the partisans of King Stephen (1135–1153) during the period of English history known as the Anarchy. His later writings reveal a consistent horror of civil war of the sort engendered by Stephen's usurpation of the throne. John was, however, sufficiently vocal in his opposition to Henry's policies towards the English church to be banished from court during 1156 and 1157. Although he was to recover favour with his monarch, he acquired a lingering scepticism about Henry's motives which was to be confirmed by later events.

Thus, it is hardly surprising that when Becket became Archbishop of Canterbury in 1162, John backed his friend's cause against the English crown. He consequently spent much of the 1160s in exile, either in France or at the papal court, lobbying on behalf of Becket and against Henry and the English bishops who backed the King. Yet as the large body of his correspondence dating from this period testifies, John felt no more comfortable with Becket's zealotry than with Henry's repressiveness. His letters often adopt an independent line and express a willingness to compromise with Henry which is in marked contrast with Becket's intransigence.

The murder of Becket did not deprive John of his career at Canterbury. Yet while he served the English church in numerous capacities during the early 1170s, and was consecrated Bishop of Chartres in 1176 (a post in which he seems to have achieved little), his waning years were peaceful and restrained after his intrigues during the era of Theobald and Becket. He died at Chartres in 1180 and is buried in the abbey church of Notre-Dame-de-Josaphat.

John of Salisbury's literary output falls broadly into two categories. On the one hand, he composed several treatises of considerable philosophical interest, most notably the *Policraticus*, but also the *Entheticus de Dogmate Philosophorum* (or *Entheticus Major*), a satirical poem about philosophers and courtiers, and the *Metalogicon*, an important discussion of pedagogy and speculative philosophy. These works all date from about the period between 1154 and 1159. By contrast, John's writings of an historical nature – the *Historia Pontificalis* and most of his letters, as well as his lives of St Anselm and Becket – were composed later in his career, during or after his association with Becket. This should not be taken as evidence that he lost interest in scholastic or theoretical disputes. On the contrary, his historical writings (and indeed many of the crucial decisions of his administrative career) often represented practical applications of the principles he had already articulated in a philosophical form. Above all, it was a constant concern to unify theory and practice that constituted the hallmark of John's political and intellectual life.

The *Policraticus*: textual history

The arrangement of the text of the *Policraticus* as we know it today does not seem to reflect either the order of its composition or the development of John's interests. John's earliest effort to treat many of the themes ultimately addressed in the *Policraticus* may be found in the *Entheticus Major*, so-called because John prefaced the *Policraticus* with another shorter and quite different poem also called *Entheticus*. Probably composed between 1154 and 1156, the *Entheticus Major* satirises many of the foibles of princes and courtiers, compares them to the standards set by the ancient philosophers, and lays down a new code of conduct for the intellectual Christian man of affairs.

What the *Entheticus Major* lacked, of course, was sustained philosophical argument of the sort found in the *Policraticus*. Thus in 1156 or 1157, during his period of self-proclaimed 'disgrace' when he was exiled from Canterbury due to Henry II's anger, John began to write a prose work which attempted to demonstrate the foundations of the good life for man and to demystify the false images of happiness propounded by those of his contemporaries who unwittingly advocated the hedonistic doctrines of Epicureanism. This treatise, which represented a sort of self-consolation (perhaps modelled on Boethius's 'Consolation of Philosophy') in a time of political disfavour, came to form the bulk of the chapters in books VII and VIII of the *Policraticus*.

After his recall to Theobald's household, John seems to have undertaken to transform his self-consolatory meditation into a full-fledged volume of advice to his fellow clerical bureaucrats about how to avoid potential misfortunes of life at secular and ecclesiastical courts. In particular, such concerns apparently stimulated John to compose the more overtly political sections of the *Policraticus* (books IV, V and VI) in which he articulates a theory of government and society which, if realised, would better preserve the physical and spiritual safety of civil servants like himself as well as their princes and subjects. John thereby broadened his concern from the good life for the individual man to the good life for the entire political body. The completion of the *Policraticus* in its final form is dated, on both internal and external evidence, to the middle of 1159.

Sources

Like most works of medieval philosophy, the *Policraticus* depends heavily upon authoritative sources as a means for extending and enhancing its arguments. Thinkers like John believed that the case for a specific claim was strengthened not only by rational demonstration but also by the antiquity and the eminence of the authorities one could adduce in support of it. Thus we encounter throughout the *Policraticus* extensive quotations from and citations of both pagan and Christian sources.

John's most important authority, in both quantitative and qualitative terms, is Holy Scripture. While his careful and often subtle use of biblical imagery and texts reveals a thorough knowledge of both Testaments, he manifests a clear preference throughout the *Policraticus* for the Old Testament, especially the books of the prophets and of wisdom. At times, the *Policraticus* even engages in extended biblical commentary. Much of book IV, for instance, is taken up with exegesis of a passage from Job, by means of which John demonstrates the salient features of the good ruler.

John is also conversant with the Fathers of the Latin Church and other early Christian authors. The *Policraticus* displays a particular fondness for St Augustine and St Jerome, and for the historical writings of Orosius, but there are few available writers of the patristic age whom John fails to cite. By contrast, he is more hesitant in referring to the writings of his contemporaries; Bernard of Clairvaux is the only recent figure upon whose work the *Policraticus* explicitly draws with regularity. More commonly, John mentions the doctrines of contemporary thinkers by means of pseudonymous references, a technique which he employs throughout his corpus when he wishes to cloak the actual identity of his opponents.

The *Policraticus* is perhaps best known, however, for the number and range of its references to the texts and doctrines of pagan antiquity. Indeed, the scope of John's learning has often earned him the designation of the best read man of the twelfth century. John's classical education was particularly thorough in the areas of rhetoric, philosophy and poetry. He seems to have been familiar with all the available works of Cicero – although not, of course, with Cicero's two major works of political theory, *De re publica* and *De legibus*, whose ideas he knew only through Christian intermediaries like St Augustine. Likewise, John integrated into the *Policraticus* many citations from the major and minor Latin poets; among his favourites were Virgil, Horace, Juvenal, Lucan and Ovid.

Yet there are good reasons for doubting whether the breadth of John's classical quotations and allusions in the *Policraticus* was matched by a thorough acquaintance with the texts to which he refers. It has been demonstrated, for instance, that his use of passages from the pagan historians Gellius, Suetonius and Frontinus does not reflect direct exposure to their writings. Rather, John relied on *florilegia* (or books of extracts) compiled by later editors which were readily available to him at the Canterbury Cathedral library. Hence, John's classical learning was not as extensive as a cursory reading of the *Policraticus* might suggest.

Of the philosophical and literary works of the Greeks, John knew little in comparison with later centuries; like virtually all Western men of his time, he read no Greek. He could acknowledge the bare existence of Homer, Herodotus, Pythagoras and Socrates, and he was occasionally able to ascribe specific doctrines to them. He knew some of Plato's thought by means of an available Latin translation of and commentary on the *Timaeus*. Perhaps most importantly, John was closely attuned to the reintroduction of Aristotle's writings into the Latin West, a process which is commonly said to have revolutionised medieval learning. He may have been one of the first in the Middle Ages to be familiar with the entirety of Aristotle's *Organon* (the six Aristotelian treatises on logic). Even though Aristotle's moral and political writings would not be circulated in Western Christendom until the thirteenth century, John was able to glean from the *Organon* many important Aristotelian ideas (such as the doctrine of the golden mean and the psychology of moral character) which he incorporated into the social philosophy of the *Policraticus*.

Yet the general absence of classical models of politics created for John something of a dilemma, since his intellectual instincts resisted the postulation of innovative concepts unsupported by long-standing tradition. His solution is one that was not uncommon in the Middle Ages: he created a bogus authority – in essence, he perpetrated a forgery – in order to legitimise ideas which were otherwise original to him. The archetypical instance of this in the *Policraticus* is his reference to a work called the 'Instruction of Trajan', purportedly composed by the Roman imperial writer Plutarch. John attributes to this treatise many of the most significant and insightful features of his political theory, especially the claim that the political system can be analysed in detail as an organism or living body whose parts are mutually devoted to and dependent upon one another. In fact, the framework for the whole of books V and VI is allegedly borrowed from the 'Instruction of Trajan'. Yet there is no independent evidence for the existence of a work by Plutarch (or some later Plutarchian imitator) as described by John, and when the 'Instruction of Trajan' is cited by authors subsequent to him, it is always on the basis of the report of the *Policraticus*. Hence, scholars now usually conclude that the 'Instruction of Trajan' was actually a convenient fiction fashioned by John as a cloak for that intellectual novelty so despised by the medieval cast of mind. Moreover, this gives us good reason to believe that when John refers to other unknown sources, he may be performing a similar sleight of hand upon his audience.

John's method: *exempla*

To the modern reader, one of the most peculiar features of the *Policraticus* is John's regular and prolonged use of *exempla*, that is, stories told to illustrate or exemplify a lesson or doctrine. Many chapters of the text are little more than a collection of such tales strung together with no apparent organisation or interconnection. The sources for these *exempla* vary widely: many are biblical, some derive from classical or patristic historians, and a few are even the products of John's own experiences at papal and royal courts. The complaint is sometimes heard that he is wholly unconcerned about the actual historical significance – let alone the accuracy – of the stories and events he recounts. John's reliance upon *exempla* does not meet standards set by modern historical scholarship.

Yet the use of *exempla* must nevertheless be taken very seriously. The *Policraticus* is as much a work of moral edification as of philosophical speculation. It is intended to have practical relevance and value by imparting to John's contemporaries a code of conduct applicable to the unsettled circumstances of the clerical administrator. Thus, John's examples are oriented to the demonstration of how abstract principles of moral and political behaviour may be employed in everyday life. Like the parables of Jesus in the New Testament, the *exempla* of the *Policraticus* teach general lessons through concrete stories. Sometimes these lessons pertain to the translation of vicious or sinful beliefs into action, while at other times they illustrate the ways in which goodness and faith manifest themselves. But in all cases, John's *exempla* are meant to help the reader to bridge the gap between abstract moral discourse, on the one hand, and the actual conditions in which human beings find themselves, on the other.

Thematic unity of the *Policraticus*

Because it was composed over the course of many years and touches upon a bewildering array of topics and issues, the *Policraticus* might appear to be more a rambling and disjointed collection of stories and observations than a focussed and coherent piece of philosophical argument. But while on initial inspection this claim seems plausible, the careful reader will discern in the *Policraticus* a number of unifying elements which lend intellectual coherence to the treatise. In surveying these themes, we may begin to grasp the nature of John's contribution to Western modes of political discussion and debate.

Perhaps the most surprising theoretical feature of the *Policraticus*, at least when judged on the basis of current attitudes towards the Middle Ages, is John's treatment of the relationship between secular and spiritual spheres and powers. John is not strictly a 'hierocratic' thinker, if that term denotes the claim that all political authority flows from God through the Church to earthly rulers, so that the use of power is always to be regulated and limited by ecclesiastical officials. Instead, he permits secular government to be conducted without direct interference by the Church. Like the soul in the body, he asserts, the priesthood fixes the general aims of the healthy political organism (namely, the conditions necessary for salvation). But the head of the body is responsible for ensuring and supervising the actual physical welfare of the organism as it pursues its path through life. Thus, there exists a common good within the community unique and distinct from, although conducive to, the ultimate spiritual end of salvation. It is the promotion of this common good – the realization of a just society on earth – that forms the primary temporal duty of princes and of all their subjects.

John's doctrine of the different but interrelated aims within the community parallels his teachings about moral goodness and personal happiness. As a Christian, he accepts that the ultimate goal of human existence is eternal life in the presence of God. But for him this does not diminish the importance of achieving goodness and happiness on earth. Rather, the *Policraticus* declares that men are morally bound to seek their own temporal fulfilment through the acquisition of knowledge and the practice of virtue; such a way of life, while it can never earn the gift of God's grace from which arises salvation, only confirms the completeness and joyfulness which is the special attribute of the faithful Christian. John consequently attempts to fuse classical and Christian values and to demonstrate a fundamental consistency between ancient moral philosophy and medieval Christian moral theology.

John believes that, at least so far as life on earth is concerned, men play an active role in creating their own happiness both as individuals and as political creatures. He claims that the political system must be guided by the principles of nature, which he regards as 'the best guide to living'. Yet nature does not strictly determine human behaviour. Rather, men must actively cooperate with nature by means of experience and practice. Human beings conform to the course suggested by nature, a feat which is accomplished by developing and perfecting their knowledge and virtue. This is true at the personal as well as the social level: just as humans cultivate their own individual qualities by improving upon their natural attributes through effort and education, so they achieve a well-ordered political community by acknowledging and performing the natural duties demanded by justice towards their fellow creatures. Nature may fix the path of the good life, but men must exercise their minds and wills so as to discover and follow this route.

It is obvious, then, that John's political and moral philosophies are inextricably interwoven. Nowhere is this more evident than in his notion of moderation. John contends in Aristotelian fashion that the golden mean is a structural feature of all the virtues which individual persons may acquire; justice, courage and the like are middle points between dual vices of excess and deficiency. For this reason, John insists throughout the *Policraticus* that while many sorts of conduct (such as hunting, banqueting, drinking, gaming and so on) are vicious if performed often or regularly, they may be condoned if done in moderation for the purpose of recreation. In sum, moderation is the touchstone of an ethically correct (and ultimately, happy) life. But moderation simultaneously constitutes the salient characteristic of the good ruler in the *Policraticus*. John's king exercises power in a moderate fashion, neither releasing his subjects wholly to the caprice of their own volition nor controlling their behaviour so strenuously that they become incapable of using their legitimate free will. Royal moderation is equivalent to respect for the proper sphere of liberty which belongs to each and every member of the political community. John stresses that even a zealous insistence upon the virtue of subjects is a violation of the terms of moderate government: the king accords his people a sufficient measure of personal liberty that they may commit errors, at least so long as their sins endanger neither the safety of orthodox faith nor the security of the temporal polity. For the ability of an individual to acquire his own virtue requires him to train and exercise his will, which means that he will make mistakes on occasion.

By contrast, immoderate conduct (especially that in excess of the mean) is regarded by John as the defining mark of tyranny. The discussion of tyranny is one of the best known and most influential features of the *Policraticus*. Unlike preceding classical and medieval authors, who conceived of tyranny purely in terms of the evil or destructive use of public authority, John identifies the tyrant as any person who weds the ambitious desire to curtail the liberty of others with the power to accomplish this goal. As a result, his theory of tyranny is generic in the sense that it permits the tyrant to emerge in any walk of life. Specifically, he catalogues three classes of tyrants: the private tyrant, the public tyrant and the ecclesiastical tyrant. Private tyranny occurs when any private person employs the authority allotted to him so as to dominate or limit the legitimate freedom of someone else. The private variety of tyrant may appear in the household, the manor, the shire or anywhere that power is wielded. The suppression of private tyranny John assigns to royal government, since the king is charged with primary responsibility for the enforcement of law and the protection of all sections of the community.

When monarchic authority passes into the hands of an ambitious man, however, the form of tyranny becomes specifically public, in so far as the office of the prince differs from other forms of power in secular society. For the prince, as the pinnacle of temporal political organisation, represents both the ordinary assurance of the security and liberty of his subjects and the authoritative source of earthly law and jurisdiction within his realm. Thus, a public tyrant is inevitably accompanied by the destruction of the other parts of the community as well. In order to combat the threat of a public tyrant, John believes that the other members of the polity are charged with a duty – stemming from the principle of justice itself – to criticise, correct and, if necessary, even to kill a tyrannical ruler. Moreover, he takes this duty to be a generalised one: it pertains not merely to royal magistrates but to all segments of the body politic, since all are equally obligated (by their membership in society) to enforce the terms of justice.

The final category of tyranny – the ecclesiastical tyrant – is perhaps the most striking one to the modern reader. John devotes nearly as much attention in the *Policraticus* to the criticism of the behaviour of clerics and priests as of temporal political officials. In particular, he realises that there is great scope for churchmen to abuse their powers and hence to become ecclesiastical tyrants whose ambition for the offices and wealth of the church requires them to disregard the spiritual nourishment of the body of Christian believers. He is less forthcoming, however, about the appropriate method for the punishment of ecclesiastical tyrants. In general he prefers to leave such correction to the determination of the Roman pontiff, although he does acknowledge that once a cleric or priest has been stripped of ecclesiastical immunity he may be prosecuted for his crimes by earthly authorities. But of more significance, John's analysis draws theoretical force from its refusal to excuse any sphere in which power is exercised from the possibility of tyrannical conduct.

The key themes of the *Policraticus* in many ways reflect the concerns of twelfth-century political, intellectual and ecclesiastical life. Indeed, John's very conception of philosophy compels us to examine his thought in relation to its historical circumstances. Throughout his writings, he stresses that philosophical inquiry ought not to be a specialised, dry and obscure pursuit, but rather an integral feature of an active and dutiful life within the political arena, a life devoted to the service of God and His children. In the conduct of his career, as well as in the political theory of the *Policraticus*, John sought above all to illustrate the principle that philosophy is an aid to achieving the good life of both the individual and the whole community. The vitality of John's political thought consists primarily of its confrontation with the practical demands of politics in relation to the requirements of living well in a moral and religious sense.

At the same time, John's work succeeds in making the philosophical analysis of politics more intellectually respectable to a medieval audience. The *Policraticus* aims to demonstrate that public affairs are not necessarily corrupt, but can instead be conducted in a philosophically satisfactory manner according to which human goodness and happiness are promoted and enhanced. Such a claim represents an important step towards the incorporation of political thought into the domain of speculative inquiry from which medieval writers had largely excluded it up to John's own day. The thirteenth century, with its full recovery of Aristotle's social and political philosophy, would complete this process. But one need not await the infusion of Aristotelian doctrines to discover an author for whom political philosophy is a worthwhile and coherent field of learning. John of Salisbury richly deserves a reputation for having restored the theoretical study of politics to a place of prominence in the intellectual system of the medieval West.

Bibliographical note

A virtually complete English translation of the *Policraticus* may be pieced together from two volumes: John Dickinson's rendering of the so-called 'political' sections of the text (books IV, V and VI, and portions of VII and VIII under the title *The Statesman's Book* (New York: Knopf, 1927)) and J.B. Pike's translation of the remainder of the work, published as *The Frivolities of Courtiers and the Footprints of Philosophers* (Minneapolis: University of Minnesota Press, 1938). The *Entheticus Major and Minor* have lately been translated into English by Jan van Laarhoven (Leiden: E.J. Brill, 1987). Until recently the standard translation of the *Metalogicon* was by D.D. McGarry (Berkeley: University of California Press, 1955); it has just been replaced by a far improved edition and superior translation by K.S.B. Keats-Rohan (Oxford: Oxford University Press, 1990). There exist good editions of the *Historia Pontificalis*, ed. Marjorie Chibnall (London: Thomas Nelson, 1956), and of *The Letters of John of Salisbury*, in two volumes: *Volume I, The Early Letters (1153–1161)*, ed. W.J. Millor, H.E. Butler and C.N.L. Brooke (London: Thomas Nelson, 1955), and *Volume II, The Later Letters (1163–1180)*, ed. W.J. Millor and C.N.L. Brooke (Oxford: Clarendon Press, 1979).

Readers interested specifically in John's political thought are advised to consult the following secondary materials. An asterisk [*] indicates an introductory work:

*Kate L. Forhan, 'A Twelfth-Century "Bureaucrat" and the Life of the Mind: The Political Thought of John of Salisbury', *Proceedings of the PMR Conference* (Villanova, Pennsylvania) 10 (1985), 65–74.
*Hans Leibeschütz, *Mediaeval Humanism in the Life and Writings of John of Salisbury* (1950); reprinted with new afterword (Nendeln, Lichtenstein: Kraus, 1968).
Janet Martin, 'John of Salisbury's Manuscripts of Frontinus and of Gellius', *Journal of the Warburg and Courtauld Institutes* 40 (1977), 1–26.
'Uses of Tradition: Gellius, Petronius and John of Salisbury', *Viator* 10 (1979), 57–76.
Cary J. Nederman, 'The Aristotelian Doctrine of the Mean and John of Salisbury's Concept of Liberty,' *Vivarium* 24 (1986), 128–142.

*'A Duty to Kill: John of Salisbury's Theory of Tyrannicide', *Review of Politics* 50 (Summer 1988), 365–389.

Cary J. Nederman and J. Brückmann, 'Aristotelianism in John of Salisbury's *Policraticus*', *Journal of the History of Philosophy* 21 (April 1983), 203–229.

Cary J. Nederman and N.E. Lawson, 'The Frivolities of Courtiers Follow the Footprints of Women: Historical Women and the Crisis of Virility in John of Salisbury', *Ambiguous Realities: Medieval and Renaissance Women*, ed. J. Watson and C. Levin (Detroit: Wayne State University Press, 1987), 82–96.

*Richard H. Rouse and Mary A. Rouse, 'John of Salisbury and the Doctrine of Tyrannicide', *Speculum* 42 (October 1967), 693–709.

*Clement C.J. Webb, *John of Salisbury* (London: Methuen, 1932).

Michael Wilks, ed., *The World of John of Salisbury* (Oxford: Blackwell, 1984).

For background reading about John's political, social and cultural world and times, the following studies are recommended. An asterisk [*] denotes an introductory work:

R.L. Benson and Giles Constable, eds., *Renaissance and Renewal in the Twelfth Century* (Cambridge: Harvard University Press, 1982).

*C.N.L. Brooke, *The Twelfth-Century Renaissance* (New York: Norton, 1970).

*David C. Douglas, *The Norman Fate, 1100–1154* (London: Methuen, 1973).

*Georges Duby, *The Three Orders: Feudal Society Imagined*, trans. A. Goldhammer (Chicago: University of Chicago Press, 1978).

Avrom Saltman, *Theobald, Archbishop of Canterbury* (London: Thomas Nelson, 1956).

Beryl Smalley, *The Becket Conflict and the Schools* (Oxford: Blackwell, 1973).

*Richard W. Southern, *The Making of the Middle Ages* (New Haven: Yale University Press, 1953).

Medieval Humanism (Oxford: Blackwell, 1970).

*W.L. Warren, *Henry II* (London: Methuen, 1973).

Principal events in the life of John of Salisbury

Policraticus

Prologue

Although pleasurable in many ways, the pursuit of letters is especially fruitful because it excludes all annoyances stemming from differences of time and place, it draws friends into each other's presence, and it abolishes the situation in which things worth knowing are not experienced. Arts would have perished, laws would have disappeared, faith and all religious duties whatsoever would have shattered, and even the correct use of eloquence would have declined, save that divine compassion granted to mortals the use of letters as a remedy for human infirmity. The examples of our ancestors, which are incitements and inducements to virtue, never would have encouraged and been heeded by everyone, unless, through devotion, care and diligence, writers triumphed over idleness and transmitted these things to posterity.

If indeed the shortness of life and the obtuseness of understanding, the negligence of inactivity and the uselessness of occupation, permit us to know little, then even this is constantly banished and torn from the soul by forgetfulness which deceives knowledge through perpetual hostility and infidelity to its stepmother, memory. Who would know of Alexander or Caesar, or would respect the Stoics or the Peripatetics, unless they had been distinguished by the memorials of writers? Whoever would have followed the footsteps of the cherished apostles and prophets, unless they had been consecrated for posterity in the Holy Scriptures? Triumphal arches advance the glory of illustrious men whenever inscriptions explain for what cause and for whom they have been erected. It is only because of the inscription on a triumphal arch that the onlooker recognises that Constantine (who was of British stock) is proclaimed liberator of his country and founder of peace. No one would ever be illuminated by perpetual glory unless he himself or someone else had written. The reputation of the fool and the emperor is the same after a moderate period of time except where the memory of either is prolonged by the beneficence of writers. How many powerful kings have there been of whom there is nowhere a word or a thought? Therefore, there is no better counsel to those who seek glory than to be worthy of the greatest thanks of men of letters and of scribes. There is nothing to be

3

gained from the excellence of their conduct, which would be enveloped in a perpetual darkness unless illuminated by the light of letters. Whatever favour or commendation is obtained elsewhere, it is just as when Echo, of whom we hear in fable, captures the applause of the theatre: the sound begins and ends instantly.

From letters, one may confidently obtain solace from sorrow, recreation from labour, satisfaction from poverty, and moderation in prosperity and in pleasure. When a sharp mind is expanded by useful reading and writing, the soul is set free from vice, and redeemed from a state of adversity by a sweet and marvellous pleasure. One will never discover in human affairs a more pleasurable or a more useful occupation – except, of course, divinely prompted devotion, pursued either by prayerful conversation with the divine being or by acceptance, through the broadening of one's charitable heart, of God into one's soul and the meditative examination of the great works which He has performed. Believe from my experience that all the sweetness of the world is bitter when compared to this discipline; it is all the more so when one has refreshed the senses and invigorated the clear judgment and acumen of one's incorruptible reason.

You should not, therefore, be amazed that I do not follow your advice to ascend to some grade upon that scale by means of which one raises one's position at present. I do not plunge into the great affairs of court; let the response to you be the words of Isocrates, who when questioned by friends about why he did not become engaged in public affairs, responded, 'Of the experiences of this place, I know not; of my experiences this place knows nothing.'[1] I despise that which the courtiers embrace, and what I embrace they despise. It may be greatly surprising that I do not break off or cut the rope – if it cannot be otherwise untied – which has in the past held me and even now holds me in obedient servitude to the frivolities of courtiers. I loathe and regret that at the moment almost twelve years have been squandered, despite extensive training for a different life; and as it were, being suckled at the teat of a more sacred philosophy, it is appropriate that one should pass into the company of philosophers rather than of courtiers. I feel that you are also in a disturbed condition, except that you are more righteous and more prudent in doing what is useful in order to stand immobile upon the solid foundation of virtue, neither a lightly swaying reed nor a follower of soft pleasures. Rather, you

[1] Macrobius, *Saturnalia*, 7.1.

command the vanity that otherwise commands the world. Thus, where diverse provinces heap well-earned praise upon you, as if they were erecting a triumphal arch, I, a plebeian man, am only capable of honouring you by making a shrill sound upon rustic pipes with the uncultured language of this book, like a pebble tossed onto your piles of honours; while it has none of the elegance that is known to please, at least it cannot displease because it is written out of devotion.

The book concentrates in part on the frivolities of courtiers, and it dwells more upon those frivolities which are more burdensome. The book also busies itself with the footprints of philosophers; it is left to the determination of the wise which footprints should be avoided and which followed in each case. And because there should be no injury to anyone, it is proper to address this work to one in whom frivolity could never be demonstrated, that is, to address you who are the most discriminating man of our times, and to describe what seems to deserve censure in those like myself. Thus, when someone recognizes his own foolishness in what is recited or heard, he should bring to mind the lesson that 'with a change of name, the story may be told about you'; this connection will be most obviously made because all know that you are occupied with many serious matters. In this way, Seneca taught others while he admonished his Lucilius. Jerome writes to Oceanus and Pammachius, yet he mainly castigates the excesses of others.

Whoever would seek to justify the foolishness of the flatterer should calculate the trouble and time involved, and (if he is a wise man) judge what is said according to the motive for the statement. If someone imagines that this sounds too harsh, it should not be thought that anything said is directed at him, but rather at me personally and at those like me who desire to improve with me, or at those who, having passed into death, suffer all censure with equanimity. One knows that the failing of Achilles is an annoyance to no one: the present generation shall be corrected while the past shall be reprimanded as it merits. Thus Horace granted his slaves the use of the December liberty in order that he might be corrected:

> That sly dog Horace touches every fault
> His friend displays, but makes him laugh withal,
> And thus admitted plays about his heart.[2]

[2] Persius, *Saturae*, 1.116–117.

I have helped the case by bringing in pertinent material from diverse authors insofar as they contribute to or support the concerns that have been introduced, occasionally making no mention of the names of the authors, not only because your experience in letters is a sign that you for the most part will recognize the bulk of them, but also so that the ignorant may be incited to more assiduous reading. If anything here departs extensively from true faith I am confident that you shall indulge me, since I am not promising that all which has been written here is true, but that, whether it is true or false, it will serve the reader as useful. I am not so silly as to ascribe truth to the tale that the winged bird was once spoken to by the tortoise or that the country mouse accepted into his poor house the city mouse, and so on; but I do not doubt that these fictions of ours are of service to instruction. For the most part, the material that is utilised comes from elsewhere, except when I make my own that which is said commonly and rightly, so that I sometimes express ideas by means of my own abridgement, while at other times I express them faithfully and authoritatively in the words of others.

And since I have started to reveal all my mental secrets at once, I shall expose my arrogance fully. All whom I encounter who are philosophers in word or deed are judged to be my clients, and what is more, I arrogate them to myself in servitude. This is so to the extent that they in their surrender hurl their speeches on my behalf against detractors. For I name them as authorities. I have seen neither Alexander nor Caesar; I have heard neither Socrates nor Zeno, Plato nor Aristotle disputing; yet from these and others just as unknown much is preserved for the utility of readers. Still one should not appear to take pleasure in contention and it is my obligation to confess to the use of lies. And if the enemy will not otherwise be quiet – since I too have my Cornificius and Lanvinus – I agree that I have told lies, for we know from the Scriptures that 'every man is a liar'.[3] So our Lanvinus shall not be rescued with his immense chest, inflated belly, swollen and reddened face, and readiness to gnaw to bits the character of others rather than correcting his own. I will say who he is unless he restrains himself from injuries, and he will clearly realise that to be aged neither confers full authority nor preserves it unimpaired. Yet should he pursue investigation of the matter, and

---

[3] Psalms 116:11.

should he refute my reason and my fictional authorities, the words of the enemy shall not deter me from making amends. Indeed, I shall call friend whoever may correct my errors.

If it is discovered that what has been written somewhere is other than its author's words, still one should not maintain that I am being deceptive, since in military affairs I have followed the historians who frequently dissent from one another, and in philosophy I am a devotee of Academic dispute, which measures by reason that which presents itself as more probable. I am not ashamed of the declarations of the Academics, so that I do not recede from their footprints in those matters about which wise men have doubts. Although this school may seem to introduce obscurity into all matters, none is more faithful to the examination of truth and, on the authority of Cicero who in old age took refuge in it, none is on better terms with progress. Therefore, in remarks that are occasionally made about providence, fate, free will and the like, it may be noted that I prefer the Academics, rather than rash assertions about those matters which are still in doubt. Also I have sometimes used the Scriptures, which are well suited to the clarification of thought. Yet nothing will be discovered which is opposed to faith and good morals, and thus, the same unalterable truth gives birth to modern thoughts as to old ones. For it is written that 'facial features are not identical in everyone, nor yet different, as is proper in sisters'.[4]

Everything has been reserved for you to examine, that the greater and more just glory should be yours for criticism than mine for authorship. Differences within the various books are to be ascribed to matters of employment, that is, those affairs of court by which I am distracted to the extent that one is allowed hardly any time to write. While you have besieged Toulouse I have started this work and removed myself for a short while from the frivolities of courtiers, because leisure without letters is the death and burial of every living man. If any like Lanvinus would slander unknown or fictional authors, he must blame the second-hand materials of Plato, Cicero's 'Dream of Scipio', and the philosophers who practise saturnalian rites, or else indulge the fictions of our authors, if they serve the public utility.

I devoutly beg of those who may read or hear this work that they

---

[4] Ovid, *Metamorphoses*, 2.13–14.

might commend me in their prayers to the compassionate Father, and strive to gain forgiveness for my errors which are multiplied beyond number. For I hope to be joined with the all-fearful Lord; with heart and words each in their turn I pray for those in need that the omnipotent and compassionate God may protect our deeds and thoughts; may the Angel of the Great Judgment deem our minds so worthy of enlightenment that those who err will not lead us into the vices.

BOOK I

CHAPTER I
What most harms the fortunate

Among all of those things that important men are used to confronting,
none of them may be thought more pernicious than that delightful
allurement of fortune which turns one aside from the vision of truth.
In so far as the world showers its riches and delights – those which
renew and inflame the vicious eagerness for sensuous pleasure – the
soul is tricked by a multiplicity of allurements into a captivity in which,
alienated from itself, inner goodness decays as the desires are
extended to the deceptions of various external things. If indeed virtue
is hostile to prosperity, then wealth applauds its own in order to injure
them; and this unhappy success follows in the path of fortune, so that
in the end catastrophe occurs. Initially they accept a drink at the
banquet and, when they have become inebriated, a lethal venom or
something worse is intermixed. The more their appearance is
illuminated, the denser is the fog that spreads across their stupefied
eyes; the prevalence of darkness is therefore the disappearance of
truth, and the virtues are cut down at the root, the vices yield a crop,
the light of reason is extinguished, and the whole man is carried
headlong into miserable misfortune.

In this way the rational creature is rendered brutish; the image of
the Creator is distorted into something resembling the character of a
beast; and man degenerates from his condition of dignity, acts in a
conceited fashion, puffs up because of the honours collected, and by
arrogance destroys understanding. Who is to be considered so
unworthy as one who condemns the possession of self-knowledge?
Who is so unworthy as one who insults the Creator by squandering
time, that which is handed out in sparing quantities for use in life and
which alone cannot be restored – its reclamation requiring someone
to pay out, in the currency of life, interest and penalties at an usurious
rate? Who is so brutish as one who, because of defective reason and

libidinal impulses, forsakes his own proper sphere, attends to unsuitable business, and not merely business, but also is constantly occupied with unsuitable leisure pursuits? . . .

CHAPTER 2

In what consists devotion to unsuitable ends

Surely an unsuitable goal [*alienum*, literally 'what belongs to another'] is that which is not dictated by natural reason or duty – if, however, it is ever correct for that which is never rightfully conceded to anyone in the first place to be called unsuitable. What is suitable by nature pertains to everyone equally; what is a matter of duty, to individuals. Therefore, the suitability which arises out of duty differs from that deriving from nature, although obligation towards natural law stems from duty. It is a species of parricide to impugn natural law, and it is as bad as sacrilege to cancel the laws of parents and not to confer due honour on the mother of all. That which reason allows on the basis of honourable intent is not an absolutely unsuitable goal. If perhaps moderate pleasure or utility occurs and no one is harmed, this may not in fact be opposed to duty or nature; but if one or the other is impugned, it is immediately and absolutely unsuitable and is completely impermissible to anyone whomsoever. And so such an inappropriate deed is always either an error or a crime.

CHAPTER 3

The distribution of duties according to the political constitution of the ancients

Worldly philosophers, forming by principle and practice that justice (which may be called 'political') according to which human republics justly exist and flourish, have determined that each one is to be content with his own situation and endeavours, prescribing to urbanite and suburbanite, and also to peasant and rustic, their particular location and endeavours. Each and all will be dutifully devoted to the public utility. Every person will receive the fruits of nature, labour and industry strictly according to merit. No one will usurp that which is another's, remaining inclined towards love of all without distinction. The foremost and central urban location is conceded to the Areopagus, from which rightful duties are channelled off, like streams of health and life, into the professions, just as reason weighs each one's duty so that the most suitable arrangement is established . . .

[John proceeds to claim that the just government advocated by the ancient philosophers necessarily prohibited noble citizens from any activity that involved the pursuit of pleasure for its own sake. Among such activities John counts hunting (chapter 4), gambling (chapter 5), musical performances (chapters 6 and 7), and theatrical amusements (chapter 8). John condemns none of these interests absolutely and without exception, however. He instead insists that when carried out in moderation and at appropriate moments, all such pursuits are permissible as forms of relaxation. Only when someone engages in these pastimes immoderately and without circumspection is it necessary for their practice to be prevented.

The remainder of book I (chapters 9–13), as well as the whole of book II, is concerned with forms of magic including soothsaying, superstitious prophecy, dream interpretation, astrology, fortune-telling and augury. The extent to which John criticises these practices is perhaps reflective of their popularity at twelfth-century courts, whether as forms of amusement or as seriously maintained superstitions. John regards all such occupation with magic to be a token of human presumptuousness, in so far as it suggests man's effort to acquire a type of knowledge that pertains to God alone.]

BOOK III

Prologue

I have become the enemy of the multitude in so far as I examine the follies of the frivolous. For this reason I might disappear into retirement or keep silent; but my tumultuous affairs prevent the first option while the impulses of my soul destroy the other. Whoever is placed beneath some authority, if he is wise, ought to comply with the commands of the governor. Yet when one is moved by the stimulus of deep feeling, one cannot dissimulate, but instead will be inspired to express one's passions. Thus, exultation is stroked by the gentle breeze of what is joyful, hope induces cheerfulness, fear yields anxiety, and grief plunges the soul into confusion. Such alternation between good and bad fortune is experienced by every particular person. In truth, the misery of bad fortune is more pronounced and more often assails everyone. Who is not more often favoured with the annoyance of bad fortune than stroked by the consolation of good fortune? Rare is someone who can protect himself totally from the full onslaught of fortune. Whoever prevails due to his own qualities of strength will be impeded by the health or fate of a friend or a relative. Although he who is not stirred by the loss of his own material goods is not very human, neither is one in a human condition who is not moved by the loss of that which belongs to another.

Those who are wise have already posed the question, however, of whether whatever belongs to man is rightfully man's own. The advance of virtues has solved the puzzle of this obscurity, since the comedian [Terence] reminds us that nothing human is alien to man and the Celestial Master teaches that a human being should love his fellow human beings just as he loves himself. And it is apparent that the disciple who does not rejoice with the truth and does not burn with anger against the enemies of public welfare is unworthy of so great a master. At least in part, the present minor effort concentrates to a certain extent upon these false disciples and will strike down their follies with the very sword that they possess and to which they have become accustomed.

CHAPTER I

Of the universal and public welfare

The public welfare is therefore that which fosters a secure life both universally and in each particular person. There is nothing worthwhile in human life which is not advantageous for a secure life. The ancient philosophers have defined human beings as consisting of a rational soul and corruptible flesh. Yet flesh takes life from the soul, since the body cannot otherwise be alive, inasmuch as that which is always inert will remain inactive unless it is moved with the aid of some spiritualised nature. This latter also has a life of its own. For God is the life of the soul, a thought which is profoundly and truly embraced by one of the moderns, although in light verse: 'God is the life of the soul, the soul the life of the body; the one dissolves when the other flees, lost when it is undermined by God.'[1] Just as the life of the body is animated – moving by means of the soul, acquiescing in its movements to the disposition of the soul itself, and harmonising with the soul in obedience to necessity – so the soul lives according to its own mode of animation, since it is surely moved by God, it yields to Him humble devotion, and it acquiesces in all things. If the soul is impaired, its very life is impaired. Likewise, the body, when its parts do not move with reference to the soul, runs up against the ultimate inactivity of death. Therefore, as long as it is wholly alive, it is disposed in accordance with a whole which is not divided between a number of parts, but which is a genuine whole in that it operates simultaneously in every part and in each.

God occupies totally the soul that lives perfectly; He possesses it totally; He rules and vitalises it in total. No corner of it is excepted. But why say 'corner' or 'part' regarding the soul? It is devoid of parts, uncompounded in nature and utterly unacquainted with duplication. Were such parts possible, they could be claimed only from the distributor of all that is good. It may be asked, what parts could be

---

[1] St Augustine, *De libero arbitrio*, 2.16.41 and *De Civitate Dei*, 13.24.6.

claimed? At minimum these would be the virtues through which the soul grows strong, functions and gives itself tests. If, therefore, it does not develop through the multiplication of its parts and quantitative extension, still it is enlarged in its reason and understanding by an appetite for the good and an aversion for the bad while retaining its uncompounded nature. When spirit fills these parts (for God is spirit), the life of the soul is completed and perfected. For when God, who is the greatest good, is understood – the sight of him apprehended as clearly as is possible and permitted – and when the good which one sees is sought by an incorruptible will, and when reason reveals the way so that no one who is attracted by a sober impulse towards the good will stray to the right or the left, then the soul attains to a measure of the glory of immortality. Perhaps this was felt by the one who, in his sweet knowledge, said: 'My heart and my flesh cry out for the living God.'[2] In any case, whoever advances along this path neither fears nor dreads, neither is saddened nor suffers as do any of those who fail by withdrawing from the supreme and true good. Perhaps faithful souls are invited by the prophet who says the words 'Turn to me with all your heart',[3] so that the angel of joy or grief, apprehension or hope, may not turn away from my face and may not displease my will. This life fills all creatures because without it no creature has substance. For all that exists shares in His existence.

But although life inheres in all natural things, it only inhabits rational creatures by reason of grace. Therefore, they exist because truth is in them; they are enlightened because wisdom is in them; they esteem goodness because the fount of goodness and love is in them. Indeed, all virtue, whether angelic or human, is a vestige of divinity impressed to a certain degree upon rational creatures. The indwelling Holy Spirit imprints sanctity upon the soul, the rivulets of which disperse it to many places, extending the diverse gifts of grace. And it appears to me that the true and unique security of life is when the mind, enlivened by the Spirit, is enlightened by the knowledge of things and is kindled by the love of honour and the cultivation of virtue. Knowledge precedes the cultivation of virtue because no one can faithfully seek that of which he is ignorant; and evil, unless it is known, cannot usefully be guarded against. Furthermore, the repository of knowledge is laid bare in two ways: with either the

---

[2] Psalms 84:2.   [3] Joel 2:12.

exercise of reason, which knows that which understanding can discover, or with the disclosure by the revelation of grace of that which has been hidden from our eyes. It is then either by nature or by grace that one can approach the recognition and knowledge of the truth of such matters as are necessary for each person. It is more astonishing that every person carries in his heart a book of knowledge open to those subservient to reason. In this are represented not only all the things visible in nature, but also all those invisible things which the Fabricator writes with His own finger. It is so much the case that God's dictates are known either by benefit of nature or by manifestation of grace that none is able to excuse himself on account of ignorance. As it is written: 'For that which is known of God is manifest in them; for they reveal God.'[4]

Yet I neither broaden the boundaries of corrupt nature nor pose an impediment to grace, as though nature possessed a goodness which was not conferred upon it, since it is certain that nothing can be done without grace. Therefore, the acknowledgement of truth and the cultivation of public virtue is the general safeguard of each and every person and of rational nature. The contrary of this is ignorance and its hateful and injurious child, vice. And ignorance is rightfully the mother of vice because it is never so sterile that it does not provide a hateful harvest of wretched objects. The ethical writer states,

> Sacrifice no incense,
> that a trifle of rectitude may cleave to the shallow fool.[5]

Awareness consists of the possession of certitude either in knowledge or faith. But the rules of faith may be deferred for a short while, since they await their proper time and place. One with certain knowledge has knowledge of himself, which cannot happen if one does not estimate one's own strength or if one is ignorant of others.

[4] Romans 1:17.
[5] Persius, *Saturae*, 5.120–121.

CHAPTER 3

That pride is the root of all evil and passionate desire a general leprosy which infects all

Pride is truly the root of all the evils that feed mortality. Streams become dry if the source of the flow is cut off; a tree will not thrive with severed roots. Vices languish if passion is banished; yet if manure is piled upon the roots, the tree will become fertile and the sterility of the desert will recede. If the source of the liquid overflows, then the increase turns into streams; if fuel is added to the fire, then the blaze of the wood is renewed. So if one fosters the poisonous vice of pride inherent in nature, not even if one wishes can one impede that virus of mortification from infecting the vital organs. Love of self is not as much akin to man as inherent in him. If someone exceeds the mean, he veers toward error. All the virtues are limited in their proper ends and consist in the mean; if one is excessive, one is off the path, not on the path.

If this self-love prevails no one may expect a cure. It is a form of leprosy, indeed, which is more incurable than any other sort of leprosy. Is one ignorant of whether passionate desire is a leprosy? Consult Gehazi. If one is ashamed to admit that from which one suffers, then convince him by the physical marks. But why do I say that Gehazi ought to be consulted, as if he were unique? Speak to the world because all are affected; interrogate me, one who is ill. Certainly passionate desire is a wretched and pitiful leprosy. Perhaps you are ignorant of what is said; you may be ignorant of the infirmity because, not being a man disposed towards passionate desire (and in this being above mankind), you are unaware of the plague; but my faithful witness in heaven asserts on my behalf that all are corrupt, and are committing abominations, so that there is none who does good, to the extent that there is not a single one. Whether you may be one you may consider. I know that Paul is not such, for it is he who proclaims and bemoans the onset of this plague: 'O wretched man that I am, who shall deliver me from the body of this death?'[6] I know that he is not such who has drunk of the spirit of truth from the river of wisdom; when he thunders against those infected with this illness, he

---

[6] Romans 7:24.

says, 'For all that is in the world, the lust of the flesh and the lust of the eyes, and the pride of life, is not of the Father, but is of the world.'[7] Whoever, therefore, does not temper his self-love may fear leprosy and is to be greatly alarmed by the dimming of vision that is imminent.

Accordingly, if they who will not restrain passionate desire, which is the source and nourishment of evil, incur the loss of salvation, what will become of those who inflame it through the stimulus of flattery and who virtually foster incitement to the vices? What can they do or endure who turn away from listening to the truth, who do not close their eyes off from admiration of those things which are corruptible and false, who open their hands and keep occupied with all manner of sensual activity? Then, as if their own malice were not sufficient for the moment, the falsehoods of one contend with the falsehoods of another. Indeed, one may make liberal use of Terence's words, in so far as the furnace of passionate desire is inflamed by the assembly of flatterers and petitioners, informers and defamers, the jealous, the ambitious, the shameful, and the violators of all the duties; it is easier to encounter these than it is to enumerate them, since they are present everywhere on the earth. All law is opposed to such persons, all legal rights stand jointly against them, and all creatures will someday take up arms against these enemies of the public welfare.

[7] I John 2:16.

CHAPTER 4

The flatterer, the toady and the cajoler, than whom none is more pernicious

The flatterer is inimical to all virtue, and like a sore upon the eye he fastens himself by his speech to those with whom he bonds. He is to be avoided all the more inasmuch as he does not desist from committing injury under the pretence of friendship, until finally he blunts the sharpness of reason and extinguishes that modicum of light which may seem to be present. In addition to this, he plugs up the ears of his audience in order that they do not hear the truth; one can hardly conceive of anything more pernicious. One may be acquainted with the remark of Laelius (or actually Cicero): 'One is to despair of the welfare of him whose ears are closed to the truth and can not hear what is true.'[8] What is more unfaithful than to circumvent him to whom one owes faith by enticing words, jocular deportment and dissimulating actions, and to propel him into sordid vices and the bottomless abyss by the blind allurement of all the vanities? What is more odious than that fraud and deceit which, under the appearance of love and faith, is exercised against the simple, the credulous and (what is most detestable) the friendly by perfidious and worthless enemies? Indeed, men of this sort all speak towards the end of pleasure, not of truth. They entreat with iniquitous and deceitful words which subvert those friends who fall into error, repeating 'Well done, well done' . . .

[8] Cicero, *De amicitia*, 24.90.

CHAPTER 6

The multiplication of flatterers is beyond number and pushes out of distinguished houses those who are honourable

This plague of flatterers has increased to the extent that – God's indignation notwithstanding – if by chance courtly opinions should come into conflict, one fears that the moderate and good man would not readily have the power to expel rather than be expelled. For disgusting uncleanliness and cancerous affliction gradually pervades everything, so that never or rarely is someone not defiled by this illness. All seek favour with those with whom they live; such is not only permissible but honourable, since all that nature brings forth obeys virtue and provides the best guide for correct living. But as soon as the seeking of favour deserts the rule of moderation, one is carried off head first into rushing between doing everything and doing nothing, between an infamous and a good reputation, a captor of favour and an incestuous solicitor of influence. Having previously bribed the friend with delights, the flatterer creeps up on his fortune in the manner of a prostitute, diminishing his faculties, accumulating the plunder from those things which belong to him, and converting everything to one's own advantage. It therefore follows that no servile obsequiousness is bothersome to the flatterer, no indulgence seems indecent, and he assumes a role in all duties, as long as he may anticipate a reward for all his fraudulence.

Who are those who rely upon their garb, who seize on to those at the top, who are surrounded by an entourage of foot servants and whitewashed by the indulgence of comrades-in-arms and attendants, who are vaunted with the first salute in public, who have the best seats at dinner, whose ears are flattered by the palliative of their title which opens the sensitive ears of the nobles, the merit of whose fortunes is born aloft and extolled to the heavens on beating wings, and for whom great houses ransack their affairs and change their conditions every which way? Unquestionably it is flatterers, who live at the beck and call of others so long as they cheat them fraudulently. Truth is harsh and very often is the parent of difficulty in so far as it will refuse to flatter anyone. For the bitter truth is more useful and more esteemed by a mind of integrity than the distilled honey of a prostitute's speech. Better indeed, testifies the holy Solomon, are lashings by friends than the fraudulent kisses of coaxers. Why not? Faith is always to be preferred to faithlessness. Faith is not maintained intact where one thing is done while another is simulated, especially if the mind and will seek injury. For if one follows the Stoics, it is said that the faithful person does as he says.

'My light', 'my salvation', 'my refuge', 'my heart and my life', 'invincible commander', 'the wisest of those alive', 'the most generous and benevolent of all', 'mirror of the virtues' and other such inappropriate ascriptions – are these not the vices of flatterers as surely as their seductiveness? For it is they who do not even shun the semblance of the clown when they are professing their friendship. 'Poison', a wise man remarks, 'is not given except when washed down with honey.'[9] No secrets are as insidious as those which are concealed by the semblance of duty or in the name of some necessity. What you believe to be obedience, assume to be friendship and judge to be attention – these are the very essence of insidiousness. As the story is told (because the fictions of poets may serve the truth), Juno could not have deceptively urged Semele into the fire if she had not adorned herself in the appearance of her nurse and pretended affection. You believe that service is meted out; you are actually subjected to an

---

[9] St Jerome, *Epistolae*, 107.6.

extreme and distressing servitude. For 'when into a ready ear is poured a little of the poison of a vicious nature',[10] you no longer prefer to die rather than to drive off all those who speak the truth and disdain to sink down into the infamy of the flatterer. Not only he who contradicts, but even he who fails to give express consent to, the delights and defilements of a powerful friend is banished from the house, and is fortunate if he is not judged to be an enemy.

And not even consent suffices for esteem, for it is necessary to approve, to commend and to applaud the insanity; after he has done all evil, he is to be lauded as though his deeds were good. For just as the identity of wills is an indication of love, so by way of dissent may one be accused of every offence of enmity. As a result, the satirist remarks:

> What is one to do at Rome? I am ignorant of deception; a book,
> if it is bad, I am unable to laud and desire; the movement
> of the stars I know not; taking a vow to murder one's father
> I neither will nor can; the internal organs of frogs never
> are inspected; to carry to the adulterous bride a message,
> or instructions, may be left to another; I assist no one
> in being a thief, and thus, for this reason nobody comes for a
>   teacher;
> it's just as though
> my useless body were crippled and lacking a right hand.[11]

I flee, therefore, the city filled with such obscenities; I abandon to their flatterers those who have been poisoned by the toxin of flattery. 'Asturias and Catulus may live in that place; they remain who transform black into white.'[12] Do not believe that the vice depicted is that of the city only; it exists throughout the whole world. What is the case generally is specifically true of the Roman world; I recall hearing the Roman pontiff routinely deride the Lombards, since it was said that they raised their hats to all those with whom they conversed, in order that they might strive for favour at the beginning of the discussion and, as they discussed matters, they would caress the heads of their fellows with the oil of commendation. 'My son', Solomon stated, 'if sinners entice you, do not consent.'[13] For they themselves 'lay in wait for their own blood, and promote deception

---

[10] Juvenal, *Saturae*, 3.122–123. [11] *Ibid.*, 3.41–48.
[12] *Ibid.*, 3.29–30. [13] Proverbs 1:10.

against their own soul . . . Restrain your feet from their path; for their feet run to evil and they hasten to shed blood.'[14]

[14] Proverbs 1:18, 15–16.

CHAPTER 10

That the Romans are dedicated to vanity and what the ends of flatterers are

. . . Romulus consecrated to his gods the city of Rome upon the auguries of sacrilegious fratricide and the shedding of a brother's blood, after which, being harassed by ghosts, he endeavoured to redeem the slaughter of his brother by the empty honour of pretending to share supreme power. The emperors, whom the Roman people by their custom faithfully murdered, were also deified with still greater faithfulness, the Romans disguising their manifest treachery with empty solace, just as if they were handing out a small curative to him whom they had slain; they pretended that the late emperors had been transformed into the status of divinities, as though the hand of the Omnipotent did not suffice to rule His heaven and His earth except with the approval of tyrants. Thus are made indigenous divinities or (as others prefer to say) heroes, to whom the faithless Romans did not even ascribe the dignity of human status. An appellation was thereby introduced according to which princes, conspicuously adorned with noticeable virtue and true faith, dared – not to mention rejoiced – to pronounce themselves divine; for long-standing and vicious habits endure in opposition to the universal faith. If it comes to words, the Romans take precedence in such matters over the Greek infidels, since it is the former who were taught the use of flattering allurements to the extent that they readily were transformed into a race of teachers themselves. This nation invented the speech by which we deceive superiors, in so far as we confer distinction on a single person by honouring him in the plural, and by the authority of their name the Romans have transmitted this technique to their neighbours and to posterity.

If you inquire into those times, direct yourself to that period when Julius Caesar's dictatorial powers were either uncovered or perfected

22

(I know not which); just as he was made all things, so he took possession of all things. My image of those times frequently presents itself in connection with the disposition of all subjects according to the pleasure of the ruling powers, and although in their souls they may have struggled against domination, they were prepared to prescribe the sentence of exile or death upon themselves. Hence arises a truly dreadful power; hence the torment of pain and the inflammation of the mind arouse a fearfulness of heart and they claim for themselves the principal authority over all matters. This is so to such a degree that, for example, priests disguise the precepts of divine law, elders are ignorant of wisdom, the judge is ignorant of justice, the prelate knows no authority, the subject knows no discipline, the freeborn disdains liberty; in sum, the whole populace despises calm and peace. For so long as all are led by a single preeminent will, they are deprived of their own free will, universally and individually. Was this not the situation during the period when

> the patricians were prepared to sit and vote,
> if he demanded a kingdom, a temple, the slaying of the Senate,
> the unspeakable prostitution of a young woman?

And so it is only fortunate, with regard to the acts of citizens, that 'there was more that Caesar was ashamed to command than that Rome was ashamed to permit'.[15] Were not the opinions of the tyrant transmitted to his successors in tyranny, inasmuch as it might be suspected that he preferred the law to be taken into his own hands rather than to be respected by humbler people? In this way, the semblance of liberty is retained, if everyone pretends to will that which has been directed – making, or by all means appearing to make, a virtue of necessity, in so far as necessity is joined to consent – and embraces gratefully that which is pressed upon one. There are no elements of true and natural liberty, however, where flattery claims everything for itself, where vanity claims everything, leaving behind nothing of either truth or virtue.

One ought not to doubt that there is flattery without deceit, although Gnato concedes on behalf of flatterers that when he is most deceptive, then he triumphs. Just as the aim of the orator is persuasive speech, and the end of a physician is a medical cure, so the aim of

---

[15] Lucan, *Pharsalia*, 3.109–112.

flatterers is sweetly spoken deception. For assuredly 'the pipe plays sweetly while the birdcatcher traps the bird';[16] and poison may be administered in a potion of honey, that it may injure sooner. Yet 'it is not always the case that the physician may comfort the patient',[17] and the orator may not always obtain his aim, when it pertains to another. Thus, at least the flatterer does not always deceive or triumph over his friend. Yet he has not abandoned his end, if he has not neglected that to which he attains. For Ulysses did not evade the invitations of the Sirens for the reason that some sweet sound was missing from their attraction, but because he opposed the incentives of pleasure and vain allurements of the prostitute with the true strength of virtue. Which of their arts of deceit did the tempting Pharisees and the ambushing Herodians not exercise in order that they might, by their deceitful speech, trap in words Him in whose mouth nothing was deceitfully contrived. Master, they said, we know that you are truthful and that you teach according to the true way of God, and neither do you care for some particular person, nor do you receive him personally. What is more alluring? But the deceit that was aimed at and the ill will that was produced were disclosed by the subject matter of the following question: whether or not it is permitted to give away tax money to Caesar? See the snare prepared for the feet of the innocent and His frustration of the traps which iniquity has set for His subversion. If He proposes that the taxes are to be given, then the special people of the Lord, the seed of the children and the distinguished heredity of the Lord, would be slavishly subjected to such obligations as the tenth and first fruits and legal ceremonies. If He would respond to those who serve the welfare and the peace of all that the tribute is to be refused, then He could justly be arrested by the publicans as a virtual author of sedition and an offender against the imperial majesty. Because they vainly set a trap before the eyes of those who possess wings, the fetters of their deceit were unleashed, in as much as when a coin of tax was brought forward, He directed that each image be restored to its own; and that which is Caesar's must be restored to Caesar, in order that God not be defrauded of His rights. Of course, it is not allotted to everyone that they should evade the traps of flattery, since some do not anticipate them, while others anticipate them but are unable to turn away. Still, there is one certainty: those who are

---

[16] Cato, *Disticha*, 1.27.   [17] Ovid, *Epistolae ex Ponto*, 1.3.17.

dedicated to vice are no more pleased by virtue than those who inhabit a kitchen smell good.

CHAPTER 15

That it is only permitted to flatter him whom it is permitted to slay; and that the tyrant is a public enemy

Still, to whom is owed that sinner's oil of which he who walks before faithful kings disapproves and for the acquisition of which the words of the Gospel sent the foolish virgins who shut themselves out? It is owed to he who is involved in vile affairs and who, by the judgment of the just God, becomes more vile yet, and who aspires to glitter in the preference of popular opinion rather than to glare in the blaze of his charitable works. In the secular literature there is even caution because one is to live one way with a friend and another way with a tyrant. It is not permitted to flatter a friend, but it is permitted to delight the ears of a tyrant. For in fact him whom it is permitted to flatter, it is permitted to slay. Furthermore, it is not only permitted, but it is also equitable and just to slay tyrants. For he who receives the sword deserves to perish by the sword.

But 'receives' is to be understood to pertain to he who has rashly usurped that which is not his, not to he who receives what he uses from the power of God. He who receives power from God serves the laws and is the slave of justice and right. He who usurps power suppresses justice and places the laws beneath his will. Therefore, justice is deservedly armed against those who disarm the laws, and the public power treats harshly those who endeavour to put aside the public hand. And, although there are many forms of high treason, none of them is so serious as that which is executed against the body of justice itself. Tyranny is, therefore, not only a public crime, but, if this can happen, it is more than public. For if all prosecutors may be allowed in the case of high treason, how much more are they allowed when there is oppression of laws which should themselves command emperors? Surely no one will avenge a public enemy, and whoever does not prosecute him transgresses against himself and against the whole body of the earthly republic.

BOOK IV

Prologue

It is certainly a difficult matter to recognise the truth and to attack those errors of obscurity or carelessness which most frequently spoil its clear expression. For truly what is more righteous than the examination of unknown matters? The knowledge of such matters, the path to which does not guide those contemptuous of them, stimulates the sting of justice in the punishment of wrongdoers. Therefore, the first step in philosophising – the very genus of those matters it is proper to discuss – is that of prudently understanding what is true of particulars; the second step is that of faithfully comprehending the truth in everything, which illuminates the particulars. But this philosophical preparation is only accessible to those who, in opposition to the kingdom of vanity, freely proclaim they are freed when they are the children of truth, and who serve the Holy Spirit by leading away iniquity and injustice yoked by the neck. For 'whenever there is the spirit of God, in that place there is liberty';[1] servility to fear and assent to vice exterminate the Holy Spirit. Furthermore, it is the Holy Spirit which speaks of and is not ashamed by equity in the inspection of rulers and which chooses between spiritually impoverished kings and those who aim to harmonise with God and who learn to know, speak and do the truth. He who does not wish to hear or speak the truth is alienated from the truth of the Spirit. But enough of this. For the moment, let us turn to understanding how the tyrant differs from the prince.

---

[1] II Corinthians 3:17.

27

CHAPTER I

On the difference between the prince and the tyrant, and what the prince is

There is wholly or mainly this difference between the tyrant and the prince: that the latter is obedient to law, and rules his people by a will that places itself at their service, and administers rewards and burdens within the republic under the guidance of law in a way favourable to the vindication of his eminent post, so that he proceeds before others to the extent that, while individuals merely look after individual affairs, princes are concerned with the burdens of the entire community. Hence, there is deservedly conferred on him power over all his subjects, in order that he may be sufficient in himself to seek out and bring about the utility of each and all, and that he may arrange the optimal condition of the human republic, so that everyone is a member of the others. In this, nature, that best guide to living, is to be followed, since it is nature which has lodged all of the senses in the head as a microcosm, that is, a little world, of man, and has subjected to it the totality of the members in order that all of them may move correctly provided that the will of a sound head is followed. The prince is raised to the apex and becomes illustrious, therefore, as a result of his many and great privileges which are as numerous and extensive as are thought to be necessary for him. Certainly this is proper because nothing is useful to the people except that which fulfills the needs of the prince, since his will should never be found opposed to justice.

Therefore, according to the general definition, the prince is the public power and a certain image on earth of the divine majesty. Beyond doubt the greatest part of the divine virtue is revealed to belong to the prince, in so far as at his nod men bow their heads and generally offer their necks to the axe in sacrifice, and by divine impulse everyone fears him who is fear itself. I do not believe that this could have happened unless it happened at the divine command. For all power is from the Lord God, and is with Him always, and is His forever. Whatever the prince can do, therefore, is from God, so that power does not depart from God, but it is used as a substitute for His hand, making all things learn His justice and mercy. 'Whoever therefore resists power, resists what is ordained by God',[2] in whose power is the conferral of authority and at whose will it may be removed from them or limited. For it is not even the ruler's own power when his will is harsh to his subjects, but a divine dispensation at His good will to punish or train subjects. From this we see that during the persecution by the Huns, Attila was questioned by the holy bishop of a certain city about who he was, to which he responded: 'I am Attila, scourge of God'; the bishop venerated him (it is written) as a divine majesty. He said, 'The minister of God is well honoured'; and also, 'Blessed is he who comes in the name of God.' The gates of the church were mournfully unbarred to admit the persecutor through whose hand martyrdom was attained. For he had not the audacity to exclude the scourge of God because he knew that His cherished son had been scourged and that there was no power to scourge him except from the Lord.

If, consequently, power is regarded as venerable by those who are good, even to the degree that it is a plague upon the elect, who ought not to venerate what is instituted by God for the punishment of wrongdoers, for the approval of the truly good, and for the enforcement of devoted service to the laws? 'It is indeed an adage worthy', as the Emperor has it, 'of the majesty of kings that the prince professes an obligation to his own laws. Because the authority of the prince is determined by the authority of right, and truly submission to the laws of princes is greater than the imperial title',[3] so it is the case that the prince ought to imagine himself permitted to do nothing which is inconsistent with the equity of justice.

---

[2] Romans 13:2.   [3] Justinian, *Codex*, 1.14.4.

CHAPTER 2

What law is; and that the prince, although he is an absolutely binding law unto himself, still is the servant of law and equity, the bearer of the public persona, and sheds blood blamelessly

Princes should not suppose that they are disparaged by the belief that the justice of God, whose justice is eternal justice and whose law is equity, is preferable to the justice of their own statutes. Furthermore, equity (as the experts in law assert) is a matter of what is appropriate, according to which reason equalises the whole and seeks just equality in matters of inequality; what is equitable to all is what grants to each person that which is his own. Its interpreter is law, inasmuch as law makes known the will of equity and justice. And thus, Chrysippus asserted that law has power over all divine and human affairs, for which reason it presides over all good and all evil and is ruler and guide of things as well as of men. Papinian, a man of the greatest experience in matters of jurisprudence, and Demosthenes, the influential orator, would seem to support this and to subject all men to its obedience because all law is a sort of discovery and gift from God, the teaching of the wise, the corrective to excesses of wilfulness, the harmony of the city, and the banishment of all crime. It is proper for all who dwell in the community of political affairs to live according to it. All are, for this reason, obligated to be restrained by the necessity of observing the laws, unless perhaps someone imagines that he is granted the licence of iniquity.

Still the prince is said to be an absolutely binding law unto himself, not because he is licensed to be iniquitous, but only because he should be someone who does not fear the penalties of law but someone who loves justice, cherishes equity, procures the utility of the republic, and in all matters prefers the advantage of others to his private will. But who in public affairs may even speak of the will of the prince, since in such matters he is not permitted his own will unless it is prompted by law or equity, or brings about judgments for the common utility? For in fact his will in these matters should have the force of judgment; and that which most rightfully pleases him in all matters has the force of law because his determination may not be inconsistent with the design of equity. 'From your visage', it is said, 'my judgment proceeds, your eyes must look at equity',[4] for indeed the uncorrupted judge is one whose determination is on the basis of the assiduous contemplation of the image of equity. The prince is therefore the minister of the public utility and the servant of equity, and in him the public persona is borne since he punishes all injuries and wrongs, and also all crimes, with moderate equity. In addition, his rod and staff, exercised with the moderation of wisdom, return all deviations and errors to the way of equity, so that the Holy Spirit may meritoriously congratulate the prince, saying: 'Your rod and your staff, they are comforts to me.'[5] While his shield is also strong, still it is a shield for the feeble and one which deflects the darts of malignance from the innocent. Those who are advanced most by his duties of office are those who can do least for themselves, and those who most desire to do harm are those who draw the greatest hostility.

That sword with which blood is shed innocently is therefore not borne without cause, so that one may frequently kill and still not be a man of blood nor incur the accusation of murder or crime. For if one may believe the great Augustine, David is called a man of blood not as the result of war, but as a result of Uriah. And Samuel is nowhere indicted as a man of blood or a murderer, although he killed Agag, the obese king of Amalek. This is indeed the sword of the dove, which quarrels without bitterness, which slaughters without wrathfulness and which, when fighting, entertains no resentment whatsoever. For since law will prosecute the blameworthy without personal animosity, the prince most properly punishes transgressors not according to some wrathful motive, but by the peaceful will of law. For although it may be seen that the prince has his own public executioners, we ought to think of him as the sole or primary executioner to whom it is permitted to allow a substitute hand. And we may agree with the Stoics, who have diligently investigated the reasons for names, when they say that 'public executioner' (*lictor*) is derived from 'stick of the law' (*legis ictor*) because it is the aim of his duties to strike down whoever the law adjudges must be struck down. And, for this reason, those officials of antiquity by whose hand the judge punished the guilty would be told, 'Comply with the will of the law' or 'Satisfy the law', when they hung the sword over the criminal, so that the grief of the situation might be mitigated by the mercifulness of these words.

[4] Psalms 17:2.   [5] Psalms 23:4.

CHAPTER 3

That the prince is a minister of priests and their inferior; and what it is for rulers to perform their ministry faithfully

This sword is therefore accepted by the prince from the hand of the Church, although it still does not itself possess the bloody sword entirely. For while it has this sword, yet it is used by the hand of the prince, upon whom is conferred the power of bodily coercion, reserving spiritual authority for the papacy. The prince is therefore a sort of minister of the priests and one who exercises those features of the sacred duties that seem an indignity in the hands of priests. For all duties of sacred law are in fact the affairs of the religious and the pious, yet that duty is inferior which executes the punishment of crime and which seems to be represented by images of executioners. And for this reason, Constantine, the most faithful emperor of the Romans, when he had convened the Nicean Council of priests, neither ventured to take the foremost position nor allowed himself to mingle with the presbyters, but occupied the hindmost seat. The decisions which were heard to be approved by them were venerated by him, just as if he supposed them to emanate from the court of the divine majesty. And when written accusations involving the crimes of priests were presented in their turn to the emperor, he accepted them and placed them unopened in the fold of his toga. After he called them back to charity and concord, he himself said that inasmuch as he was a human who was subject to the verdict of the priests, it was not allowed for him to examine divine cases which none except God alone could adjudicate. Those rolls which he had accepted he consigned to the flames uninspected, fearful to publicise the crimes or abuses of the Fathers and to incur the same curse as Ham, the reprobate son, who did not share in the reverence of his forefathers. And thus, in the writings of Nicholas, the Roman pontiff, it is narrated that the same Constantine had said: 'Truly if my own eyes had seen a priest of God or any of those who wrap themselves in the robes of the monastery sinning, my cloak would have been stretched out and would have covered him up, so that no other would see him.'

The great Emperor Theodosius was suspended by the priest of Milan from the use of regalia and imperial insignia because he deserved punishment (although not on account of a serious error), and the emperor patiently and solemnly did the penitence for homicide imposed upon him. Indeed, according to the useful testimony of the Teacher of the gentiles, he who blesses is greater than he who is blessed, and he who is in the possession of the authority of conferring a dignity takes precedence over him who is himself conferred with a dignity. Furthermore, by the law of reason, whoever wills is he who nullifies, and he who can confer rights is he who can withdraw them. Did Samuel not impose a sentence of deposition upon Saul by reason of disobedience, and substitute for him the humble son of Jesse atop the kingdom? If the properly constituted prince administers faithfully the office undertaken, such honour and such reverence are exhibited for him as to match that superiority which the head has over the other members of the body. In addition, he administers his office faithfully when, mindful of his special situation, he remembers to cherish the unique character of the community subject to him, and when he is cognizant that he does not owe his life to himself but to others, and when he allots things to them according to the order of charity. Therefore, he owes the whole of himself to God, most to his country, much to his parents and relatives, and less (although still a little) to foreigners.[6] He is thus duty bound 'to the wise and to the foolish, to the insignificant and to the great'.[7]

Inspection of such persons is common to all prelates, both those who administer care in spiritual matters and those who exercise temporal jurisdiction. Consequently, we have Melchizedek, the first whom Scripture introduces as king and priest (making no mention at present of the mystery by which he prefigures Christ, who was born in heaven without a mother and on earth without a father). It may be read of him, I say, that he had neither father nor mother, not that he was deprived of either one, but because according to reason, kingship and priesthood are not generated of flesh and blood, since in founding either one, respect for lineage should not prevail apart from respect for the merits of the virtues, but the desire for the benefit of faithful subjects should be prevalent. And when someone ascends to the summit atop either mountain, he must be oblivious to carnal desires and must do only what is demanded for the welfare of those subject to him. Accordingly, he is father and mother to his subjects or,

---

[6] Cicero, *De officiis*, 1.45.160.   [7] Romans 1:14.

if he knows of a more gentle form of affection, he should use that; he desires love more than fear, and reveals himself to his subjects as someone whose life they would out of devotion prefer to their own, so that they count his safety as equivalent to the life of the people; and then all affairs will proceed properly for him, and a small body of obedient guards will prevail (if necessary) over innumerable adversaries. For love is stronger than death; and the military formation that is tied together by the bonds of love will not break easily.

Before the Dorians fought the Athenians, they consulted an oracle regarding the outcome of the battle. It was responded that they were to be victorious, unless they killed the king of the Athenians. When they reached the point of making war, their soldiers were commanded before all else to safeguard the king. The king of the Athenians at that time was Codrus. It was he who, deliberating upon the response of the deity and the command to the enemy, changed his royal dress, entering the encampment of the enemy carrying kindling around his neck. The throng there blocked his way and he was slain by a soldier whom he had struck with his pruning hook. Once the body of the king was recognised, the Dorians departed without a battle. And thus in this way the virtue of the Athenian leader, by which he offered his own death in exchange for the safety of his country, delivered Athens from war. Similarly, Lycurgus during his reign laid down decrees affirming the obedience of the people to their princes and of the princes to rulership in accordance with justice; he abolished the use of gold, silver and all other wicked materials; he consigned the safeguarding of the laws to the Senate and the power of choosing the Senate to the people; he resolved that virgins should marry without a dowry, so that wives would not be chosen for pecuniary reasons; he willed that the elderly should have the greatest honours on account of the status of their age; certainly in no other place on earth did the elderly have such great honour. Then, in order that his laws should be bestowed eternally, he placed the city under the obligation of a solemn oath that they would not change one of his laws until after he had returned. He departed afterwards for Crete, went there into a perpetual exile, and commanded that upon his death his bones be thrown away in the sea so that the Lacedaemonians would not suppose that the bonds of their sacred oath were dissolved by the return of his remains. I use these examples so freely because I find that the Apostle Paul used them while he preached to the Athenians. That remarkable preacher strove to impress Jesus Christ and His crucifixion upon their minds, so that by a multitude of gentile examples, they would learn that deliverance is obtained solely through the ignominy of the cross . . .

It is recurrently mentioned that the Roman commanders dedicated themselves to the proper training of their troops. Thus, Julius Caesar is reported to have said, 'The commander who does not labour in order that he may be loved by the soldiers does not know the weapons with which to arm them and does not know that those opposed to the humanity of a commander towards his corps are the real enemy.' Similarly, he never said to his troops 'Go here', but 'Come with me'; for this was said because labour in which the commander shares will seem less laborious to the soldier. Moreover, on the same person's authority, the pleasures of the body are to be shunned; for it is asserted that in war the human body is injured by the sword, whereas in peace it is injured by pleasure. For as a conqueror of peoples, he had perceived that pleasure is never so easily vanquished as when it is shunned, if only because he personally, who had dominated peoples, was ensnared in the bonds of Venus by a shameless woman.

CHAPTER 4

That the authority of divine law consists in the prince being subject to the justice of law

But why do I stoop to examples of human improvement, in spite of the fact that they are numerous, when everyone can be more appropriately propelled towards action through laws than through examples? One ought not, however, to hold the opinion that the prince himself is constantly released from law. Attend to the law which is imposed upon princes by the Greatest King who is an object of fear over all the earth and who takes away the breath of princes: 'When you have come to the land which the Lord your God will give you, and have possessed it and dwelled therein, you will say, "I will select a king over me, like all the nations that are around me"; you will select him king over you whom the Lord your God will choose from among one of your brethren. You cannot make a foreigner – someone who is not your brother – king over you. And when he has been selected, he should not multiply horses for himself, nor return the people to Egypt in

35

order that he may multiply the number of horses; for the Lord has said to you that you shall not henceforth return that way any more. He should not have many wives who will improperly influence his mind, nor should he have a large weight of silver and gold. And afterwards he will sit upon the throne of the kingdom and he will write for himself a copy of this law of Deuteronomy in a book, drawing from the exemplar of the priests of the tribe of Levi, and it will be with him and he shall read therein all the days of his life, that he may learn to fear the Lord his God, and to keep all His words and ceremonies which are prescribed by the law. His heart should not be lifted up haughtily above his brethren, nor should he incline in his direction to the right or to the left, in order that he and his children may reign a long time over Israel.'[8] Need one ask whether anyone whom this law constrains is limited by law? Certainly this is divine and cannot be dismissed with impunity. Each word of this text is thunder in the ears of the prince if he is wise. I keep silent about selection and its forms, which is required for the creation of the prince; my attention is turned for a brief period to that formula of living which is prescribed for him.

It is said that when someone is empowered who declares himself a brother of the whole people in matters of religious worship and in the feeling of charity, he should not multiply his horses, since the greatness of their number is a burden to subjects. To multiply horses is really to collect more than necessity requires, whether by reason of vain glory or because of another error. For 'too much' and 'too little', if one follows the Prince of the Peripatetics, signify the excess or diminution of legitimate quantities within particular genera of things.[9] Is it to be permitted, therefore, to multiply dogs or birds of prey or savage beasts or any monstrosities of nature you please, when horses, which are necessary for military purposes and useful in all aspects of life, are limited in number to a legitimate quantity? Certainly there is no mention made in the law of actors and mimes, clowns and prostitutes, pimps and similar prodigal men whom the prince ought rather to exterminate than to encourage; not only are all these abominations to be excluded from the court of the prince, but they are to be eliminated from the people of God.

The name 'horses' may be understood to include everything useful

---

[8] Deuteronomy 17:14–21.
[9] Cf. Aristotle, *Topics* 107a11–13, 113a3–7 and 123b27–30; and *Categories* 14a2–6.

for the household and all of its necessary supplies; a legitimate quantity of such things is that which is rationally demanded by necessity or utility, provided that the useful and the honourable are made equivalent, and that a civilised person always chooses what is honourable. For philosophers were long ago satisfied that no opinion is more pernicious than the opinion of those who separate the useful from the honourable; and the truest and more useful judgment is that the honourable and the useful may at all times be converted into one another. Secular histories report that, when it was observed that Dionysius, the tyrant of Sicily, surrounded his person with guards, Plato inquired: 'Have you committed so much evil that you need to have so many guards?' This is in no way fitting for the prince, who in doing his duty so wins the affection of all that every one of his subjects would expose his own head to imminent peril for him – just as nature urges the limbs to expose themselves for the relief of the head – and would sacrifice his own skin for the sake of the royal skin; and all that a man has he will give up for the life of the prince.

It is stated next that 'he should not return the people to Egypt in order that he may multiply the number of horses'. Indeed, all who are established in roles of authority are to take precautions with the greatest diligence in order that inferiors may not be corrupted by their example, nor by their abuse of things, nor by following the path of pride or luxury which returns the people to the darkness of confusion. For frequently it happens that subjects imitate the vices of superiors because the people strive to be in conformity with their magistrates, and everyone aspires to that which is perceived to be illustrious in others. The thoughts and words which the great Theodosius expresses are celebrated by that eminent versifier:

If that which one has decreed is commanded in common,
one ought first to order one's own subjection; then, greater
    observance of equity
by the people will occur, nor will they refuse, when they see for
    themselves
the author subjected to his own dictates. The world is arranged
after the example of the king, nor is an effect upon the judgments
of men a matter of powerfulness of edicts instead of the life of the
    ruler.
The changeable masses are always altered by the prince.[10]

[10] Claudian, *Panegyricus de iv consulatu Honorii*, 296–302.

37

The actual wealth of individuals is by no means comparable to the wealth of all. Any given person spends out of his own private coffers, but the ruler draws upon the public treasury or riches; if perhaps there should be a deficit, he has recourse to the wealth of individuals. It is necessary, however, that private persons be content with their own goods. Should these be diminished, he who at present aspires to the splendour of the powerful would blush bright red at his own sordid poverty. For from the decree of the Lacedaemonians, the parsimony of rulers in the use of public goods is ordered, while the common law nevertheless permits the use of their inheritance and those things that fall upon them by adornment of fortune.

CHAPTER 5

That the prince must be chaste and shun avarice

. . . It is stated next: 'Do not have a large weight of silver and gold.' For God forbids rulers to gather for themselves treasure of silver and gold, acquiring wealth by means of deceit, seeking abundance in the poverty of others, procuring affluence from rapine, and erecting their own individual happiness upon the ruin of the multitude. But someone may respond with reference to the great wealth of Solomon. This is granted, yet princes are not forbidden riches but only avarice. Were not gold and silver worthless at the time of Solomon? These would not have been worthless, however, if, there being a large weight of them which exceeded usefulness, a greedy king had hoarded them for himself. He could have buried them in the earth, that they would be more desirable for having been removed from human familiarity.

In Petronius, Trimalchio recites the tale of the craftsman who made glass vases of such strength that they would not shatter any more than gold or silver. When, therefore, such a vase of purest glass was fabricated – one only (it was supposed) worthy of Caesar – he went to Caesar with his present and was admitted. The beauty of the gift was lauded, the handiwork of the creator was commended, and the devotion of the giver was approved. In order that the admiration of the onlooker should be transformed into astonishment, and that he should procure for himself the greater appreciation of the emperor, the craftsman asked to get the vase back from the hand of Caesar, and he threw it down powerfully upon the floor with such force that not even the most solid and most stable material of bronze would have remained unharmed. Caesar was not so much astonished as horrified by this. Yet when it was picked up off the ground, it was not broken but dented, as if the material of bronze was adorned by the appearance of glass. Then, bringing his small hammer out of his breast pocket, he most suitably corrected the defect, and he repaired it with repeated blows just as if it were a dented bronze vase. When completed, he judged himself to possess Jupiter's heaven because he believed that he had earned himself the close friendship of Caesar and the admiration of all. But it happened differently. For Caesar inquired whether anyone else knew the circumstances surrounding this glass. When he answered negatively the emperor proclaimed that he should be quickly beheaded because, if this skill should become widely known, gold and silver would become as worthless as mud. Whether the tale was related truly and faithfully is uncertain, and different people hold different views regarding Caesar's action. While not prejudging the interpretations of those who have greater wisdom, I think that the devotion of an able craftsman was badly repaid, and that the prospects of the human race are ill-served when an outstanding skill is eradicated in order that the kindling of avarice, the nourishment of death, and the cause of contentions and battles – in sum, money and the materials out of which money is made – may be preserved in value, because without diligence men would be possessed of nothing, since without diligence there can be nothing which is of value. Thus,

Net worth is now valuable; the tax-bracket confers honours,
the tax-bracket confers friends; the poor are everywhere despised.[11]

More useful are those who strive to exterminate all bases of dispute and causes of enmity from their public affairs in order that the malicious effect may disappear with the abandonment of its cause;[12] of such a kind were the decrees of Lycurgus over the Lacedaemonians, and the lessons of Pythagoras of Samos (which was once in ancient Greece, but now is part of Italy) who is reported to have served the whole of Italy through the strength and virtue of his constitutions. If gold as well as silver became worthless, then virtue

[11] Ovid, *Fasti*, 1.217–218.
[12] Aristotle, *Metaphysics* 1014a.

and those things which nature (the best guide to living) commends as useful would alone be valuable. Accordingly, the pauper would not be despised, nor would only the wealthy receive honour as a monetary distinction, so long as everyone is valuable or worthless on the basis of his own personal endowments. Furthermore, some things have value in themselves, whereas some things are dignified by the opinions of others. Bread and victuals, which are composed of necessary nourishment and clothing, are everywhere on earth dictated by nature as valuable. All things are naturally favoured which delight the senses. What more need be said? Those things which are natural are not only uniform, but are also esteemed by all; those which follow from considered opinion are uncertain; and to the extent that some things arise from personal preference, so they will disappear by personal preference as well.

The ruler should therefore have no fear lest the medium for commercial exchange become extinct, because market relations are frequent even among those who are ignorant of money. I know that Solomon had such wisdom that he would never have been apprehensive lest gold and silver would be denounced by his posterity, whose natures would seem to be greedy and to hunger for the most part after nothing other than money. For this reason, according to the inspiration of wisdom, the preeminent king condemned this blight, so that the example of his contempt towards money would be an invitation to his posterity. Thus, while it is expedient for the king to be extremely wealthy, still he must count his wealth as the people's. He does not, therefore, truly own that which he possesses in the name of someone else, nor are the goods of the fisc, which are conceded to be public, his own private property. Nor is this a surprise, since he is not his own person but that of his subjects.

CHAPTER 6

That the ruler must have the law of God always before his mind and eyes, and he is to be proficient in letters, and he is to receive counsel from men of letters

'When he sits upon the throne of his kingdom, he will write for himself a copy of this law of Deuteronomy in a book.' See that the prince must not be ignorant of law and, although he takes pleasure in many privileges, he is not permitted to be ignorant of the laws of God on the pretext of the martial spirit. The law of Deuteronomy, that is, the second law, is therefore to be written in the book of his heart so that the first law, which is impressed upon the page, corresponds to the second, which is recognised by the mystical intellect. The first could be written on stone tablets; but the second was not imprinted, except upon the purer intelligence of mind. And the prince properly writes Deuteronomy in a book because he may thus reflect upon the law in his reason without the letter disappearing from before his eyes. And hence, the letter of the law is followed in such a fashion that there is no divergence at all from the purity of its spirit. For in fact the letter destroys, while the spirit confers life, and with the ruler rests the moderate interpretation of human law and equity in accordance with necessity and general circumstance.

'Taken', it is said, 'from the exemplar of the priests of the tribe of Levi'. Surely this is fitting. All censures of law are void if they do not bear the image of the divine law; and the ordinance (*constitutio*) of the prince is useless if it does not conform to ecclesiastical discipline. Nor did this escape the notice of the most Christian prince, who proclaimed that his laws were not to disdain imitation of the sacred canons. And not only should one aspire to be ruled by the examples of priests, but the prince is dispatched to the tribe of Levi in order to obtain its benefits. For the legitimate priests are thus to be heeded, so that the just man shall shut off his hearing to all reprobates and those who thrive at the expense of their opponents. But who are the priests of the tribe of Levi? They are those without an avaricious motive, without an ambitious impulse, without a disposition towards flesh and blood – those whom law has introduced into the Church. This refers not to the letter of the law, which mortifies, but to its spirit, which stimulates the qualities of sanctity of mind, cleanliness of body, sincerity of faith and charitableness of works. For just as the law of the shadow both regulated all affairs figuratively and expressed to the priests its preference for a single line of flesh and blood, so after the cessation of the shadow, when truth was disclosed and justice from heaven was seen, those who were commended by their meritorious lives and the scent of good opinion, and who were set apart for the work of ministry by the agreement of the faithful or the diligent prudence of prelates, were attached by the Spirit to the tribe of Levi and were consecrated as legitimate priests.

It is added: 'And it will be with him and he shall read it all the days of his life.' Note how diligent in guarding the law of God should be the prince, who is commanded to hold it, to read it and to reflect upon it always, just as the King of Kings – created from woman, created under law – carried out the whole justice of law, to which He was subject not by necessity, but by will because His will is law, and He meditated day and night on the Law of God. But perhaps someone will suppose that we ought not to imitate Him who embraced the faith of the poor rather than the glory of kings and who, assuming the form of a servant, did not seek a place on earth to lay His head and who confessed under interrogation by a magistrate that His kingdom is not of this world. To such an argument, we may respond with the examples of illustrious kings who are remembered in our blessings. From the strongholds of Israel proceed, therefore, David, Hezekiah and Josiah and others who believed the glory of their kingship to consist in this: that they and their subjects were to be fastened by the bonds of divine law if they were to seek God's glory. And lest these examples appear to be remote, and less follow from them because we seem to depart appreciably from their laws and tradition of conduct and religious worship and profession of faith (although their faith and ours are the same, with the exception that what they had expected in the future, we for the most part rejoice in and venerate in completed form, since the figures of the shadow have been tossed aside by that truth which arose from the earth and is revealed in the sight of the gentiles) – lest, I say, their examples be disparaged as somewhat foreign or profane, Christian princes can be instructed by our Constantine, Theodosius, Justinian and Leo and other most Christian princes. For in fact they gave particular effort in order that the most sacred laws, which bind the lives of all, should be known and upheld by all, and that no one was to be ignorant of them, except if either the cost of the error is compensated by some utility to the public or the legitimate sting of harshness is avoided by reason of pity for the aged or the infirmities of gender. Accordingly, their deeds are incitements to virtue; their words are so many lessons in moral matters. Ultimately their lives, in which vice was subdued and captured, have been constructed like triumphal arches consecrated to posterity: arches which list their magnificent virtues, proclaiming in everything the faithful acknowledgement that all these excellent acts were done not by our hands, but by the Lord's.

Of course, Constantine is distinguished by perpetual benediction for founding and endowing the Roman Church, not to speak of his other eminent deeds. It is clear who Justinian and Leo really were from the fact that they strove to sanctify the whole globe as a sort of temple of justice by cultivating the most sacred laws. And what is to be said of Theodosius, whom the others cherished as the exemplar of virtue, and who is venerated by God's Church not only as an emperor but as a high priest, on account of venerable religiosity and widely known justice, as well as his still unsurpassed patience and submissive humility towards priests? How patiently he who produced laws bore the sentence of the Milanese priest! And lest one imagine that the sentence was made by a soft presbyter and one who had commanded the applause of princes, the prince was suspended from the use of his regalia, excluded from church and was forced to discharge a solemn penance. But what subjected him to such a requirement? Only a will subjected to God's justice and obedient constantly to His law. And unless one has contempt for that which is written of rulers with metrical levity, one may perceive in a few words how he stood out in the sanctity of his character from a passage in Claudius Claudian's writings where he instructs his sons.

As for the rest, when I reflect upon the words of the previously set out law, each seems full of meaning to me and they are presented to the mind as though fertilised by the spirit of intelligence. 'He will therefore', it is stated, 'have the law with him', making provision lest, when it is necessary to have it, it be held against him towards his own damnation. For in fact 'the powerful will suffer powerful torments'.[13] And it is added: 'He must read it.' It indeed seems too little to have the law in one's purse, unless it is also faithfully protected

---

[13] Wisdom 6:7.

in one's soul. It is to be read, therefore, all the days of his life. As a result of this, it is clearly accepted that it is necessary for princes, who are commanded to reflect daily upon the text of the divine law, to be proficient in letters. And perhaps you do not commonly find that priests are commanded to read the law daily. Yet the prince is to read it each and every day of his life because the day that the law is not read is not a day of his life, but the day of his death. Of course, an illiterate would not be able to do this without difficulty. And thus, in a letter which I recall that the King of Romans transmitted to the King of Franks, who was exhorted to procure for his offspring instruction in the liberal disciplines, it was added elegantly to the rest that an illiterate king was like a crowned ass.

Yet if, by reason of a dispensation on account of the merit of preeminent virtue, a prince happens to be illiterate, then it is necessary that he receive the counsel of those who are literate, in order that his affairs proceed properly. Let him, therefore, stand beside the prophet Nathan and the priest Zadok and the faithful sons of the prophets who will not permit him to be diverted from the law of God, and when what is before his eyes is not manifested in his soul, the men of letters are to introduce it through speech into the opening of his ears. Accordingly, the mind of the prince is to read through the tongue of the priests, and anything illustrious he observes in their moral conduct he is to venerate as the law of God. For the life and speech of the priesthood is like a book of life set before the sight of the people. Perhaps this is what was in mind when it was commanded to receive the example of law from the priests of the tribe of Levi, since their proclamations should moderate the governmental power of the commissioned magistrates. Nor is he totally devoid of reading who, although he does not read himself, hears what is read by others of the faithful. But if he does neither one by what means will the dictates of a precept held in contempt be faithfully performed? For in fact the onset of wisdom is the coming together of all that is desirable. Was not Tholomeus of the belief that something was missing from the sum of his happiness up to the time when, receiving seventy interpreters, he shared the laws of the Lord with the Greeks, even though he himself was a gentile? For it does not matter whether the interpreters examined the matter in an enclosed room or whether they reached their conclusions in separation, so long as it is accepted that the king, solicitous after the inquiry into truth, had translated the laws of the Lord into Greek.

In the 'Attic Nights', I recall having read that, when Philip of Macedon's notable moral qualities were singled out, among other things his devotion to studies had coloured his conduct of war and exultation of victories, the liberality of his dining table, the refinement of his performance of duty, and whatever was said or done splendidly or courteously. And this, through which he was acknowledged as more excellent than others, he took pains to transmit, as the foundation of his bequest of worldly goods, to the only person he expected to be heir to his kingdom and promising future. For this reason, he was seen to write a letter to Aristotle expressing the hope that the Philosopher would instruct the recently born Alexander . . . I do not recall that Roman emperors or commanders were illiterate, so long as their republic prospered. And I do not know the precise way in which it happens that, by the languishing of the virtue of letters among princes, the hand of the military arm is impaired and government itself is virtually cut off at the root. Yet it is no surprise, since without wisdom no government is able to endure or exist. Socrates was judged by the Apollonian oracle to be the wisest person, and it was he who beyond dispute excelled incomparably over those who were called the seven sages not only in esteem for wisdom, but for virtue; he asserted that republics would be happy if, and only if, they were ruled by philosophers or if their leaders would aspire to study wisdom.

And (if you view the authority of Socrates with contempt), Wisdom states, 'Through me kings rule and makers of law discern the just; through me princes govern and the powerful discern justice; I love those who love me, and those who seek vigilantly after me will find me; riches and glory are with me, genuine wealth and justice; my fruit is better than gold and precious stones, my gems better than choicest silver; I walk the path of justice in the midst of the road of judgment, in order that those who love me may prosper and replenish their treasuries.'[14] Likewise, 'Counsel is mine and equity is mine, mine is prudence, mine is strength.'[15] And elsewhere, 'Receive discipline and not silver, learning rather than choice gold. For wisdom is better than all the most precious wealth gathered together, and all desirable

[14] Proverbs 8:15–21.   [15] Proverbs 8:14.

45

things cannot be compared to it.'[16] Although the gentiles believed that nothing was to be done without a sign from the gods, they still honoured one thing like a God of gods and ruler of all, namely, wisdom, for the reason that it surpasses all else. Accordingly, the ancient philosophers proposed that the gates of all temples should depict the image of wisdom and that these words whould be written:

I am born of Use, perpetuated by Memory;
the Greeks call me *Sophia*, you *Sapientia*.[17]

And likewise this: 'I hate foolish men and ignorant works and philosophical aphorisms.' And certainly it was elegantly devised that, although the ancients did not know the truth fully, still they struck upon it to some extent, inasmuch as they supposed wisdom to be the guide and ruler of all things which are done properly, since they accurately prided themselves on the fact that among all nations and peoples, from the beginning wisdom has held primacy – its own proper virtue trampling the necks of those who are most proud and most arrogant. Solomon even confesses that he loves it above his own welfare and all beautiful things, and that with it all good things were brought to him.

[16] Proverbs 8:10–11.
[17] Aulus Gellius, *Noctes Atticae*, 8.8.

CHAPTER 7

That the fear of God should be taught, and humility should exist, and this humility should be protected so that the authority of the prince is not diminished; and that some precepts are flexible, others inflexible

It is stated next: 'That he may learn to fear the Lord his God, and to keep all his words which are prescribed by law.' The law itself adds the reason for the observation of legal tenets: 'That he may learn', it states. For in fact a diligent reader is a disciple of the law, not a master; nor does he distort the law as a captive to his own discretion, but he accommodates his discretion to its meaning and integrity. But what does this disciple learn? He surely learns to fear the Lord his

God. Properly so because wisdom begets and fortifies government; and fearing the Lord stimulates wisdom. Whoever, therefore, does not start at the level of fear aspires in vain to the summit of legitimate rulership. Legitimate, I say, because it is written of certain rulers that, in so far as they are hurled down from their elevated position and are cast headlong into greater misery, 'they have become kings, and not by me; they have become princes and I was ignorant';[18] and elsewhere: 'The handlers of the law are unaware of wisdom.'[19] The prince is, therefore, to fear the Lord and he is to profess his servility to Him by an evident humility of mind and by the performance of pious works. For indeed a lord (*dominus*) is the lord of a servant. And so the prince serves the Lord provided that he faithfully serves his fellow servants, namely, his subjects. But it is to be acknowledged that the Lord is God, towards whom is to be exhibited no more fear by reason of majesty than love by reason of piety. He is also a Father and one to whom no creature can deny feelings of love because of the merits of His deeds. 'If I am Lord', it is said, 'where is my fear? If I am Father, where is my love?'[20] The words of the law are also to be safeguarded as one proceeds forward in the happy ascent from the first level of fear, like a sort of ladder of virtue. 'Love of Him', it is said, 'is guardianship of law,'[21] 'because all wisdom fears the Lord'.[22] Furthermore, 'Whoever fears God will do good, and whoever is holding fast to justice will apprehend it, and it will meet him like an honoured mother.'[23]

But what words are to be so diligently safeguarded? Above all they are the precepts of the law, so that by means of the prince strict obedience to law does not vanish from earth because he exempts neither his own hands nor the hands of his subjects. Yet there are certain precepts which have a perpetual necessity, ones which are lawful among all peoples and which cannot be broken at all with impunity. 'Before the law, under the law, under grace',[24] one law is binding upon all: 'What you would not have done to yourself, do not do to others'; and 'What you would have done to yourself, this do to others'. Now may the whitewashers of rulers proceed, now may they whisper or, if this is too little, publicly proclaim that the prince is not

---

[18] Hosea 8:4.
[19] Jeremiah 2:8.
[20] Malachi 1:6.
[21] Wisdom 6:19.
[22] Ecclesiasticus 19:18.
[23] Ecclesiasticus 15:1–2.
[24] St Augustine, *De doctrina Christiana*, 2.16.25.

subject to law, and that his will has the force of law not only in establishing legal right according to the form of equity, but in establishing anything whatsoever. If they wish and they dare, they may make the king, whom they remove from the bonds of law, an outlaw; yet I assert that kings must keep this law – protesting this loudly not only against their denials but to the world. 'For with that judgment', says He who neither deceives nor is deceived, 'by which you judge, you shall be judged'.[25] And certainly the most grave judgment is to be made against those who preside, in so far as their own good measure – in compressed, coagulated and overflowing form – will ultimately be poured down into their deepest recesses. Not only do I remove from their hands the power of directing the law, but I think that precepts and prohibitions to be maintained perpetually are by no means subject to their pleasure. And so, in the instance of those laws which are flexible, the ruler may be allowed some direction over their terms, yet still the integrity of the law must be conserved through the rational balancing between the honourable and the useful.

'They do not,' it is stated, 'lift up their heads haughtily above those of their brethren'. Since it is especially necessary, this rule is repeated frequently, because humility never seems sufficiently commended to princes and it is most difficult for one to ascend through the ranks of honour without engendering imprudence in the soul. 'God above all opposes the haughty and He gives grace to the humble.'[26] The provident ruler, therefore, prays that haughtiness will not enter his path, since those who do iniquitous works are injured by them, are expelled and are not able to hold their ground. Accordingly, he is not to be haughty above his brethren; but inasmuch as his brethren are to be remembered, he is to accord fraternal affection to all his subjects. And certainly prudence commends to princes the qualities of humility combined with discernment and charity because without these princes cannot subsist at all. Whoever, therefore, loves the eminence of his own rank should maintain with the greatest diligence the utmost humility of moral character. For those who retreat from the works of humility fall from the summit of their dignity because of their swollen weight. For it is perpetually maintained that 'whoever humbles himself will be exalted and, reciprocally, whoever exalts himself is pressed down'.[27] Haughtiness made Tarquin the last king

[25] Matthew 7:2.   [26] James 4:6 and I Peter 5:5.   [27] Luke 14:11.

of the Romans, and it substituted for him magistrates of greater indispensability because of their humility. When do you read that a haughty man reigned for any long period? History is well supplied, in fact, with examples of those who were injured by their haughtiness.

Yet one should not shun haughtiness to the degree that one falls into contempt, since just as much as exaltation is to be deflected, so is baseness. And also, in Roman Law there is the caution that those who pronounce judgment are to make themselves readily accessible for consultation, yet are not to expose themselves to contempt; and the directive is also added that those who preside over provinces in outlying districts should not allow provincials on to intimate terms because contempt for dignity is born of the equality of social intercourse. Therefore, the governor publicly venerates the majesty of the people in his private capacity and he also treats them according to their rank. This is made known in the lessons of the ancient philosophers themselves . . . I think that magistrates in general are to be persuaded of this: that in the dignity of their public splendour they are to remember their own personal condition, and thus, they are to attend to the circumstances of their own personal condition in such fashion that they do not disfigure the dignity of their public rank. Further, one preserves the integrity of the honours placed upon one in such a fashion that the dignity of others is not diminished; and thus, one is to control one's private dignity so that it does not create injury to the public power.

CHAPTER 8

Of the moderation of the prince's justice and mercy, which should be temperately mixed for the utility of the republic

What obtains for the prince ought to obtain for everyone: no one is to prefer his own affairs to the affairs of others. Yet truly the amount of that affection, with which subjects are to be embraced like brothers in the arms of charity, must be confined to the limits of moderation. And thus, for him to love his brothers, he must correct their errors in medical fashion; he must acknowledge the flesh and blood in them so that he may subject them to the words of the Spirit. It is above all the habit of physicians that when they are not able to cure an affliction with palliatives and gentle medicines, they employ harsher cures, as for example fire or iron. They would never use the harsher ones except when they have despaired in their desire to promote health gently. And thus, when mild power does not suffice for the ruler to cure the vices of inferiors, he properly administers intensely painful blows of punishment; pious cruelty rages against the evil, while the good are looked after in safety.

But who is so strong as to amputate a part of his body without pain? He grieves, therefore, when he is asked for the required punishment of the guilty, yet he executes it with a reluctant right hand. For indeed the prince has no left hand and in tormenting the parts of the body of which he is the head, he serves the law mournfully and with groans. Philip, when he heard that Phicias, a good fighter, felt alienated from him, because in his poverty he barely supported his three daughters and he was not aided by the king, was admonished by friends to be on guard for him. 'What', inquired Philip, 'if a part of my body had an illness, ought it to be cut off when it is possible to care for it?'[28] After being approached privately and in a friendly way, Phicias procured sufficient money to satisfy the necessities of his household difficulties, and also he had greater loyalty towards the king than he did before he took offence. Also Lucius asserts that 'a prince must be of a moral character of one of advanced years and should follow the counsel of those who are moderate, and perform the duties of the physician who cures disease sometimes by starvation of the overfed, sometimes by refreshment of the malnourished, and who sedates pain sometimes by cauterising tissue, sometimes by poultice'. Moreover, he is to be affable in speech, generous in support, and is to preserve entirely the dignity of his authority in matters of moral character. For indeed good speech and a gracious tongue result in a reputation for benevolence. Goodwill will extract the most faithful and most constant love even from the obdurate and that which has been created will be fostered and solidified. And subjects owe reverence to men of moral dignity.

Trajan, the best among the gentile emperors, responded eminently to the arguments of his friends that he was too intimate with everyone and went beyond what was decent for emperors. For he wished to be

---

[28] Frontinus, *Strategemata*, 4.17.

an emperor to private persons of such a kind as he had wanted the emperors to be when he was a private person. And it is related that when Pliny the Younger, who at the time was appointed among other judges as persecutor of the Church, so advised him, Trajan withdrew the sword of persecution from the slaying of martyrs, having tempered his edicts. And perhaps he would have dealt with the faithful more mercifully, except that the laws and examples of his predecessors and the prudence (as it was supposed) of his counsellors and the authority of his judges had urged him to annihilate a sect which the public believed to be superstitious and inimical to true religion. Although I do not commend totally the justice of a man who was ignorant of Christ, still I extenuate the guilt of him who had departed from the influence of others and had indulged his own pious instinct towards kindness and compassion; by nature he was merciful towards everyone, yet tough with those few whom it was wrong to spare. I submit that in the course of his entire imperial reign only one of his nobles or senators of the city was punished, although it might have been discovered that many more had transgressed seriously against him. Moreover, Trajan was unaware of that senator who was punished. For he had said that one is insane who, if he has bleary eyes, chooses rather to gouge them out than to cure them. He had asserted that the fingernails, if they are too sharp, are to be cut, not torn off. For if the cithern player and other minstrels manage by great diligence to curb the fault of a wayward string and restore it to harmony with the others, producing the sweetest consonance of dissidences not by breaking the strings but by stretching or relaxing them proportionally, then how much more should care be taken by princes to be moderate – at one time by the vigour of justice, at another by the forgiveness of mercy – so that subjects are made to be of a single mind as in a household and the works of peace and charity create one perfect and great harmony out of pursuits which appear discordant.

But this is certain: that it is safer to relax strings than to stretch them too tensely. For of course the tension of relaxed strings may be regained by the skill of the craftsman and they should regain their pleasing sounds; but those which are once broken no craftsman may repair. Indeed, if a sound is required which they do not have, then they are stretched in vain and frequently soon come to nothing rather than to that excess which was required. As the moralist has it:

> The prince is reluctant to punish, quick to reward,
> and is saddened whenever he is thought to be fierce.[29]

For justice is one matter, piety is another affair, yet both are so necessary to the prince that anyone without them claiming not only princely power but even magistracy ridicules himself to no avail, and yet others are also provoked to laughter, contempt and hatred towards him. 'Compassion and truth', it is stated, 'should never desert you, bind them about your neck, and write them upon the tablet of your heart, and you will find favour and respect in the heart of God and men'.[30] For indeed compassion is owed favour, justice is owed respect. Above all the favour and love of subjects, which is produced by divine favour, is the best instrument of all governance. And yet love without respect is not advantageous because the people will retreat into illegalities once the stimulus of justice ceases. The prince must, therefore, perpetually meditate on wisdom, and on the basis of it he must perform justice, although the law of mercy is always to be upon his tongue; and this mercy will temper the vigour of justice, although his tongue will pronounce just judgment. For truly his office translates justice into judgment, which is necessary to him inasmuch as he is not permitted to be free of his duties if he has not also divested himself of the honour set upon him. For indeed the honour of the king esteems justice and restricts the faults of wrongdoers with tranquil moderation of mind.

A book about the moderation of magistrates, which is entitled *Archigramaton*, is reported to have been written by Plutarch. He is said to have instructed through word and example the magistrates of his own city in the practice of patience and justice. Also he had a slave, a worthless and insolent man but outstandingly erudite in the liberal disciplines and well experienced in philosophical disputation. It happened that Plutarch had ordered that his tunic was to be removed and he was to be beaten for some offence (I know not what). The blows of the whip had already harshly begun when, still denying his guilt, he said that he had not done evil, he had not committed a crime, and he reproached Plutarch that his many services did not merit a flogging. In the end, when he made no headway, he began to cry out and in the midst of the flogging struck out, not lamenting and

---

[29] Ovid, *Epistolae ex Ponto*, 1.2.123–124.
[30] Proverbs 3:3–4.

moaning and wailing but in solemn and rebuking words: Plutarch was not conducting himself in the fashion appropriate to a philosopher; it is shameful to be angry, particularly when he had frequently argued against bad temper and had written a most honourable book on patience. He added that it was disgraceful that he had impugned his teaching by his conduct because, through a lapse of intellectual integrity in which he let loose and flew into a rage, he had beaten an innocent person with many blows. To this Plutarch slowly and quietly and with the greatest seriousness replied: 'Does it seem that your flogging is because of anger? Is it a result of my anger if you receive from me what is owed? Whether from my expression or my voice or my colour or even from my words, do you discern that anger has corrupted or seized me? It is my opinion that my eyes are not wild nor my face upset, nor am I shouting frightfully, nor am I beginning to erupt with frothing and redness, nor do I speak scandalously or obscenely, nor finally do I quiver all over with rage or gesture wildly. All these, of course, if you are unaware, are customary signs of anger.' And then, turning to the one who was beating, he said: 'During the time that he and I dispute, you do your work; and without my wrathfulness, beat out his slavish insolence, and teach him to regret his iniquity rather than to quarrel.' Thus speaks Plutarch who bequeathed some little erudition to all who are in the seat of rulership.

<hr style="border-top: 3px double;" />

CHAPTER 9

*What it is to stray to the right or
to the left, which is forbidden to the prince*

It is stated next: 'He should not incline in his direction to the right or to the left.' To stray to the right is to insist vehemently upon the virtues themselves. To stray to the left is to exceed the mean in the works of virtue, which consists in the mean. Truly all vehemence is inimical to salvation, and all excess is in error; an excess of goodness and of habitually good deeds is very evil. The moralist says:

The wise man acquires a reputation for folly, the equitable for
    iniquity, if he strives for virtue itself beyond what is sufficient.[31]

[31] Horace, *Epistolae*, 1.6.15–16.

53

And the philosopher says: Beware that which is excessive because if one abandons this cautious moderation itself, to that extent does one withdraw incautiously from the path of virtue. Solomon also says: 'Refuse to be excessively just.'[32] What, therefore, is advanced by excess, if the queen of the virtues, justice, perishes in its excessiveness? Also, elsewhere it is stated: An excess of humility is pride in its greatest measure. To stray to the left is to stray or to deviate from the path of virtue towards the precipice of vice. In just this fashion, he is diverted to the left who is excessively inclined towards punishing the faults of subjects; and he is turned along a course to the right who is excessively indulgent out of mercifulness towards evildoers. In addition, both routes are off the path; but that which veers to the left is more pernicious.

[32] Ecclesiastes 7.16.

CHAPTER 10

What utility princes may acquire from the cultivation of justice

But where is the utility in such observation of statute? It is above all furnished at once by the words of the prophet. For it is asserted that 'he and his children may reign for a long time over Israel!' Observe that the reward for such great troubles is found in the future, in so far as the paternal kingdom will be preserved in the sons for a long time. For indeed the virtue of the parents will extend the succession of the sons and the fortune of successors will be shortened by the iniquity of their forebears. For the Holy Spirit is reliable testimony to the fact that 'the unjust will be destroyed all together and the descendants of the impious will be slain. Yet the salvation of the just is from God, who is their strength in times of tribulation'.[33] But since the eternity of the whole of time – however great it is – is extinguished by the minutest moments, and within the whole nothing except a very brief moment subsists, what can be 'long' within it when all these, if they were gathered into one, would not equal the place of a certain point

[33] Psalms 37:38–39.

compared with true eternity because there is nothing in the finite world comparable to infinity?[34] Surely there is proportion – although small, nevertheless some – between the centre and the periphery of circumference, as many agree; there is none between eternity and time. What, therefore, is 'long' in that whole which is brief? Or what temporal happiness will seem durable to the soul, if one's faithful and perpetual soul is deprived of a far greater expanse of time?

But on this matter I think – speaking without prejudice to the judgments of the more expert – that 'reign for a long time' refers to the lifetime of the unfailing soul which will be crowned with the glory of eternal happiness as reward for a well-administered kingdom. For since it is certain that God will reward the works of individuals and of everyone in abundant compassion and plentiful justice, who is to be looked upon in a brighter light: those who perform justice in all matters or those who drag down everyone with themselves into death? Just as, therefore, 'the powerful will suffer powerful torments', so they will delight in the rewards of justice if they exercise powers correctly; and they will possess greater glory in the afterlife compared to their subjects in so far as in their great freedom to do harm they surpass the virtue of subjects. 'One is able', it is written, 'to transgress, and does not transgress; to do evil and does not do it; thus are his good deeds founded upon the Lord.'[35] For indeed princes are reputed for justice even when they refrain from injury; and their faculty for harm is the very substance of their merit. To refuse evil is a great thing in them, even if they do no great goodness, provided that they still do not permit their subjects to indulge in evil. Is it not a great thing that the happiness they seem to have is promised to them perpetually if they behave properly? Certain people say that it is impossible both to flourish in this world and to rejoice in eternity with Christ; and surely this judgment is true, if flourishing in the world includes the enticements of vice. Nevertheless, kings can both flourish and abound with the most sweet worldly things and yet can pick the most useful fruits of eternity. Besides, what is more magnificent than if princes were transported from riches to riches, from delights to delights, from glory to glory, from things temporal to things eternal?

[34] Cf. St Augustine, *Confessio*, 11 and Boethius, *De consolatione philosophiae*, 2, pros. 7 and 4, pros. 6.
[35] Ecclesiasticus 31:10–11.

CHAPTER I I

What are the other rewards of princes

Yet I do not exclude what is prima facie promised literally: that both
the father is promised a lengthy reign and his succession is held out to
his sons who are his successors in eternal happiness just as in the
temporal kingdom. For I know that the law was addressing a carnal
people who still had a heart of stone, who were mentally (if not
physically) uncircumcised, who were for the most part ignorant of
eternal life, and who exulted if the goods of the earth were given or
promised for their sustenance. Accordingly, to those of carnal
wisdom was given a carnal promise, and a long duration of time was
promised to those who had not yet conceived of the hope of eternal
happiness; and the succession of their sons to the temporal kingdom
was held out to those who had not yet contemplated eternity. The
father was, therefore, to be succeeded temporally by the son, if the
justice of the father was copied. 'Take away impiety from the
presence of the king', Solomon says, 'and his throne will be founded
upon justice.'[36] For if impiety departs from his presence, that is, from
his will, the works of the entire kingdom are directed by the sceptre of
equity and the practice of justice. He further says: 'The king who sits
on the judgment seat disperses all evil with his gaze.'[37] Look at how
princes delight in those privileges through which (to make no mention
of eternal happiness) the glory of the kingdom is perpetuated by their
body and blood. The Lord will pride Himself that He has
encountered a man after His own heart and, when He has lifted him
up rapidly to the apex within the kingdom, He will offer the kingdom
to him perpetually through the succession of the line of his sons. 'Of
the fruit of your body', it is said, 'will I place upon your throne'; and:
'If your sons will keep my commandments and my testimony that I
shall teach them through myself or my vicars, both they and their sons
will sit upon your throne';[38] and 'I will make his seed to endure forever
and his throne to last as the days of heaven. If his sons forsake my law
and do not walk in my judgments, if they profane my justice and do
not keep my commandments, then will I visit their transgressors with
the rod',[39] in the sense that the kingdom is translated from family to

[36] Proverbs 25:5.   [37] Proverbs 20:8.
[38] Psalms 132:11-12.   [39] Psalms 89.29-32.

56

family and those heirs to his seed who seem to be followers of the flesh are eradicated; the succession will be transferred to those who are ascertained to be the inheritors of faith and justice. And for that reason, the truth of the promise is abiding, and that which proceeds from the mouth of the Most High is judged permanent because the faithful seed of just kings keeps up the succession for eternity. I even think that this perpetuation also obtains quite literally, so that sons succeed parents if they are faithful representatives of the commandments of the Lord (which is to say nothing at present about Christ who, created of the seed of David according to the flesh, is King of kings and Lord of lords). This is so to the degree that, although everything might be disposed properly and there would seem to be no concerns or duties at all for a governor, it is generally accepted that those who at one time receive a prince into their midst will not be without a successor of his seed. And this is evident from the examples in the histories . . .

But because men desire nothing more than to have their sons succeed them in their goods – inasmuch as those who foresee mortality as their own proper condition perpetuate their lives by means of the progeny of their flesh – this is promised to princes. For this reason it is demanded that they make the greatest effort to cultivate justice. It will happen that those who are unconcerned about themselves are constantly anxious about the circumstances of their sons. In this regard, charity of an inferior sort is observed because the love which the father owes principally to country and parents is poured out from father to son, until the father's affection for his offspring drains completely the storehouse of his heart. Sons in return respond to their parents in a wholly deserving way, sharing that love with their own offspring which is received from their parents. Yet the good order of charity demands a different arrangement, which is prudently expressed by the most learned of the poets. For indeed upon the fall of Troy the aged Anchises is set upon the shoulder of his pious son, the right hand of Ascanius is given to the parent Aeneas, and the wife Creusa clings to her husband, following the footprints of those coming before her by reason of the infirmity of women. All his compatriots were given a leader, a man of arms and illustrious piety. For another leader would have been ineffective, since kingdoms are not able to be acquired nor justice to be preserved without those who are virile. At the present time, everyone is concerned about one thing:

to distinguish their children, regardless of the sort they are, by acquiring riches and honours rather than virtue. For it is disregarded that burdens are imposed by the republic.

After the expulsion of Tarquin the Proud, who was the very last to reign in the city, when the first consul, Brutus, had found his children deliberating about recalling the kings to the city, he had them dragged before the forum and in the middle of the assembly ordered a cane beating followed by decapitation so that he would be seen by the entire public to have adopted the role of parent to the people instead of to his own children. Of course even though the killing of relatives makes me shudder, it is not possible not to approve of the faithful consul who preferred to jeopardise the welfare of his own children instead of the welfare of the people. Whether he did the right thing, wise men may judge. For I realise that this field lies broadly open to orators, and that the rhetoricians have toiled frequently over both sides of the argument, inasmuch as they labour for the absolution of the killing of blood relations by reason of faith and attempt to extinguish the merit of faith with the impiety of killing relatives. If you urge me towards an opinion on the matter, I offer the response that I find Gaius Dolabella had been offered by the Areopagites in a Smyrnian case. When he held the imperial proconsulship of the province of Asia, a Smyrnian woman was brought in confessing that she had slain her husband and son by secretly giving them poison because they had insidiously and vilely slain her son from another marriage – a fine, exceptional and most innocent youth – and claiming herself to be permitted by the indulgence of the laws and to be ignorant of legal right and to be avenging so atrocious an injury against herself and her family and the whole of her republic. The matter of legal right was external to the case because there was agreement regarding the facts and there was question about the law (*iure*). When, therefore, Dolabella handed over the matter to the council, there was none who, in a case that was considered to be ambiguous, dared either to acquit manifest poisoning and the murder of blood relations or to condemn vengeance which succeeded against the impious and murderers. Consequently, the matter was referred to the members of the Athenian Areopagus, as the more venerable and more experienced judges. However, upon examination of the case, they ordered the return of the plaintiffs and the woman in a hundred years. This, therefore, was neither an absolution of the poisoning, because it is not permitted by law, nor a punishment of the offending woman, whose pardon could be indulged, according to the judgment of many. This may be found in the ninth book of Valerius Maximus' 'Memorable Words and Deeds'.

Certainly one might easily agree that both Brutus and the woman transgressed because

> the medicine exceeded the mean, and was following too nearly
> the direction of the illness[40]

and, although the crimes were great, it would be more admirable to have punished them without the punishment having been a crime. And thus, even the laudatory poet cites Brutus as evidence of infelicity; for Virgil says in the sixth book.

> The offspring stirring up new wars, the
> father by punishing them for the glory of liberty is called
> unfortunate, no matter how inferiors extol his deeds.[41]

Yet the following verse excuses this unfortunate murder and demonstrates the empty glory of vanity, saying: 'Love of country conquers him and a great passion for praise.'[42] But it ought not to be feared in vain that some will henceforth imitate Brutus, preferring the people to one's children, since even the vices of children are preferred to the welfare of the republic, although the welfare of the people ought certainly to go before the children of everyone. In the Book of Kings it is shown that when a vow was made to a day of fasting (involving punishment of those who partook of food before night-time contrary to the vow) and Saul's son Jonathan sampled honey that had touched his sceptre, that is, his spear, the king spared his son in violation of the vow of religion, impelled by paternal feeling; this transgression is seen to have brought to ruin the people of Israel that day. Also Eli, although it may be read of him that he was holy, spared the vices of his sons, and was ruined when his throne was overturned and he broke his neck and died. To remain silent about others, I ask how much was the public welfare of men loved and desired by 'Him who did not spare His own Son, but delivered Him up for us all',[43] to the extent that He might in freedom and innocence sustain the bondage and beating and crucifixion and most dishonourable death

---

[40] Lucan, *Pharsalia*, 2.142–143.　　[41] Virgil, *Aeneid*, 6.820–823.
[42] *Ibid.*, 6.824.　　[43] Romans 8:32.

which we had earned and to which we were condemned? Scrutinise the histories of kings, you will find that a king was sought from God for the reason that he might lead in the sight of the people and might fight their wars and might sustain the burdens of the whole people in the manner of the gentiles. Still he was not necessary, except that Israel was a transgressor in the manner of the gentiles, in so far as it did not seem to be content with God for its king. For if the people of Israel had lived according to justice, if they had walked faithfully in the commandments of the Lord, God would have freely humiliated their enemies and would have laid His hand upon their afflictions, so that by the routine aid of God one man would have overtaken a thousand and two thousand would flee before two.

I recall that my host at Placentia, a man who possessed the most noble blood as well as a wordly prudence founded in the fear of God, had said that it was famous from the recurrent experiences of the Italian cities that so long as they cherished peace and cultivated justice and refrained from perjury, they enjoyed fully and rejoiced in such liberty and peace that there was nothing at all, or very little, which disturbed their calm. Yet when they fell into fraudulence and were divided in themselves by the unstable paths of injustice, immediately the Lord called upon them either the arrogance of the Romans or the furore of the Germans or some other punishment, and His hand remained extended until the time when they withdrew themselves from their iniquity by means of penitence; by this remedy alone do all disturbances in their vicinity cease. He had also added that the merits of the people cancel all princely regimes or they are administered with the greatest mildness because, on the contrary, it is certain that God permits a hypocrite to reign on account of the sins of the people, and it is impossible that a king long rejoices who exults in the humiliation of the people and in his own too haughty summit. This was said by my host at Placentia; and, as I believe, it is consistent with faith.

Such things may also be found in the writings of the past. For when Helius had performed the prefecture of Rome in splendid fashion, he was chosen emperor from among the senators; when the Senate begged that his son Caesar be pronounced 'Augustus', he stated: 'It should be sufficient that I myself have ruled although not deserving it. But rulership should not be by blood, but by merit; and he reigns uselessly who is born king without meriting it. And without doubt he has violated parental feeling who destroys his children with an overwhelming load that cannot be borne. This is surely to suffocate children, not to improve them. They are first to be raised with and instructed in the virtues; and, when they are proficient in them, so that they are demonstrated to excel in virtues those whom they must excel in honours, they ascend by invitation and they never turn aside their pledge to their citizens. For who doubts that those are preferable who are glorified by the privilege of a sort of natural integrity, who have been summoned to virtue by the renown of their ancestors, and who on the same grounds make others confident of the benefits of their future goodness?' These words he said. And of course he expresses elegantly the privileges of the prince, whose sons indubitably succeed him on the basis of God's ancient gift, unless iniquity subverts their rulership.

CHAPTER 12

By what cause rulership and kingdoms are transferred

It is well known from Wisdom that 'kingdoms will be transferred from dynasty to dynasty on account of injustice and injury and abusiveness and diverse forms of deceit'.[44] Do you not see how rapidly was subverted the throne of the first king of the people of God? Saul and Jonathan, as well as the other sons, were destroyed in the mountains as their sins demanded in order that he who was called from tending ewes in lamb might be confirmed in their throne. Skim through the course of all the histories and you will see briefly the succession of kings and the Lord's cutting them off like the cutting of the warp in a loom. And the more glorious the kings are, the sooner their seed is stamped out if they rise up against God. 'There is no wisdom, there is no prudence, there is no counsel opposed to the Lord',[45] certainly there is no courage. If He arises, if He gives chase, one resorts in vain to the correcting favour of the sacraments and to the protection of walls. Who was greater in Greece than Alexander? And yet one may read that he was succeeded not by his own flesh, but by the son of a dancing girl. Who is unaware of the line of the house of Caesar? Few

[44] Ecclesiasticus 10:8.   [45] Proverbs 21:30.

61

or none of them bequeathed their inheritance to their sons, and, in brief, after their various perils and murders of many family members, all were eradicated as if in an instant by diverse and usually ignominious deaths and, descending into hell, they had as their successors either enemies or base men.

I ask: what so rapidly subverts and transforms powerful kingdoms? Certainly the indignation of God will be provoked by multiple injustices against Him. Injustice is (as the Stoics agree) a mental disposition (*mentis habitus*) which removes equity from the realm of morals. For indeed the soul is proclaimed to be deprived of justice by reason of the privative suffix. Moreover, justice consists chiefly in this: do not do harm and prevent the doing of harm out of a duty to humanity. When you do harm, you assent to injury. When you do not impede the doing of harm, you are a servant of injustice. Furthermore, abusiveness is when mental passion is accompanied by actions which result in manifest harm to others. And it serves iniquity because it insolently rises up against one to whom reverence is owed by reason of status, office or natural bond. Finally, deceit is (as Aquilius defines it) when one thing is done and another is pretended; whenever it is performed with the intention of doing harm it is always bad. Deceit differs in many ways from abusiveness, which is haughty and palpable, whereas deceit does harm fraudulently and virtually by means of a trap.

These vices are the ones which, when they occur, subvert all power everywhere because the glory of princes is perpetuated by their contraries. For indeed deceit encompasses the mark of weakness represented by timidity, and is most opposed to courage. Prudence curbs abusiveness, repeating constantly: 'Why are dust and ashes arrogant towards dust and ashes?' Temperance does not admit of injury, refusing to submit others to that which it would itself refuse to suffer at the hands of another. And justice excludes injustice, at all times doing to others those acts which it wishes done by others to itself. These are the four virtues which the philosophers have called 'cardinal' because they are believed to flow like the main channels from the primary fount of honour and to propagate from themselves all the streams of goodness. Perhaps these are the four rivers which depart from God's paradise of delights, so that they irrigate all the earth, which in its own time will bear desirable fruits . . . I believe that neither leaders nor powerful men are excepted from this because the glory of kings is to be transferred if they are found to be unjust, injurious, abusive or deceitful, since 'the mouth of the Lord has spoken it'[46] . . . For the prince is master of all and is seen to be the author of all because, when he can correct all, he is properly a participant in that which he refuses to amend. For since he is the public power (as we said previously), he draws strength from all and, lest it wane in him, he must procure the safety of all the members. Moreover, as many offices as exist in the administration of the princely government, such are the number of members of the prince's body. Hence, provided that each individual office is conserved in the integrity of virtue, and in a high degree of esteem, the health and fitness of these royal members is in a way procured. Yet when by negligence or dissimulation on the part of the ruler, virtue and renown are lost from these offices, it is as if illness and blemishes have attacked his own members. Nor does the head subsist safely for long when weakness pervades the members.

[46] Isaiah 1.20.

BOOK V

Prologue

Those empowered by anointment are not inclined to survey their realms without delay, nor is it easy to traverse the length and breadth of the provinces in a short period. Yet this great deed is summarily toasted on occasion by the wise, and by no means may this toast be explained completely by the excessive pressures of stylistic expression. For what in human affairs is greater than princely government, whose duties in a certain manner encircle, complete and penetrate everything and which bears the troubles of the whole republic with its immovable strength? And as a result, the prince has scrutiny over his territory and he avoids delay in surveying it not only on account of his rank but also because of the composure with which the frivolities of all are to be scrutinised by the head of the republic. We will therefore concentrate upon the inspection of his body with moderate brevity, and we will moreover heed what Plutarch proposes about this matter. Subtracting the superstitions of the gentiles, there is validity in the judgments, in the excellent words and the sacred morals of so great a ruler as can readily be perceived in the commands of Trajan. Yet if anyone disputes Trajan's faith or morals, these could be ascribed to the times rather than to the man. If Virgil was permitted to acquire the gold of wisdom from the clay of Ennius, in what way is it hateful for us to share in our own learning from what is written by the gentiles? Abandoning such objections to the ash heap, let us proceed.

CHAPTER I

Plutarch's letter instructing Trajan

There exists Plutarch's letter instructing Trajan, which describes the idea of a certain sort of political constitution. It is said to be thus: 'Plutarch sends greetings to Trajan. I know that in your moderation you do not desire rulership, which yet it is always merited by devotion to good morals. You are of course judged so much the worthier in so far as you are seen to be more removed from the accusation of ambition. I accordingly congratulate your virtue and my fortune, if you yet administer carefully that which you properly merit. I do not doubt that you are in other respects subject to danger, and that I am subject to the angry tongues of detractors, since not only does Rome not suffer the weaknesses of emperors, but also common gossip is accustomed to refer the transgressions of disciples back to their teachers. Hence, Seneca was slandered by the tongues of his detractors for the offences of Nero, the recklessness of Quintilian's young charges was referred back to him, and Socrates was accused of being too indulgent towards his pupils. Yet you administer everything most correctly if you do not desist from knowing yourself. If you first of all compose yourself, if you dispose all your affairs towards virtue, everything proceeds properly for you. I have written out for you the strengths of the political consitution of our forebears through which you will have Plutarch as an advisor in living if you comply with it. Otherwise, I invoke the present letter as witness that you do not advance the advice of Plutarch in the destruction of the empire.'

CHAPTER 2

According to Plutarch, what a republic is and what place is held in it by the soul of the members

The parts of this political constitution follow thereafter in a pamphlet entitled 'The Instruction of Trajan', which I have sought to incorporate partially into the present treatise, yet in such a way as to reproduce the outlines of its meaning rather than its actual words. It is first of all required that the prince evaluate himself entirely and direct himself diligently to the whole body of the republic, whose condition he enjoys. For a republic is, just as Plutarch declares, a sort of body which is animated by the grant of divine reward and which is driven by the command of the highest equity and ruled by a sort of rational management. By all means, that which institutes and moulds the practice of religion in us and which transmits the worship of God (not the 'gods' of which Plutarch speaks) acquires the position of the soul in the body of the republic. Indeed, those who direct the practice of religion ought to be esteemed and venerated like the soul in the body. For who disputes that the sanctified ministers of God are his vicars? Besides, just as the soul has rulership of the whole body so those who are called prefects of religion direct the whole body. Augustus Caesar himself was constantly subject to the sacred pontiffs until the time when he created himself a Vestal pontiff and shortly thereafter was transformed into a living god, in order that he would be subject to no one.

The position of the head in the republic is occupied, however, by a prince subject only to God and to those who act in His place on earth, inasmuch as in the human body the head is stimulated and ruled by the soul. The place of the heart is occupied by the senate, from which proceeds the beginning of good and bad works. The duties of the ears, eyes and mouth are claimed by the judges and governors of provinces. The hands coincide with officials and soldiers. Those who always assist the prince are comparable to the flanks. Treasurers and record keepers (I speak not of those who supervise prisoners, but of the counts of the Exchequer) resemble the shape of the stomach and intestines; these, if they accumulate with great avidity and tenaciously preserve their accumulation, engender innumerable and incurable diseases so that their infection threatens to ruin the whole body. Furthermore, the feet coincide with peasants perpetually bound to the soil, for whom it is all the more necessary that the head take precautions, in that they more often meet with accidents while they walk on the earth in bodily subservience; and those who erect, sustain and move forward the mass of the whole body are justly owed shelter and support. Remove from the fittest body the aid of the feet; it does not proceed under its own power, but either crawls shamefully, uselessly and offensively on its hands or else is moved with the assistance of brute animals.

In this manner, Plutarch asserts much more about the qualities of the body, which he develops diligently throughout the tract towards the end of teaching the republic and instructing magistrates. One who follows everything in the text syllable-by-syllable is a servile interpreter who aims to express the appearance rather than the essence of an author. And because much in him regarding the worship and praise of gods, which he had thought to press upon the religious prince, is examined according to superstition, let us disregard that which pertains to the practice of idolatry. Instead, we may touch briefly upon the ideas of the man when he instructed the prince and officials of the republic in the practice of justice.

CHAPTER 3

What is principally directed by Plutarch's plan . . .

In total, therefore, there are four precepts he endeavours to inculcate within the rulers of the republic: reverence for God, self-discipline, education of officials and those in power, and love for and protection of subjects. He thus asserts in the first place that God is to be honoured; then each person is to cultivate himself to the extent that, according to what the Apostle observes (although he was not familiar with the Apostle), each one will possess the vessel of his own body 'in holiness and honour';[1] afterwards the education of the whole household is redolent of the education of its head; and in the end the community of subjects is exalted by the advantage and security of the head itself. Also, the strategies and stratagems of great men are used, which, if they were inserted one by one, would be tedious for the reader and might, in part, even undercut the sincerity of our faith. Certainly, because the holy fathers and the laws of princes seem to adhere to the same path as Plutarch – yet in the absence of his faithlessness – we may touch upon his teachings in succinct and catholic speech, adding sections of his stratagems. Once again, his starting point is from reverence for the gods, whereas ours is from God who is to be loved by all men without distinction and is to be venerated with all their heart, all their soul and all their strength . . .

[1] 1 Thessalonians 4:4.

CHAPTER 6

Of the prince who is the head of the republic, and his election, and privileges, and the rewards of virtue and sin; and that blessed Job should be imitated; and of the virtues of blessed Job

It follows that in imitation of Plutarch's path, we must scrutinise the members of the republic. It is said that the prince occupies the place of the head, and is regulated solely by the judgment of his own mind. And so, as was said already, divine disposition places him on top of the republic and prefers him over others, at one time on the basis of the mystery of His secret providence, at another time just as His priests have determined, while at still another time he is put in charge when the wishes of the whole people concur. And for this reason, it may be read in the Old Testament how Moses, when ordaining him who should preside over the people, had assembled the whole synagogue in order that the ruler might be selected while standing before the people, so that there would remain neither any grounds for later retraction nor any lingering doubts. It may be read in the Book of Kings how the future king, Saul, appearing in front of the people, had been lifted up over the community of the people upon their shoulders. For what reason, I ask, unless because he who ought to preside over others must extend his heart and head almost as if he were able to embrace the whole breadth of the people in the arms of good works and to protect them – indeed, just as if he were more learned, more holy, more circumspect, and more distinguished in all the virtues? For the Lord said to Moses: 'Take Joshua, son of Nun, a man who has the spirit of God in him, and lay your hands on him, and set him before Eleazar the priest, and give him commandments in the presence of the whole synagogue, and give instructions about him publicly, and you will set your distinction upon him in order that the children of Israel will listen to him.'[2] Evidently, we are listening to the ordination of a prince of the people, so clearly described that it almost does not need exposition. Yet if you question its clarity, I will explain it to you on the authority of the Lord, adding the significance of the vestments and some aspects of the sacraments, when enjoined at the proper

[2] Numbers 27:18–20.

place and time. Yet plainly there was never popular acclamation here, never the rationale of blood ties, never was there contemplation of nearby relatives. Upon the death of Zelophehad, his children claimed their paternal inheritance before Moses. God Himself testifies that their petition was just; for in fact relatives are to be left the hereditary lands and estates and as many public functions as possible. Still, governance of the people is handed over to him whom God has elected, namely, such a man who has in him the Spirit of God and in whose sight are the commandments of God, one who is well known to and familiar with Moses, that is, in whom there is the distinction and knowledge of the law, in order that the children of Israel might listen to him.

Nevertheless, it is not permitted to withdraw in preference to new men from the bloodline of princes who by divine promise and genealogical right are owed the privilege of the succession of their offspring, if (as was previously written) they have walked in the justice of the Lord. Moreover, if they have for a short time deserted the path, they should not immediately be cast entirely aside, but should be admonished patiently about injustice, until finally it becomes conspicuous that they are firm in their evil. For Rehoboam was not immediately removed from his father's throne for the reason that, disregarding the counsel of older and better men, he departed from the path of Solomon, seeking to impose an insupportable burden upon the shoulders of the children of Israel. But his kingdom was split with the departure of the ten tribes behind Jeroboam, the servant of Solomon, and the kingdom was divided in so far as Judah and Israel each had a kingdom. He therefore felt the punishment for his obstinacy, as well as the mercy of the grace of God and the privilege of blood, inasmuch as he at least remained king but the greater part of the kingdom was cut off. For what reason did this happen to him? Because he adhered to the counsel of the young, disregarding the ways and precepts of prudence. For it is impossible that he should dispose rulership advantageously who does not act upon the counsel of the wise. 'Woe', it is written, 'to the land whose king is a child and whose counsellors feast in the morning; blessed is the land whose king is noble and whose princes eat at the correct time for nourishment and not for luxury';[3] for in the former place there cannot be

---

[3] Ecclesiastes 10:16–17.

wisdom. Thus, the holy Job says, 'Where shall wisdom be found, and where is the place of understanding? Man does not know its value, nor is it found in the land of those living pleasantly.'[4] Nothing corruptible may be compared with it, for wisdom is received from hidden places.

Rehoboam might more usefully have disdained the young counsellors, acquiescing to the counsel of older and better men and holding up the life of the blessed Job as the very blueprint of ruling. Listen, therefore, to what Job declares about himself: 'When I went out to the gate of the city and they prepared my seat in the street, the young men hid themselves, and the elders stood up for me. The princes refrained from talking and put a finger to their lips. The voices of the rulers were silenced and their tongues stayed still in their mouths. The ears hearing me blessed me, and the eyes seeing me paid testimony to me because the poor man who cried out and the orphan who had no one to aid him were set free. The blessing of the dying was claimed by me, and I was the consolation of the widow's heart. I am clothed in justice and my judgment is my vestment, like cloak and crown. I was eyes to the blind and feet to the lame; the poor had a father and the causes about which I did not know I diligently investigated. I broke the jaws of the iniquitous, and I stripped the prey from their teeth. And I said: In my nest I shall die, and I shall multiply my days like the palm tree. My root is spread towards the waters, and in my fronds the dew shall be accumulated; my glory shall always be renewed, and my bow is restored in my hand. Those who heeded me awaited my opinion, and they kept attentively silent for my counsel. They did not risk adding to my words, and my eloquence descended over them . . . If I laughed at them, they did not believe it, and the radiance of my features did not descend to earth. If I desired to go among them, I was seated first; and when I was seated like a king with his army, I was the consoler of those still sorrowful.'[5] Look at how the formula for ruling well is expressed in great measure in the just man, whose virtues, if we wished to pursue them individually, would fill up entirely one or a series of pages in a large book.

The diligent reader dissects each individual word because in all of them no detail is unrelated to the mystery of salvation. Still, I might touch, however briefly, upon a few matters which stand out from the surface of the words themselves. 'When', it is said, 'I washed my feet

---

[4] Job 28:12–13.   [5] Job 29:7–22, 24–25.

with butter and the rock poured rivers of oil out for me; when I went out to the gate of the city and they prepared my seat in the street, the young men hid themselves and the elders stood up for me'. He intimates, therefore, that material affluence and the receipt of blessings does not compensate for his prudence, but its authority over him in all things continued undisturbed by reason of his conscience and the evidence of good works. For he who had marched out to the gate was not in need of concealment, and he who was worthy of a seat of learning stimulated the prudence of the elders as the frivolous young men hid themselves.

'The voices of the rulers were silent and their tongues stayed still in their mouths', not daring to speak of important matters and to impose on the shoulders of men those insupportable burdens which they are not used to touching with even the tips of their fingers. For Job taught that all praiseworthy virtue consists in action, and the splendour of words which are not supported by solid works is empty. 'In all work', Solomon says, 'there will be abundance; where there are many words, however, there is frequently deprivation.'[6] Surely princes and leaders are to precede others along the path of morals – not to intone haughtily about what others are to do.

'The ears hearing me and the eyes seeing me blessed me.' He elegantly describes the apparatus of the body, through which the soul's perception principally flourishes; for in fact knowledge of the external world passes into the soul most faithfully by means of the eyes and ears, and the incautious tongue too frequently divulges the treasures of the heart. Yet because 'hearing' and 'seeing' are added, he expresses something like the judgment of the wise man: 'Happy is he who speaks into a listening ear.' And thus, he does not say that human tongues, which are frequently impelled either in the direction of love or of hate, bless him. The testimony of his own conscience suffices, especially since it is strengthened by wise judgment.

For that reason, it is said, 'the poor man, the orphan and the dying were set free; and I was the consolation of the widow's heart'. For in this does princely authority, which was instituted by God for the repelling of injury, become manifest. Indeed, these are the works of mercy, and the name of the actor will be praised for generations. But lest you believe that the laxity of mercy warranted the audacity of vice,

---

[6] Proverbs 14:23.

it is said: 'I am clothed in justice and the crown of my judgment; causes about which I did not know I diligently investigated.' For the judge must examine matters tenaciously and dissect the sequence of events by full inquiry, nor ought he to oppose anyone whose case has yet to be settled by the most thorough legal reasoning. For as one moralist asserts, whoever judges rapidly will hasten to repent of it.

'I broke the jaws of the iniquitous.' The iniquitous man is whoever in matters of law pursues profit rather than a just cause, and who loves reward to the extent that he strives for retribution. And although it is equitable that one judges in terms of monetary values, the servant of avarice advances towards death. And so it follows: 'And I stripped the prey from their teeth. And I said: In my nest I shall die.' Accordingly, composure of mind will be his who is content with the magnitude of his material goods. He is not pressured by that stimulus of avarice or ambition according to which some men would connect together house to house and field to field, straight up to the boundaries of space, as if they alone inhabited the face of the earth.

'And I shall multiply the days like a palm tree.' Aristotle in Book Seven of the *Problemata* and Plutarch in Book Eight of the *Memorabilia* both report a surprising thing: they say that if you set a great weight on top of the trunk of a palm tree, and also bear down such a heavy burden upon it that it is not able to bear the magnitude of the burden, it does not yield downwards and bend into the ground, but rises up against the weight and strives upwards and is bent back into shape. As a result, Plutarch says, the palm is chosen to be the symbol of victory in battles, since the nature of the tree is such that it does not yield in the face of pressure and encumbrance. Likewise it is reported that the branch of the palm, which the Greeks call 'royal', cannot be pulled out if it is dragged downwards, but yields if you remove it upwards. It is also generally accepted that the trunk or stock of the palm is curtailed at the root but spreads out at its upper reaches. It is different from any other tree, which grows so much more stout as its stock approaches closer to the ground. By the palm, therefore, is signified invincible justice, which does not know descent but which only advances towards the higher reaches. For this reason, 'the just man will flourish like the palm . . .'[7]

'If I desired to go among them, I was seated first', since he who

[7] Psalms 92:12.

preceded others by such great measure on the path of virtue was worthy of the most eminent chair. When he was seated like a king surrounded by servants, he dried the tears of the sorrowful. Surely the conclusion is pleasing, since the public power strives to preside in such fashion that he does not permit any sorrows to exist in his community. In regard to the art by which this circumstance is created, the field subjected to good morals is accompanied by so many delightful flowers and abundant fruits that, if someone were to enter it, he would rejoice in the presence of the delights of Paradise itself. Perhaps you marvel and are stunned with astonishment at how in this exile of the flesh so great a sweetness may be shared and how one may be a fellow citizen of the citizens of heaven; but whether this is possible you may discern for yourself by reference to the works of the just man. 'If I have withheld that which the poor desire, and have caused the eyes of the widow to dim; if I have eaten my morsel alone, and the orphan has not eaten of it, since from his infancy my mercy grew upon him and from his mother's womb he has been guided by me; if I have despised the passer-by because he did not have clothing, and the poor man because he was without shelter; if his flanks have not blessed me, and he is not warmed by wool from my sheep; if I have lifted up my hand over the orphan when at the gate I considered myself superior to him – then may my shoulder be removed at its socket and the bones of my arm be broken. For I have always feared God like a flood swelling over me, and I could not bear His weight. If I supposed my strength to be gold, and called fine gold my confidence; if I am delighted because of my great wealth and because my hand obtains much; if I saw the sun when it shined or the illumination of the advancing moon, and my heart was enticed in secret, and I kissed my hand with my mouth, which is the greatest iniquity and a denial of the Highest God; if I was joyful at the destruction of him who hated me, and exulted that evil came to him; . . . if the men of my tent did not say "Who would give of his flesh that others may be satisfied?" (the stronger did not lodge outdoors, my doors were open to the traveller); if I have hidden my sins like the first man and concealed my iniquity within myself; if I am fearful of an excessive multitude, and the contempt of relatives terrifies me, and I have not instead kept silent or departed through the door; . . . if my land cries out against me, and when its furrows lament with it; if I have eaten the fruits of it without payment, and have assailed the livelihood of the peasant –

then may my wheat rise as thistles and a thorn for barley.'[8] Do you not believe him to walk in the richness of God's delights who from pure heart and good conscience and genuine faith acknowledges these things about himself under a curse of such proportions? Who desires any interpretation of these statements or does not see clearly such great virtue? Obviously he for whom these words are not self-evident is extremely stupid or naturally obtuse.

There are gathered here many facets into a single whole, whereas each one singly would suffice to illuminate the world. If princes despise more reading or listening, they may at least read, hear and dissect by diligent examination this small passage in order that they may imitate it. For it follows in the same work: 'If kings hear and observe the voice of God, they will spend their days in goodness and their years in glory; if they do not listen, they will pass away by the sword and be consumed by folly.'[9] Do you not see the dual end of useless kings? For either they pass away by the sword or they are consumed by folly. And correctly are they said to pass away, rather than to be finished by the sword, because their sword is like a sort of passageway to the place where the powerful are punished powerfully according to the number and magnitude of their iniquities. Yet folly also consumes the impious because the strength of the prince is weakened in the oppression of the people; and indeed a worn down people cannot and will not support the strength of the prince.

[8] Job 31:16–29, 31–34, 38–40.   [9] Job 36:11–12.

CHAPTER 7

What bad and good happens to subjects on account of the morals of princes; and that the examples of some stratagems strengthen this

'He who gives honours to the unwise', it is said, 'is like he who casts a stone upon Mercury's pile.'[10] This is explained in different ways by different people. Requesting the indulgence of wiser men, I believe that Mercury's pile consists in the calculation of accounts, since

[10] Proverbs 26:8.

Mercury is the deity of those who are occupied with business affairs and who keep diligent watch over their ledgers. Therefore, to cast a stone upon the pile, which aids in the calculation of accounts, is to upset totally the computation of the accounts, and to confer honour on the unwise is to subvert the life of the republic. And it is impossible that one governs others usefully when one is subverted by one's own errors. For it is said: 'Where there is no governor, the people are brought to ruin.'[11] And elsewhere: 'An unwise king is the ruin of his people, and cities will be inhabited according to the judgment of the prudent . . . All the powerful are short-lived, a languishing illness lays down the physician. The physician cuts off the illness rapidly; so whoever is a king today will be a corpse tomorrow. For when a man dies, he will inherit serpents and wild beasts and worms.'[12] To what purpose, I ask, are the poor oppressed with injuries, enfeebled by exactions, despoiled by extensive pillaging, commanded to meet peoples in battle and to terrify the world, except in order that the powerful may be succeeded by their heirs? For in fact their heirs succeed to everything according to their right; they do not even require a solemnised will and testament, for they put themselves forward on the basis of intestacy; wish it or not, you will have these heirs.

In the field of secular literature, Plato has said: 'When the magistrate oppresses subjects, it is just as if the head of the body had swollen up so that it is impossible for the members of the body to endure it either at all or without difficulty. It is impossible, however, to tolerate or cure this affliction without the most extreme pain among the members. Yet if the affliction would be incurable, it is more miserable to live than to die. For nothing is more useful to those in misery than to end their misery, no matter how.' It is read that the same writer also has said: 'When an official brutalises subjects, it is the same as if a legal guardian had persecuted his ward, or if you had slaughtered with his own dagger someone for the sake of whose defence you had been handed and had accepted his sword. For indeed, it is a very celebrated fact that the public enjoys the rights of a ward, and public affairs do not proceed well until the time when it is acknowledged that a head is useless to them unless he faithfully coheres with the members.' These are Plato's views, which are

---

[11] Proverbs 11:14.   [12] Ecclesiasticus 10:3, 11–13.

elegantly and truly expressed. But, as it appears to me, there can be no faithful and firm coherence where there is not a tenacious unity of wills and a virtual joining together of souls themselves. If this is missing, men harmonise their works in vain, since deceit advances into catastrophe without an attitude of helpfulness. 'Deceivers and cunning men', says Job, 'provoke the wrath of God, and they ought not to complain when they are vanquished; their souls perish in calamity and they live among the weak.'[13] For works are sometimes manifested by reason of shame, or occasionally fear. But the most solid union is the one which proceeds by the openness of faith and love, and subsists solely upon the foundation of virtue. Yet works, because they are a sign of character, generate favour, since there is nothing more useful and more efficacious for the status and the improvement of magistrates . . .

What might I say about continence and the contempt of worldly things, inasmuch as several stratagems from Plutarch have been promised? Marcus Cato was reputed to have been contented with the same wine as his oarsmen. Attilius Regulus, after he had been in command of affairs of the greatest importance, was a pauper to such an extent that a small field which was cultivated by a single estate labourer supported him, his wife and children; upon hearing of the death of his worker, he wrote to the Senate about the creation of his successor on the grounds that the death of his slave left his affairs unmanaged and his presence was necessary at his farm. Gaius Scipio, after his deeds made public affairs prosper in Spain, died in the greatest poverty, not even leaving sufficient money for his daughters' dowry; hence, by reason of their need, the Senate endowed them from the public purse. The Athenians performed the same deed for the offspring of Aristides after he died in extreme poverty while he had administered affairs of the greatest substance.

Hannibal, who was in the habit of getting out of bed before dawn, would not sleep before nightfall, he would call his companions to dinner precisely at twilight, and they would never recline themselves upon any more than two couches. Similarly, when he was a soldier under the command of Hasdrubal, he would elect to sleep upon the open ground covered by his cape. And the same is told about Alexander of Macedon. Augustus Caesar ate small portions and also

---

[13] Job 36:13-14.

simple foods. He would long greatly for second quality bread and small fish and hand-pressed porous cheese and the biennial green fruit of the fig tree, and he would have his meals before dinner time, wherever and whenever his stomach desired; thus, one of his letters remarks: 'No Jew, my Tiberius, is more diligently observant of the Sabbath than I have been observant today when I consumed two mouthfuls in the bath after the first hour of evening before I had begun to be anointed.' His anger would also slacken off very rapidly, in so far as he realised that one who commits an injury immobilises his soul, and, just as he would himself say, they are cooked faster than asparagus; for he was accustomed to expressing this phrase whenever the hasty made haste . . .

As is evident from a number of stratagems, constancy was also greatly apparent among the virtues of the Romans. In fact, if all the histories of peoples are reviewed, nothing shines more brightly than the magnificence and virtue of the Romans. This is proclaimed by the fullest splendour of their empire, so that the human memory can record no empire which was lesser at its beginnings nor which proceeded to more greatness through continual enlargement and extension. And indeed, they possessed such peaceful liberty, cultivated justice, reverence for law, friendliness towards neighbours and foreign peoples, maturity of counsel, and dignity of words and deeds that they subjected the entire world to their commands. But because we started with their constancy, one of Julius Frontinus' 'Stratagems' may in the meantime take the place of many examples. And so, when Hannibal besieged the walls of the city, they deployed through a different gate reinforcements for the armies which they had in Spain in demonstration of their confidence and devotion to obligation. Likewise, when the owner (*domini*) of the fields in which Hannibal was camped had died, they were brought to market and sold for the same price which had been received for the land before the war. Finally, while they were besieged by Hannibal and were themselves besieging Capua, they determined that their army was not to be recalled except upon the city's capture.

CHAPTER 8

Why Trajan seems to be preferable to all others

Now, in addition, in order that among Plutarch's stratagems the example of Trajan may be cited, here we have one who was so brave and civilised that he spread in all directions the boundaries of the Roman Empire, which after Augustus were more frequently defended than nobly extended. Yet he would subdue military glory with moderation, conducting himself as the equal of everyone in Rome and throughout the provinces, attending often to the circumstances of the health of his friends, or having common banquets on feast days or with those who were sick, regardless of social distinctions, using the carriages and garments of all ranks equally, enriching all people publicly and privately, dispensing exemptions generously to cities, relaxing provincial tributes, oppressing no one, being loved by all, to such a great extent that in our own period princes are acclaimed in their councils by nothing else than: 'May you be luckier than Augustus and better than Trajan!' Consequently, his memory is conveyed in this way and his reputation for goodness is made so powerful that he stands out to friendly admirers and flatterers alike as the most magnificent of all examples.

It is fitting that one laud Julius for the greatness of his invincible spirit and of his powerful works, since his mind and valour were sufficient to do impossible feats. Not only the first subjection of the Gauls and the Britons by him, but his whole fortune in the civil war and the fortune of the dynasty of the house of Caesar – these all testify to the greatness of his military prowess. He was so diligent in literary matters that he would dictate four letters simultaneously. That he was proficient in civil law is indicated by the old law of the Romans. How unceasingly he exercised the strength of his powerful genius in philosophy is proclaimed and extolled if only by his invention of the intercalary day. Yet (what above all things is most wonderful!) he gave the same effort to affairs of love and to business, and to each project that he would undertake, he was so devoted that he might be thought to be free for it alone. Too, the whole world repeats the praises of Augustus, and happy memory venerates Titus for his love of and delight in the human race.

In comparison to all these, I do not hesitate to prefer Trajan, who

79

built the majesty of his reign solely upon the practice of virtue. This is akin to the remark of the moralist that 'he who does right may be judged king'.[14] Something similar to this is recommended by Claudian (under the guise of Theodosius):

> Although you rule widely even to the end of the Indies, and the
> Mede, the gentle Arab, the Chinese adore you,
> if you fear, if you desire evil, if you are led by anger,
> you will bear the yoke of slavery, you will tolerate within yourself
> iniquitous laws; then will you have rights over everything,
> when you can be king of yourself; use is more inclined to make
>   things worse, and licence exhorts luxury
> and, favouring no restraints, you will be led astray; then is living
>   chastely
> more difficult, when Venus prompts; hence anger is harder
> to control, when punishment is accessible; but curb emotions;
> and it is proper that not what is permitted but what one should do
> occurs to you; and your mind is mastered by respect for honour.[15]

But in order that those who are of the opinion that others are to be preferred to Trajan may more readily acquiesce to his praise, it is read that his virtues were commended by the most holy Pope Gregory and that the pope, shedding tears for the emperor, held him back from the fires of hell; the Lord in His rich mercy rewarded the justice which Trajan had displayed towards the crying widow. For when the remarkable emperor had mounted his horse to depart for battle, a widow, seizing his foot and wailing miserably, petitioned him to do justice to those who had unjustly murdered her son, an excellent and most innocent youth. 'You, Augustus', she said, 'are Emperor. Must I endure so atrocious an injury?' 'I', said the Emperor, 'will satisfy you when I return.' 'What', she responded, 'if you do not return?' 'My successor', Trajan asserted, 'would satisfy you.' And she retorted, 'How are you improved if someone else does good? You owe this to me; you are brought rewards according to your works; it is above all fraud not to render that which is owed. Your successor will be obligated on his own account for those who endure injuries; the justice of another will not release you; it goes well for your successor if he is released from his own debts.' Moved by these words, the emperor descended from his horse and immediately had the case

---

[14] Horace, *Epistolae*, 1.1.59–60.
[15] Claudian, *Panegyricus de iv consulatu Honorii*, 257–268.

examined and the widow was consoled by the satisfaction she wholly deserved. Moreover, it is reported that the most blessed pope poured out tears for him for so long a time until finally he was informed in a revelation that Trajan was freed from the penalty of hell, yet under the condition that he would not presume to solicit God further on behalf of any other infidel. Hence, he is deservedly preferred to others whose virtue pleases the saints so far above anyone else that he alone is freed by their intercession. And this also is to be said of the head of the republic.

CHAPTER 9

Of those who hold the place of the heart, and that the iniquitous are prevented from counselling the powerful, and of the fear of God, and wisdom, and philosophy

The place of the heart, on Plutarch's authority, is held by the senate. Yet the senate, as the ancients concur, is the name of an office and has maturity of age as its distinguishing mark; for in fact it is called 'senate' from '*senectus*', the Latin for 'old age'. The Athenians had called it the Areopagus because the virtue of the whole people consisted in it and, although many famous discoveries were made by them, nothing more glorious was instituted than their senate. For what is more noble than a meeting of elders who, having completed their service, are transformed from ordinary offices to the office of counsel and rulership and in shrivelled bodies exert strength of mind? The more they are adapted to the business of wisdom, the less they are able to exercise their bodies. Their honour above all stood out so far among the Greeks that the leaders of the republic proceeded nowhere, and nothing of importance was accomplished, except after the established elders had examined and approved it. What is more, from the foundation of Rome their names were written in letters of gold script, and they were addressed by everyone as '*patres conscripti*' [literally, enrolled fathers] who preceded others in wisdom, age and paternal affection. In their possession was the authority for counsel and all public administration. Although their name was seen to be born from their age, in other respects I believe that this was as much mental as physical age. For indeed the age of the mind is that wisdom in which consists the distribution of all duties and the complete art of living. And in truth the art of living well (as the Stoics agree) is the art of arts.

That there is no art to the greatest of matters, when it is evident that there is an art to lesser matters, is an opinion of 'men speaking from too little deliberation and erring in matters of the greatest significance'[16] – all the more because they are supporting arbitrary will instead of truth. Yet there is, as the ancients concurred, a ruling wisdom in divine and human affairs, as well as a science of things to be done and to be omitted. To persist on this course is to philosophise, because philosophy is 'devotion to wisdom' (*studium sapientiae*).[17] As the ancient philosophers therefore have it, philosophy pounds at the gate of wisdom and, when it is opened, the soul is illuminated by the sweet light of things and the name of philosophy vanishes; or, just as it is seen by those of insight, the appetite of the will is satisfied when the blossom of study turns into fruit; for the end of philosophy is wisdom. But I do not know the means by which one may engage in the end at present when we have not yet identified the beginning, which in all things is judged to be the most influential part. Still, he who knows the end cannot be ignorant of the beginning, since the root of the beginning passes along through the path of the multiple virtues straight up to the crown of the end and into the sweet fruit of its own durability and stability.

'Behold', says blessed Job, 'that the fear of the Lord is wisdom itself and to withdraw from evil is intelligence.'[18] Nowhere else do I find any other root of wisdom, since all agree in this: that the beginning of wisdom is the fear of the Lord. Fear therefore is the beginning, and in fear is progress, and the culmination of all the virtues, regardless of whether you call it charity or wisdom, is not always a stranger to fear. One separates servile from filial fear; in the one is the beginning, in the other is erected the perfection of wisdom. Whatever the manner in which the luxury of words embellishes itself, it is true that wisdom begins in fear and that the holy fear of the Lord persists in generation after generation. And so the root endures and, becoming strong with the growth of grace, it progresses towards the branches of virtue, and its strength extends straight out to the fruit of perfect charity, which is

---

[16] Cicero, *De officiis*, 2.2.6.   [17] *Ibid.*, 2.2.5.   [18] Job 28:28.

unfamiliar with the sting of punishment since in charity there is no terror which performs a penal function. And it is an indication of this fear that it performs good works continually and, embracing justice, grasps it firmly. Terror is, therefore, seen to cease, while grace advances towards virtue because now one does not fear in that servile manner which had incited one's filial affection towards reverence and good works. 'Always', says blessed Job, 'have I feared God like a flood swelling over me, and I could not bear His weight.'[19] He says above all that he did not fear Him sometimes but always, and one ought not to doubt the perfection of the speaker, whom the Lord Himself testifies was a man unequalled on earth. Nor is it credible that he had refrained from evil in the absence of charity for fear of punishment when there was no question that he was consummate in the perfection of his justice.

Up to the present point, the argument has proceeded by commendation of fear, although the nature of fear itself has not yet become clear. But if only that name which is so often repeated by the mouth might also dwell in the heart! For if it has touched the mind, the tongue will discuss matters more effectively and to greater self-advantage. For one vainly tumbles about words in one's mouth if the works of virtue are lacking. But the fear of God means never disregarding those things that one is required to perform, just as the most blessed Pope Gregory asserts. To disregard something is above all not to carry it out either in practice or in will. For whatever you will and are unable to do, God reckons as accomplished because a fulfilled will achieves a reward equal to the entire work. Thus, it is certain that he who fears God neglects nothing and does the good. He who diligently investigates all matters, and who knows and executes the things which are to be done, is without doubt the wise man and the most appropriate counsellor for the prince. Where such great dignity of character becomes known, one disputes in vain about physical age. For the one who is older is he who is chosen counsellor by his demonstration of wise advice. For it is asserted: 'Old age is neither venerable according to its days nor computed in numerical years.'[20] 'Grey hair is the glory of the old.'[21] 'Grey hairs are a man's judgment, the advancement of age is an unblemished life.'[22] Entirely blessed is

---

[19] Job 31:23.   [20] Wisdom 4:8.
[21] Proverbs 20:29.   [22] Wisdom 4:8–9.

one who embraces old age in this way, so that by the testimony of his own conscience he may rejoice in his blameless life.

But perhaps you will say: 'Who is this man? We will praise him.'[23] I do not believe that the granting of counsel must await one who has never committed a sin, but rather one who is not glad to sin, who hates sin, who rejoices in virtue and yearns for it with great desire, a man of manifestly good will. But this is not to limit one to perfection; as the old saying states, 'Better the kindness of Minerva', who is seen to be blameless not on her own terms but in comparison to others. For who will brag that his heart is kept constantly chaste, since even the stars are not clean in the gaze of Him who discovers wickedness in His own angels?

The iniquitous are therefore to be kept at a distance, as well as those who are arrogant and greedy, and all such forms of human contagion. For nothing is more pernicious than an iniquitous advisor to the wealthy. It is written: 'Protect your heart with all care, for out of it proceeds life.'[24] And so the ruler is to provide for his advisors in order that they do not need, lest they desire immoderately what belongs to another. Likewise, this extends to those who hold office throughout the interior of the body of the republic, whom we know to be treasurers and record keepers and counts of privy affairs. For all these are to be recompensed to a sufficient extent, and this ought to be interpreted by reference to necessity and usage, calculated according to the special qualities of different persons. For if the more avaricious sorts are fully recompensed and too few rewards are dispersed, disorders will be generated that are cured with difficulty or not at all. In fact, it is impossible to pursue both justice and money at once; for either a person will adhere to a particular one of them and scorn the other, or the worse will twist him free of the better. 'The greedy man', Wisdom accordingly testifies, 'is more wicked than anyone, and nothing is more iniquitous than to love money; for this person puts his life up for sale and in his life he forsakes even his own entrails.'[25] And perhaps for this reason nature, that most diligent parent, has shielded the entrails by means of the rib cage of the chest and the solidified ribs and the enclosure of the outer skin, so that they may be safer against all external violence. Nature supplies that which is necessary for them, since they are not at any time exposed to the external world

---

[23] Ecclesiasticus 31:9.   [24] Proverbs 4:23.   [25] Ecclesiasticus 10.9–10.

without loss to their health. Likewise, it is necessary in the republic to preserve this design of nature's fabrication and to supply from public funds for the provision of the necessities of life.

CHAPTER 10

Of the flanks of the powerful, whose needs are to be satisfied and whose malice is to be restrained

But even in the flanks – namely, those who ought to assist princes – this formula of nature is to be preserved. For it is generally accepted that moral character is formed from close association. 'He who touches pitch is dirtied by it';[26] and 'contact with one bunch of grapes produces spoilage in another'.[27] Do not believe justice or truth or piety to be at home among those you observe to be selling everything. Christ Himself is excluded and, if He knocks at the gate, it is not opened to Him; they who do everything for a price and nothing for free flee from and put to flight divine grace. If requests are to be presented, if a case is to be examined, if the execution of a sentence is to be ordered, if bail is to be rendered – in all cases money talks, truth is blind, piety is crippled, while

> whatever amount of money one keeps in one's safe,
> such is the extent of one's faithfulness . . .
> The pauper is believed to scorn
> the thunderbolts of the gods, and the deities are his pardoners.[28]

He who is more corrupt in his morals and who is more corrupted by bribes is all the more blessed among those like himself.

If you wish to evade the hands of the prince, a long, narrow and steep road remains for you; before you pass beyond the final torturers, you will be drenched in sweat. See how Cossus completes your documents; if you are permitted to pay a visit to him, consider this great luck. If you have not brought your transit papers, you approach him in vain. Yet if you have brought them, it is still of no use, for he will not acquiesce to dishonour noble hands with your vile parchment. What more? It is necessary to buy his efforts, since neither work nor

---

[26] Ecclesiasticus 13.1.   [27] Juvenal, *Saturae*, 2.81.
[28] *Ibid.*, 3.143–144 and 3.145–146.

pen nor the various inks come without price. But he will distort even the letters and syllables, unless you make him benevolent towards you, and he lays so many verbal snares for you that a document may seem friendly but implicitly writes war for peace and quarrel for quiet. If perhaps a beautiful belt is yours, or a suitable knife, or anything in the way of a decent small possession, number it among his goods, unless you wish your work and expense to come to nothing. For either precious objects will be extorted or you will forestall this by your liberality. Finally, your friend will carry away even your hat, of whatever kind it is, in memory of you.

Once you have departed from Cossus, the fires of purgatory menace you, for Vegento remains, whom you must entice incessantly and arouse by means of grandly improvised gestures, supplications and presents 'in order that he may turn his attention towards you with closed lips'.[29] He then will enter into consultation about individual words, schedule times for deliberations, and consider in the balance the most minute of details. Unless you flatter him in advance, it will be objected that the sequence of events is inappropriately drafted, or that the style reflects lack of cultivation, or that the notary or scribe departs (through benign or negligent disregard for the law) from the standard form; and some problem always requires money for its resolution. It may indeed trouble you least that you will be tormented by lengthy waits, in so far as what cannot be refused you is deferred. Believe an expert, I have fallen into their hands on innumerable occasions, and (to improve somewhat on the fable) the stern ferryman Charon, who never spares anyone, is far more clement than they; he was accustomed to being content with mere small change. By contrast, these magistrates command a pound multiplied over and over again.

But why is it that I protest about the venality of everything among courtiers when those things which cost nothing, such as the lack of some act, are subject to sale? No deed and no word is free of charge, no one keeps still except for a price; and thus, silence is a thing for sale. This was perhaps learned from Demosthenes, who had asked the thespian Aristodemus how much money he had received in order that he would act in a play, and who had been given the response: 'A talent.' 'And I', said Demosthenes, 'have received more to keep

---

[29] *Ibid*, 3.185.

silent.' For indeed the tongues of lawyers are harmful unless, as it is customarily said, you bind them with cords of silver.

It is not advantageous to entrap a single magistrate with presents unless perhaps he is of the greatest power, because the one who is favourably disposed to you will arouse the envy of others. For they suppose themselves to be deprived of that which is dispersed to others. Furthermore, this passes from the greatest to the least, who, unless they are flattered by abasement and invigorated by presents, suspect that an injury has been done to them. 'Every great house is full of boastful servants',[30] and likewise it is full of covetous and greedy ones. Yet among all courtly fools, those who do harm most perniciously are those who are accustomed to glossing over their wretched frivolities under the pretext of honour and liberality, who move about in bright apparel, who feast splendidly, who often urge strangers to join them at the dinner table, who are courteous at home, benign when abroad, affable in speech, liberal in judgment, generous in the treatment of kin, and distinguished for the imitation of all virtues. For as the moralist says, 'Of all injustices, none are more serious than those in which, when a person is most deceitful, he behaves in such a fashion that he appears to be a good man.'[31] He above all commits acts of licence under the guise of virtue; and, for this reason, he pursues glory through means which are scarcely appropriate to the expectation of pardon. The greatest amount will be extorted with impunity by those who cannot, or indeed disdain to, be content with a little. It is a notable and popular proverb that 'he will be enslaved forever who does not know the usefulness of a little'.[32]

Yet, lest you suppose me to be engendering inexorable hostility with regard to this matter, courtiers may lawfully accept presents so long as they are not impudently extorted. Shame is surrendered, however, as soon as one is greedy for exactions. It is said that the words 'I ask for' are to be spoken modestly and softly by the supplicant; and one is not freely offered that which is accepted when a request has been made. For he who asks buys twice; he trades his modesty for the price of the object or the hope of possessing it. One incurs no just mark of censure, however, for presents which are bestowed out of devoted liberality, for they are not extorted by the depravity of those who beg. Yet the presents of the iniquitous are not

---

[30] *Ibid.*, 5.66.   [31] Cicero, *De officiis*, 1.13.41.   [32] Horace, *Epistolae*, 1.10.41.

to be accepted, since it would be ungrateful of a man not to hold to promised obligations, and the Lord Himself says that it would be iniquitous to pardon the impious in exchange for presents. In any case, to accept a subvention is to sell one's liberty; and it is improper for those who must rule over others to be enslaved. There is to be concern both for the case and the persons, so that presents are not to be accepted from a dishonourable person and in a dishonourable way because time and place and means ought to be investigated extensively. For presents are illustrious or sordid generally according to their source and their motive, and occasionally according to their time, place and means. Moreover, the depravity of courtiers is known to such a great extent that it is in vain for anyone to rely upon the testimony of one's conscience, the fame of one's moral character, the fragrance of one's reputation, the sincerity of one's cause, or the outpouring of one's eloquence – unless a bribe has intervened.

> Although you yourself might come, Homer, accompanied by the Muses,
> If you bring nothing, Homer, you will be turned out the door.[33]

Orpheus is said to have tamed lions and tigers with the help of his eloquence, but in the presence of Dis himself he pleaded with a sweetly resonant voice and his case prevailed so favourably upon the three-headed dog that he was permitted for a single time to lead Eurydice out of the underworld, contrary to custom. Yet although you may be Orpheus or Arion or he who is said to have softened rocks solely by the sound of his lyre, still you will accomplish nothing unless you soften their leaden hearts on the anvil of vanity or appetite with a golden or silver hammer.

Everyone abhors the severity of Cerberus; I believe I have observed minor officials of more callousness than Cerberus. Still there was one Cerberus in the underworld; there are as many Cerberuses at court as there are officials. You will have to hold at bay these stewards and their servants who always bite or bark at you. No doubt all have heard the saying among physicians: 'When it hurts, accept treatment'; likewise, courtiers are prepared, if they believe it to be expedient for them, to cause pain to what is healthy. Yet in one way you will be astonished at how conscientious they are: how happily they listen to quarrels, encourage the cases of the humble, and continuously

---

[33] Ovid, *Ars Amatoria*, 2.279–280.

patronise those who are afflicted, so long as they empty out the coffers of the wealthy. For regardless of the way in which the case turns out, it always happens that they fatten their own purses, although their avarice cannot be satisfied. Whoever is placed in their hands, if he seeks penitence, is in my opinion tormented by them sufficiently that he can be pardoned. There is nothing so serious that this cannot atone for it. For what is more miserable than to camp outside the doors of the proud, to tolerate the scorn of passers-by, to be trampled on by the contempt of the contemptible, to endure the hindrances of outcasts, and to bear any indignity whatsoever from those without dignity? Socrates, when Alcibiades questioned him about why he did not drive Xantippe – a wholly bad-tempered and argumentative wife from whom womanish complaints gushed day and night – out of the house, responded: 'When I put up with such behaviour at home, I become accustomed to and experienced in suffering more readily the insolence and injury of others in public.' The old proverb is frequently repeated that the petition of an empty hand is thoughtless; and he is a truly unfit supplicant who believes that things are given in return for words. For it obtains among courtiers and physicians everywhere:

> For words alone we employ mountain herbs;
> For things of real value, pigments and spices.

Still, there are among the others some more benevolent persons who can do a little, although nearly all are prone to do injury, which is far easier than to do good. Therefore, they may keep occupied with their trade, empty out the coffers of others, stuff themselves, possess as much as Pacuvius, pile up mountains of gold; they neither love anyone nor are beloved by anyone, they are admired by those who do not know them while they are loathed and despised by those in their household. You will encounter such things in the old writings of the Romans. When Publius Cineus Graecinus (or another name if it is said instead) was censured by his friends for divorcing a beautiful, chaste and noble wife, he responded: 'And this shoe which you see is new, elegant and pleasing to the gaze of everyone, but no one except myself alone knows where it chafes me.' We read in the Book of Numbers that by fornicating with the women of Midian, Israel had provoked the indignation of the Lord, until finally Phinehas plunged a raised sword through Zimri, son of Salu, in the presence of a

Midianite concubine and stilled the anger of God by killing the wicked. The Lord then spoke to Moses, saying: 'Take away all the rulers of the people and hang them against the sun on gallows.'[34] The people had sinned, of course, and the fornication of the rulers was not described, yet it was commanded that the rulers were to be dragged off to the gallows and in their punishment calm was restored to the delinquent people because the excesses of subjects are most frequently born of the negligence of governors. And so it is important to restrain the malice of those in power and to provide for them from the public treasury so that all opportunity for corruption may be removed. And it is stipulated in the ancient law of the Romans that someone who neglects to correct himself when he has overlooked a duty is seen to be the author of a misdeed.

The more distinguished and powerful a court is, the more plentiful and pernicious are these scourges of mankind and torturers of the innocent. For in fact it is a frequent occurrence that a court either receives or creates vicious men, among whom transgressions increase in audacity since their vices are indulged by reason of their intimacy with the powerful. And also it is useless to take for granted whatever was done earlier in life, since it is hardly possible to retain one's innocence among courtiers. For who is it whose virtue is not cast aside by the frivolities of courtiers? Who is so great, who is so resolute, that he cannot be corrupted? He is best who resists for the longest time, who is strongest, who is corrupted least. For in order that virtue be unharmed, one must turn aside from the life of the courtier. He who said the following providently and prudently expressed the nature of the court: 'He departs from court who wishes to be pious.'[35] For this reason, the court has been compared to the infamous fountain of Salmacis, which is notorious for weakening virility. For, as the story is told, its waters are beautiful to sight, sweet to taste, agreeable to touch, and most pleasant to all the experiences of the senses. But those who enter it are enervated to such a degree of weakness that like effeminate men they are deprived of the nobler sex; and none stepped out from it other than those who were stunned and distressed to be changed into women. For either their sex, vanishing entirely, had degenerated into the inferior gender or they retained enough of the vestiges of their former dignity to assume the identity of

---

[34] Numbers 25:4.   [35] Lucan, *Pharsalia*, 8.493–494.

an hermaphrodite, who, by a sort of foolish error of nature, exhibits the likeness of both sexes, yet retains the true qualities of neither of them.

This obscure poetic fiction represents the likeness of the frivolities of the courtiers, which weaken men by the debasement of their virility or pervert a retained likeness of virility. He who engages in the trifles of the courtier and undertakes the obligations of the philosopher or the good man is an hermaphrodite, whose harsh and prickly face disfigures the beauty of women and who pollutes and dishonours virility with effeminacy. For indeed the philosopher-courtier is a monstrous thing; and, while he affects to be both, he is neither one because the court excludes philosophy and the philosopher at no time engages in the trifles of the courtier. Yet the comparison does not apply to all courts, but merely those which are mismanaged by a foolish will. For whoever is wise drives away frivolities, orders his house and subjects everything to reason. For as Wisdom says: 'What does a holy man share with a dog or the light with the dark? Every animal prefers its like and every man, he who is closest to himself. All flesh is tied to its like and every man will associate with his like. If ever the wolf should unite in common with the wolf, then will the same happen to the sinner and the just man.'[36]

[36] Ecclesiasticus 13:19–22.

CHAPTER II

Of the eyes, ears and tongue of the powerful, and of the duties of governing, and that judges ought to have a knowledge of right and equity, a good will and the power of execution, and that they should be bound by oath to the laws and should be distanced from the taint of presents

Next follows the contributions of the eyes, ears and tongue, which were said above to consist of the governors of provinces. Accordingly, a governor is one who governs the province by conferring legal right. Thus, he should have knowledge of equity and iniquity, and his skills and mind are to be directed to the execution of justice. For while the physician should not be blamed for the eventual outcome of death, still, if something mournful happens as the result of one's rulership, one is deservedly blamed. If a person knows something and does not act upon it, he is accused not by reason of ignorance but by reason of malice. Indeed, the end of either one is damnation, although the punishment of ignorance is more mild, except perhaps for that ignorance which has arisen from negligence. For if ignorance is unalterable, it does not carry the penalty of death but is excused by innate dimness. Still if a governor knows and wishes to serve equity but cannot, the fault is the prince's and not the governor's. But most assuredly, the judge is to incline towards the direction of his sacred calling, since he ought to have his own knowledge of right, a good will and the powers of execution; and he should be obligated by sacred oath to the laws so that he will recognise that it is illicit for him to diverge in any matter from their integrity. For Wisdom teaches us about his wisdom. 'The wise judge', it says, 'will judge his people, and the government of the prudent man will be stable. As the judge of the people is, so his ministers will be; and however is the rector of the city, such will be the inhabitants of it.'[37] Yet it also does not deny that power is necessary, saying: 'Do not seek to be made judge unless you are equal to the strength to attack iniquities, lest perhaps you tremble before the faces of the powerful and set in readiness your own scandal. Do not sin against the multitude of citizens and do not lower yourself among the people; do not be guilty of the same sin twice, for you will not be immune even once. Do not be petty in your spirit; do not despise to pray and give alms. Do not say: "God will consider the great number of my gifts and when they are offered by me to the Most High God, He will accept my gifts." Do not laugh at a man in the sadness of his soul; for it is God the circumspect who humiliates and exalts.'[38] From this the diligent reader encounters the fact that a good will is no less necessary for a judge than is knowledge or power, since he is held at fault not only for himself but for others, and he bears the burden twice for himself and others to the extent that he will not be trusted before God on the basis of the multitude of his gifts apart from the cleanliness of his will.

For this reason Plato both excellently and clearly asserts (if one would yet listen) that those who contend for holding the magistracies

---

[37] Ecclesiasticus 10:1–2.   [38] Ecclesiasticus 7:6–12.

of the republic thereby thrash amongst themselves in exactly the way that sailors in reaction to a tempest might fight about which of them ought to be able to steer.[39] In the reckonings of fortune, little or nothing is so reckless as he who appropriates a magistracy without talent or strength. And in my own time, I have seen nothing more miserable than judges ignorant of the science of law and devoid of a good will, which their love of presents and compensation proves beyond all doubt; the power which they have is exercised in the service of greediness, ostentation, or their own flesh and blood, and they are absolved from the necessity of a sacred oath to the laws. From this it is evident that princes who have conferred upon them ordinary jurisdiction are either ignorant or contemptuous of legal right. But, regardless of what we say about legal proficiency or the powers of execution, a judge must be an extremely religious person and one who hates all iniquity more than death itself.

Because, therefore, governors have ordinary powers to pronounce on matters of legal right, one rule is to be preserved by them and by other judges; and whatever is said of them transfers readily in its implications to the others. And so, what is first of all indicated to each by the necessity of their duties is that justice is to be served in all matters and none of the things which they are to do are to be done for a price. For what is unjust is at no time permitted; injustice is not to be done even for the price of one's temporal life. Yet what is just does not need the aid of remuneration, since it must be done for itself and it is iniquitous to offer for sale that to which one is obligated. It is iniquitous, therefore, to offer justice for sale; it is madness as well as iniquity to sell injustice. For the latter is in fact so disapproved of everywhere that it ought to exist nowhere; the former is so obligatory everywhere that it cannot be sold without the commission of a crime. For Balaam was culpable not for the reason that he had damaged the cause of the people of God when he had spoken in a way other than that which had been inspired by the Lord, but because he was so blinded by avarice that, supporting the cause of the infidels, he had been directed by malice to arrange that Israel would transgress in order that the anger of God might be provoked. He therefore inquired into the means by which he might justly vindicate the cause of impiety and withdraw the grace of God from His elect by a sort of

---

[39] Plato, *Republic* 488b cited by Cicero, *De officiis*, 1.25.87.

trick. Or, if he could not vindicate the opposing cause, he at least had acted in order that God would withdraw from them. For in a fight between the iniquitous, those accustomed to winning (it is said) are those who are superior in strength. You will see Balaamites who, although they refuse to make iniquitous judgments, still are so corrupted by presents that they endeavour by every trick in the book to transfer the justice from one party to the other.

I do not say readily which among these persons is more evil, although the seller of equity colours his malice with a more deceptive paint. Yet one can see that he is more evil who markets his duty to his king and queen, to whom he owes fealty, like merchandise in a doorway, and thus unfaithfully sells his lord into slavery. For indeed every magistrate is the servant of justice. Moreover, it is beyond doubt that equity is alienated by the seller, although it does not cross over to the buyer; and bought iniquity crosses over to the buyer in such a fashion that the seller receives nothing at all for it. And the only one who sells justice is one who does not have it, something which is not found in other contracts. Indeed, the seller relinquishes it before the sordid trade. Is he not sordid who pollutes his conscience and has sold not so much justice as his very soul – all for the acceptance of the promise of filth? The teacher of the gentiles disparaged riches, honours and all the varied furnishings of the world as excrement, in order that he might earn Christ alone, reasoning that everything which contributes to the loss of salvation adds to the heap of sordid things. Surely this is right and faithful because nothing clean, nothing honourable and nothing decent impedes salvation: only what is disgraceful, which, as it degenerates, is both impure and unquestionably useless. It causes such great damage that it is not able to be compensated by any temporal benefit.

For what does it profit a man, if he wins the whole world while doing detriment to his soul? And the world is not said to be useless only when salvation is utterly lost, but also when glory is diminished. Jewels may shine in their many facets, gold may glisten and everything alluring may smile its approval upon the world. Yet whatever thwarts man's cleanliness is sordid; what extinguishes the refinement of the soul is shameful; what subverts honour is ignominious. For this reason, among all the ancients, even though they were ignorant of the truth of salvation, it was counted among the forms of sordid behaviour if one did for a price that which ought to be free on the basis of the obligations of office. Also, they broadened the interpretation of this 'price' to the extent that it encompassed not only all kinds of money, but also all services and works that were not otherwise owed. For how is that which arises from filth to be anything except filthy? A bad tree cannot yield good fruit, for the forces of nature depend upon the principle that like proceeds from like. Certainly, since we have said from the start that the community is to be inspected by governors and other judges, they are all ministers of equity and public peace. Hence, they ought to be especially circumspect and cautious and take great care, in so far as their examination is reserved to Him whose prudence cannot be circumvented and whose justice cannot be corrupted. He insists that they will be judged according to the judgments by which they have judged, and they will receive from the absolutely just judge the measure of their goodness – stuffed full, concentrated and overflowing into their chests.

CHAPTER 15

What pertains to the sacred calling of proconsuls, governors and ordinary justices, and to what extent it is permitted to reach out for gifts; and of Cicero, Bernard, Martin and Geoffrey of Chartres

In addition, it pertains to the sacred calling of the governor to take precautions lest the more powerful men assail the more humble and lest the defenders of the innocent persecute their wards with false accusations of crimes. He will also prohibit the introduction of exactions and acts of violence and sales extorted out of fear and pledges of security without price or payment. He will not burden his province with publicly subsidised hospitality, and finally he will be on guard lest anyone profit from iniquity or suffer damage. For the good and dignified governor agrees to take care that his province is peaceful and quiet; this will easily be preserved if, moved by solicitude, he searches the province for bad men and removes them. For he ought to round up the sacrilegious, the bandits, the thieves, the plunderers and, just as he clears away all these offenders, so he ought to turn his attention to those who shelter them and without whom the bandit cannot long escape detection. Surely, everyone who pronounces judgment is to observe the principle that ready consultation with him is permitted, but he is not to suffer any humiliation. For that reason, the command is added that no governor may admit provincials into any further intimacy; for contempt for dignity is born out of equality of social intercourse. And, in summary, he should pronounce judgment so that his authority is augmented by the dignity of his temperament.

This means that in the process of the investigation, he ought neither to be inflamed against those whom he thinks evil, nor to weep over the petitions of the victims of calamity; for he whose face reveals the motions of his soul is not a steadfast and upright judge. What is more depraved in a man of importance than if his cheeks change colour like the wind, his skin pulls tight into wrinkles, his ears throw off sparks, his face is agitated; or if anger inflames the blood in his face and drives it to the surface, his lips contort with foam, his arms are tossed about, his feet spring up, his body trembles and his whole manner expresses not so much anger as insanity? Certainly, when I see such conduct I feel pity for them and yet I fear for myself, recalling the men living in Africa who are described by Pliny in the book 'Natural History'. For they are said to charm with their voice and tongue so that if one perhaps greatly praises their beautiful trees, abundance of crops, auspicious children, exceptional horses, and finely bred and fed cattle, he is immediately killed or destroyed. Enchantment with the eyes is also fatal. The same book refers to men living among the Illyricians who kill by looking at those whom they have long viewed with anger, and says that those men and women who do harm by their gaze have two pupils in each eye. Apollonides also asserts that women are born in Scythia who are called Bithiae, and who likewise are seen to have two pupils in their eyes and to kill whoever angers them if the person catches their gaze. I fear lest wrathful judges are related to these creatures. After all, physiognomists report that those who have speckled eyes are more inclined towards wickedness.

What is said about governors and other justices ought, of course, to hold also among proconsuls, who are commonly called itinerant justices by our fellow countrymen. Although a misnomer, since it does not suit the office, it still suits the personnel, who stray from the path of equity, chasing after their own desires in the pursuit of avarice and the plundering of the people. All duties should be freely performed so that nothing is either demanded or received beyond the fixed amount. But perhaps you ask what the fixed amount is. It is contained in the people's ordinance that none who governs is to accept a present or gift, except of food or drink, and this also is to be used in the days immediately following. This applies also to proconsuls and other magistrates created by the prince's command. Yet they ought not to refuse gifts entirely but to exercise moderation. That they are neither to refrain from gifts totally nor to exceed the mean greedily – these principles are stated in a letter by the deified Severus and the Emperor Antonius. The words of the letter are these: 'Hear what we judge as it pertains to the quantity of gifts. There is an old proverb: "Not all things, not at all times, not from all persons." For it requires an inhuman strength to accept from no one; but to accept indiscriminately is most vile; and for all things, most avaricious. It is contained in our commands that the proconsul and those in other offices will accept no donation or present, or purchase anything, except by reason of daily nourishment, which does not pertain to perishable gifts but to those which exceed useful edibles. But these gifts are not to take on the character of remuneration.'[40]

Although an advocate can justly sell his ability to plead and a counsel his sound knowledge of legal right, it is never permitted to sell judgment to anyone. Cicero, when he wanted to purchase a house on the Palatine and did not have the money at the time, accepted a secret present of two million sesterces from Sulla, who was then party to a lawsuit. Before it was purchased, the affair was uncovered and disclosed, and he was accused of having accepted money from a litigant for the sake of buying the house. Then Cicero, disturbed by the unexpected scandal, denied that he had accepted anything, saying that he was not purchasing the house; and also he said: 'What you charge is so false that if I acquire the house, it is true that money has been accepted by me.' But, when later it was purchased and this lie was exposed by his enemies in the Senate, he laughed heartily and said, between his laughs: 'You must be imprudent men if you do not know that to be a prudent and cautious head of household is to deny that one wishes to buy something when competing purchasers are nearby.' And so, that which he could not disclaim he wiped away by an urbane and humorous saying, making the matter more worthy of

---

[40] *Corpus Iuris Civilis, Digesta*, 1.16.6.

laughter than indictment. Indeed, it had been his custom that, whenever he could not deny a scandalous charge, he eluded it with a jocular response.

The Supreme Pontiff Eugenius of cherished memory and inimitable holiness, whom you have seen, never received gifts of any sort from men who were litigants or whom he supposed to be imminent litigants. For this reason, when at the beginning of his pontificate a certain prior of modest wealth, whose case had not yet been heard, quite insistently offered him the devotion of a gold mark, Eugenius said: 'You have not yet entered the house and already you endeavour to corrupt its lord?' For indeed the holy man held to be corrupt whatever was offered to a judge while a suit was pending. Bernard, monk of Clairvaux, and deacon of Saints Cosmas and Damian, and cardinal, resided by himself in the hills near Rome, banishing from his possession all presents, so that no one was yet born whose gold or silver he allowed into his hands. Should I mention Martin, returning poor from a legation contrary to custom, who, when a companion needed a horse, accepted it under duress from the Bishop of Florence, but restored it to the donor once it was known that he who first gave the present had a case in motion before the Roman Church? Holy Bernard, abbot of Clairvaux, who knew him thoroughly, relates this story more fully in the instructive book he wrote for holy Eugenius, entitled 'On Contemplation or Deliberation'. I pass along without comment that the venerable father Geoffrey of Chartres, legate of Aquitaine, did not receive presents from the provincials, except in cases of food and drink, and these with the greatest frugality; but everything that was offered in the way of a gift he disparaged as excrement. The holy man of Clairvaux testifies that Geoffrey declined to accept a free fish, which is commonly called a sturgeon, from a devoted cleric in his own legation and afterwards he only acceded to the rejected offering once he had paid out the price of the gift.

CHAPTER 17

Money is condemned in favour of wisdom; this is also approved by the examples of the ancient philosophers

... One who is wealthy and prosperous in his external trappings is judged wise and happy. Towards this end, one man takes a wife, another buys five head of oxen or a villa, exchanging their souls for these. On the other hand, some are reckoned among the blind and lame and feeble, those upon whom the world does not smile at all, yet whom wisdom invites to the wedding banquet from which the wealthy are expelled, where the elect are inebriated upon the abundance of God's house and get drunk on a torrent of eternal pleasures. In the present world, whoever does not have riches is stupid, asinine, a dummy, a blockhead, leaden, or, if nothing else, he is insensate. If anyone is a pauper, he is, therefore, stupid and unhappy. Also, a man cannot be loved by someone who is weighed down by bad fortune because 'no one who is loyal ever chose the unhappy as friends';[41] and one is justly supposed to bear on one's own whatever evils one sustains.

And so the kingdom of money increases to the extent that one despairs of a faithful judge who rejects offerings of presents. If you refuse support, you are seen to have loathing for the case of the one who offers it; and possibly you will be thought to have been bribed already by presents or love, if you wish to remain uncorrupted. The thoughts and ideas of philosophers have entirely vanished, while everyone struggles after wealth, as if relief from labour and solace from anguish could not be found elsewhere, as if shipwrecked people would be able to escape more easily from the sea by swimming if they were burdened with a heavier load. But what sore-ridden person ever accumulated thorns in order that he might lie more comfortably at rest by twisting around upon them? Surely, if one is to believe perfectly him who asserted 'Riches are thorns',[42] then the wise men of our time should seek out material goods with far less devotion. Therefore, as Publius Carpus asserts, the rich are more miserable than the poor because they depart farther from wisdom. The appetite for wealth excludes wisdom and drives off virtue; the fruit of manhood, poverty, imitates nature, the best guide for living well, and

---

[41] Lucan, *Pharsalia*, 8.535.   [42] Matthew 13:22.

is the parent and custodian of virtue, and alone begets that security which is utterly unaware of the provocations of war. He does not have quarrels who is ignorant of the causes of contention. The world is agitated, and only the pauper does not fear the hand of Caesar.

If, in any case, riches were not driven off or despised for any other reason, except because they hedge the path of wisdom with thorns, it would be necessary not to love them. Yet lest those who are ashamed to become filthy from the vileness of poverty form a bad opinion of philosophers, philosophy does not proclaim that one is to drive away wealth, but that one is to inhibit the appetite for it. It demands a mind which is self-composed and self-sufficient in all reckoning of fortune, so that its sufficiency is still from God. Thus, one will use gold just as clay, and clay like gold. For, just as riches are allowed on the basis of utility, so abuses are to be scorned by the wise man. But perhaps lowly furnishings will appear ignominious to magnates and meagre possessions will stain the splendour of honour; nevertheless the splendour of morals is far superior to that of material objects, and the beauty of physical goods will never glorify him who is dishonoured by the blemish of his own shamefulness.

It is said that the King Agathocles dined on clay pottery,
and that his board was frequently burdened with Samian clay.
When asked the reason he responded: Although I am King of Sicily,
I am born the son of a potter.
Have reverence for fortune, whoever suddenly advances to riches
from a wretched house.[43]

And so the vices are not in the objects but in their uses.

And the fruit of the philosophical soul is a nobly generous equanimity of mind; for, if it is out of stupidity that one bears everything with equanimity, still sound virtue degenerates on account of a troubled mind. Indeed, although there are many ways of philosophising, the one that seems to me to be the nobler and more laudable is that

which lunches patiently on a simple diet, in order that one may come
to know
useful things, and things which one busies oneself about in practice,[44]

that one that is carefully taught not to feel disgust for garden

---

[43] Ausonius, *Epigrammata*, 2.　　[44] Horace, *Epistolae*, 1.17.13–15.

vegetables and any other gifts of the extremely poor. For indeed, the outstanding fruit of philosophy is that one knows the way in which abundance and scarcity are born, so that one opposes every obstacle with a solid virtue which disarms fortune. Certainly, whoever is a devoted servant of this will neither fear nor dread; and before him the infirmities of fortune always collapse. What, inquires a curious examiner of philosophy, has philosophy conferred upon you? And Aristippus responds: 'To converse intrepidly with all men.' If it were honour or money or some other object of desire, he could hardly respond this truthfully.

The road to salvation is still safest for whoever is free of riches and other material possessions. For it is most difficult for those who possess objects not to be impeded by them on their passage. Who is unaware that Hippodamia had flown before the others to the palm of victory in so far as she was able to retard the progress of the opposing suitors by throwing gold?[45] And so the virgin remained invincible until finally someone who was a despiser of money came along, one who by his scorn for gold defeated the virgin, earned the gold, and from this (as was represented) he made waxen axles for the maiden who was his rival, so that love of money was engulfed by love of incorruptibility. Is not the latter commended by the judgment of God and the former made contemptible because the iniquitous overflow with material objects while the good are destitute? Yet it occasionally happens – by what means I do not know – that wealth is thrust upon just men towards their subversion; and the more diligently it is pushed away, the more zealously it pounds at the door of the contemptuous. The more carefully blessed Eugenius turned away presents, the more did they stream into him from everywhere. Also, it happens nearly everywhere that things flee so long as they are sought out and they hasten forward so long as one is fleeing from them. And this surely is the shortest and most honourable path to riches. For when one is prudently cut off from wealth, it happens that both eternal life is acquired and riches accumulate.

Even if this is seen as excessively arduous for others, it must be carried out by judges, ecclesiastical as well as temporal, who are obligated to justice by either profession or oath. Indeed, Samuel is the model for both sorts, since he so supervised the sacrifices that he did

---

[45] John confuses here two tales from classical mythology: that of Hippodamia and Pelops, and that of Hippomenes and Atlanta.

not spare the blood of the impious and so executed both sorts of judgment that no one was oppressed and nothing was accepted from the hand of anyone. This was attested by Samuel's conscience and by the people, and yet his scrupulous conscience would not be satisfied unless the people strengthened their testimony with an oath. 'For he asserted: The Lord is my witness against you and His anointed is witness on this day that you have not found anything in my hand. And they said: He is witness.'[46] Whoever is called upon by the provincials to furnish such testimony resembles the omnipotent and all-knowing judge, God. For he who introduces into consideration his conscience and daily humanity, of which the Judge on high is aware, plans his case providently. Those who, unlike Samuel, do not discuss their judgments in this fashion, but who are quick to make excuses for their sins, as though washing their hands with Pilate, proclaim: 'I am clean of the blood of this just man'; because they have sinned contrary to the law, they will be condemned according to the law. And also those men who could have constrained them, yet chose not to, will share in this condemnation. And enough has been said about these matters for the wise man. Let the pen, therefore, pass over to what Plutarch introduces about the analogy to the hands.

[46] I Samuel 12:5.

BOOK VI

Prologue

It is widely known from the moralist that

Near the school of Emilia the solitary craftsman
both shapes fingernails and has imitated in bronze the softness of
    hair;
his work is most unfortunate because he is unable
to form the whole. If I took the trouble to create anything myself,
I would not wish to be him any more than to live with a deformed
    nose,
or to be stared at because of black eyes and black hair.[1]

Inasmuch as I follow closely the footsteps of Plutarch in the 'Instruction of Trajan', I think that this image addresses my own situation, and I will be ridiculed by everyone unless I diligently complete what is started. For I am acknowledged to be dependent upon him at the present moment. Therefore, I follow him and descend with him from the head of the republic all the way to the feet, yet on the condition that, if in this section I appear too caustic to those who are permitted to be ignorant of legal right, then it will be ascribed not to me but to Plutarch, or preferably to those themselves who refuse to discern the rules which they follow and according to which they are living. For what is said about fellow countrymen has been added with the single intention that they will return to the path of virtue, even unwillingly. Indeed the purpose of helping them towards action is served as much by the examples of the ancients as by the greatness of an invincible prince, whose titles I now compile into one, so that when the trumpets and clarion and all manner of musical instruments of others cry out together at the same time his praises, I, a plebeian and uneducated man, may in a similar fashion spread his praises far and wide with my whistling pipes. For who expects the music of the copper-joined flute and the most sublime trumpet to be emulated by a half-rustic man?

[1] Horace, *Ars Poetica*, 32–37.

Still, I will approach and will thrust myself into such solemnity; and what is absent in inborn talent will be furnished by the abundance of devotion.

> While the wild boar is married to the mountain, while the fish will
>   love the river,
> and while bees feed on thyme, the tree cricket on dewdrops,
> always will his honour and name and praises endure.[2]

If great men think that anything is said in injury to them, they may learn from the prince that disagreeable medicines are administered not for the destruction of the sick but for their health. Setting this statement in advance, let us proceed to the remainder of the political body.

[2] Virgil, *Eclogae*, 5.76–78.

CHAPTER I

That the hand of the republic is either armed or unarmed; and which one is unarmed, and regarding its duties

And so the hand of the republic is either armed or unarmed. The armed hand is of course that which is occupied with marching and the blood-letting of warfare; the unarmed hand is that which expedites justice and attends to the warfare of legal right, distanced from arms. For the soldiers of the republic are not only those who, protected by helmets and breastplates, turn loose their swords or spears or whatever other weapons against the enemy, but also advocates of cases who invigorate the weary and, relying upon the fortification of an illustrious voice, lift up the fallen; and no less do they provide for mankind than if, working with the armour of life, hope and posterity, they provided protection from the enemy. Even tax collectors and public servants and all officials of courts of law are soldiers. For just as some are offices of peace and others are offices of war, so likewise it is necessary for some to arrange the first sort of task, others the second.

And so the armed hand is exercised strictly against enemies, but the unarmed is extended also against the citizen. In addition, discipline is necessary for both because both are notoriously accustomed to being wicked. The use of the hand testifies to the qualities of the head itself because, as Wisdom asserts, the iniquitous king has entirely impious ministers; 'and of whatever kind is a city's leader, of the same kind also are its inhabitants'.[3] Censuring his colleague Sophocles, Pericles said that it is necessary that not only the hands but also the eyes of the governor have continence. For the continence of governors is laudable when they restrain their hands and hold back the hands of others from exactions and injuries.

Still, the hand of both sorts of soldiers, namely, armed and unarmed, is the hand of the prince; and unless he constrains both, he is not very continent. And surely the unarmed hand is to be curbed more closely because while the armed hand is commanded to abstain from exactions and rapine, the unarmed hand is also prohibited presents. Yet if a lawful penalty is imposed upon someone, if what is fixed or conceded by legal right is exacted or accepted, then there is to be no punishment or blame at all. For whatever it is, it does not receive the name of an 'exaction'; nor does it fall into the kind of present that officials are prohibited from accepting.

Because the licence of officials is greater, inasmuch as they can plunder and molest private persons under the pretext of official business, any encroachment contrary to duty is to be punished with a heavier penalty. For the blessed Laurence, Bishop of Milan, asserts: 'What is a tax collector? Is he not a source of rapine and violent law? What is a tax collector? A plunderer without shame, a physician of extermination. Is not a tax collector more frightful than a thief? For in truth a thief steals apprehensively; yet the tax collector transgresses with assurance.'[4] The thief fears the snare of law; the tax collector thinks that law is whatever he does. Law deters thieves from illicit acts; the tax collector derives the law from iniquity for his own malicious advantage.

Who is more iniquitous than he whose words of justice condemn justice and whose weapons of innocent pillage injure and murder the innocent? Above all, he destroys law by law and is beyond the law, even while he burdens others with the law. 'For as the governor, even when he decides wrongly, proclaims right (*ius*), still having respect for what he ought to do but not for what was done, so the tax collector,

[3] Ecclesiasticus 10:2.
[4] Laurence of Milan, *Homilia de muliere Chananea*, in Migne, *PL* 66.118.

even when he transgresses, is seen to carry out right, regarding the duty of the office, not the malicious motive.'[5] But what is the duty of the tax collector? We learn from the report of Luke that tax collectors came to John in order that they might be baptised by him; and they said: 'Master, what should we do?' In response, he said to them: 'You must exact nothing more than that which is assigned to you.'[6] Behold the duties of the tax collector: to exact and receive that which is appointed. Whatever is more, however, results from the evil of the exactor and the accepter, not the giver. In addition, it is extended to the officials of all magistracies that nothing more is to be exacted by them.

And so public servants lawfully exact what is owed to them from fees, and all orders of military officers justly accept their arranged salaries. Yet it is not permitted to intimidate and molest in order that presents be extorted. 'Fire', says blessed Job, 'will engulf the tents of those who accept presents readily. Their assembly fosters pain and is determined by iniquity, and their womb prepares malice.'[7] All tax collectors, from the greatest down to the lowest, only have time these days for extortion rather than justice, and so rage against the people to the extent that what one of them leaves behind, the others do not hesitate to remove, as if they were instituted according to the lament of the prophet, that what the locusts have left over, the wingless grasshopper called the *brucus* devours. And, in order that there might be greater licence for him to do harm, he accumulates for himself several offices, so that what he does not acquire from one office is removed by means of another. The physiologists teach that from the locust is born the *brucus*, which is so-called until the time it has wings. Next, when the wings are grown and it learns to fly, it is called an *athelebus*. And when it is fully able to fly, a locust is brought forth once again; and the *brucus* is much more serious than the locust and *athelebus* because it lacks wings and cannot depart rapidly. And for this reason, whenever it arrives, it consumes the fruit of the earth entirely. Whenever the locust and the *athelebus* come they perhaps do damage in very many places, but still less than the *brucus*, which does not move once it settles into position, until the time it devours all the labours of men. And among officials you meet the very same *brucus*, *athelebus* and locust, who harm those near and far, and these

---

[5] *Corpus Iuris Civilis, Digesta*, 1.1.11.   [6] Luke 3:12–13.   [7] Job 15:34–35.

creatures, once settled into place, devour fortunes and do not depart before they have carried off all riches. Who can count the number of wards most dutifully defrauded and the number of farms that injury has forced on to the market and the number of us who by the licence of such men have been plundered of our goods under the semblance of religion or some other pretext, not as travellers to Rome or pilgrims so much as exiles? Above all, these acts are done publicly, and neither governors nor proconsuls restrain them because (as it is customarily said) the work of the wolf is congratulated by the raven, and the unjust judge applauds the minister of iniquity.

Moreover, it may be noted on the basis of everyone's experience that wherever princes are infidels and companions of thieves, they hasten to embrace those whose misdeeds they observe, adding their own share of iniquity in order that they may receive a portion of any profit. If you were to pity a pauper, if you shed tears about the death of justice, if you decide to lend assistance, if you dare to mutter so that you do not respond 'Bravo! Well done!' to each thing that they either say or do, you will have to represent your case in the court of the governor in defence of accusations by these Herodians of high treason. Unless you bend to the governor in all matters, and repeat anything at all – unless his every movement is imitated – you contradict Caesar and are opposed to the person and crown of the king. The clamour of officials rises up, is redoubled and ascends to the clouds repeating in a great voice: 'We accuse this man of the subversion of the people and the prohibition of grants of tribute to Caesar and the denial that Caesar is king and that everything is rightfully permitted to his ministers; we accuse this man of the cancellation of the laws of our fathers, the introduction of new laws, and the rejection of the very oldest habits; we are witness to these things.' But if you wish to declare your innocence or to add anything for the sake of justice, if you say that the king is Christ whom it is more necessary to obey than men, if you mention any of the privileges of His Church (which is most hateful to them), they will immediately thunder forth, proclaiming loudly: 'What further witnesses do you desire? Behold, you hear the blasphemy for yourselves; whoever asserts such statements contradicts Caesar.' Yet if the judge, seeing innocence and respecting justice, were to dissimulate, they will shout from all directions: 'If you release this man, you are not Caesar's friend. In order that the punishment of one may be the liberation of many, take this man and eradicate him so that Barabbas may live and enjoy good health.' For as their manifest works demonstrate, they are like the members of one body which was fathered by the devil. The blessed Job eminently asserts about them: 'Their body is like a shield made of cast and tightly packed scales which have been joined together; one is connected to the other, and not even a breathing space comes between them; one has been glued to another and, holding fast, they will not be separated from each other.'[8] They stand beside each other because they 'unite as one in opposition to the Lord and in opposition to His anointed'.[9] And their authority has such great force that whatever they say prevails as if it was found in the public registry. Their testimony prejudices the truth.

There is no one besides the prince who is permitted to resist their judgments. Unless they are restrained by the prince, there is no peace, or it is only that peace in which there is the most bitter of bitterness, although everyone says that it is peace. For while it is otherwise lawful to repel force with force without blame if one has safeguarded moderation, it is not permitted to murmur about their intimidations, their robberies and their tortures; for in fact they are seen to be the ministers of legal right. He is excused who does anything for the protection of his own body; yet if he resists the various injuries of these plunderers, he is judged worthy of any punishment. If they mess up your hair by dirtying and dishevelling it, if they pluck your beard, if they pull on your ears as though they were too short, if they give you a slap on the head or impiously hit you with a fist, if they pluck out one or another of your eyes, patiently tolerate it (unless you prefer to lose both of your eyes) because whatever they take for granted they boast is done with the right hand of Caesar. If you wield a sword in your hand, if you decline voluntarily to offer up your neck, then they expose their stomachs, reveal their throats, and challenge you, if you dare, that you might lay open Caesar's intestines with your sword and let go a hand that would touch Caesar in any way; for they brag that they bear the person of Caesar. Yet if this is the right hand of Caesar, what might the left hand be? Surely their conduct does not execute justice but abuses it, and does not carry out law but cancels it, although a few fraudulently defend their errors in opposi-

[8] Job 41:15–17.
[9] Psalms 2:2.

tion to the intent of the law by the terms of their prerogative; for 'they are wise in the doing of evil'.[10]

Yet while these are harmful pests to the provincials, no one can be more harmful than the prince. Everything which is granted to the provincials is subject according to legal right to the needs and uses of the prince. The whole province is like the money box of the prince; anyone who exhausts it transgresses most seriously against the prince, whose wealth is reduced. For the provincials are like those who are located on someone else's land (*superficiarii*) and, whenever the ruler claims use, they are not so much lords (*dominii*) as custodians of the property. Yet if necessity does not pressure the members, then the goods of provincials are their own, of which the prince himself may not legally make use. For if 'it concerns the republic that no one should misuse his own possessions',[11] then it is not permitted for what belongs to another to be constantly abused. Moreover, when a province is exhausted by these ministers of iniquity and wickedness and retainers of Satan – these Herodian men – what will the prince use if necessity impends? Therefore, if he is wise, he reins in their jaws with bit and bridle, lest in the fashion of wolves whose gluttony is driven on by an enormous belly they might devastate and destroy the provinces and exhaust the total strength of the republic to the injury of the prince. Besides, the despoiler himself falls into poverty, is hated by all of the provincials, and must make a case to his own judge, to be examined with severity on the basis of the works of his hands and the injuries of the provincials, whom under the pretext of his protection he has unjustly and almost fraudulently plundered and destroyed with his unarmed hand.

[10]Jeremiah 4:22.   [11]Justinian, *Institutes*, 1.8.2.

CHAPTER 2

That military service requires selection, knowledge and practice

There remains the armed hand which is occupied (as was said) with marching and the blood-letting of warfare. The wisdom and justice of the prince appears mainly in his moderate use of this hand. For as

Vegetius Renatus asserts, there is no one who ought to know either more or better than the prince, whose learning should be advantageous to all his subjects. For since the works of peace and likewise of war should be moderated, he ought to have proficiency in law and matters of war. And while some remarks were stated above about the endeavours of peacetime, it is at present the moment to discuss the armed hand, which does not flourish without selection, knowledge and practice. For whenever these qualities are not present, a useless hand yields no advantage; yet among these, knowledge and practice are the most useful. For knowledge of matters of war nourishes boldness in battle. Nobody fears to do that which he is confident he has learned well. For indeed a few who are trained in the conflicts of warfare are more prone to victory than a raw and unlearned multitude which is always open to massacre.

For what made the Romans the conquerors of all nations? Above all it was knowledge, practice and the loyalty devoted by the selected men to the republic by reason of their oath. For how else would a few Romans have prevailed against the multitude of the Gauls? How else could such diminutive men have been so courageous when confronted with the height of the Germans? It is evident that the Spanish were superior to the Romans not only in numbers but also in strength. They always came out unequal to the craftiness and wealth of the Africans. Because of all this adversity, it was advantageous to select skilled recruits and, as it is thus said, to teach them the law (*ius*) of arms, to strengthen their learning with daily practice, to calculate the likely results on the field of combat by the analysis of effective techniques during rehearsal of the battle formation, and to punish the lax severely.

The already mentioned author testifies to this, adding in nearly these words that it is useless to keep a soldier well-fed and accustomed to riches, preferring as more appropriate rural plebeians who were raised under the heavens and upon hard work, enduring the sun, indifferent to shade, unfamiliar with bathhouses, ignorant of luxury – in sum, simple souls, contented with little food, inured to all the labours that their limbs endure, for whom it is a habit of rural life to bear a sword, to construct trenches and to carry heavy burdens. Do you think that singers, gamblers and fowlers would, when they are needed, be found fit for these activities? Clearly both they and fish mongers, confectioners, clothiers and all who have transactions in anything that would seem to tend towards servility are kept away from military duty, whereas simple craftsmen, blacksmiths and likewise carpenters, hunters of deer and wild boars are considered qualified for military purposes.

For Gideon – not touching on matters of figurative meaning – was prohibited by the command of God from having faith in a fearful and inexperienced multitude and was ordered to bring forth against the Midianites only those whose strength of soul and physical experience was proven. Therefore, when Gideon proclaimed for the hearing of all together that 'whoever is timid and afraid may turn back', 22,000 men among the people retreated and only 10,000 stayed behind. But out of this ten thousand the Lord selected as more ready for warfare only those who, like dogs in their thirst, quickly lapped up water by throwing it into their mouths from their hands, whereas those who drank with their knees bent were left behind. And so with three-hundred men was achieved the liberation of the people, the killing of the enemy, the capture of their kings, and the destruction of the princes of not so much a 'militia' as a 'malice'; and Gideon killed Zebah and Zalmunna with the edge of a sword, and carried off the ornaments and baubles with which they were accustomed to decorating the necks of the royal camels, as well as the ornaments, jewelry and clothes of purple which the kings of Midian were in the habit of enjoying, and from the whole booty he reserved for himself only the golden earrings of the Ishmaelites, distributing the rest according to the interest of the people. Therefore, he conquered an innumerable multitude of enemies with a small group of strong men who, I should suppose, had not readily learned how to lap up water while partaking of the luxuries of cities or the feasts of kings and daily banquets, for which reason the Lord thought to elect them in preference to others.[12]

Even though necessity occasionally requires city dwellers and more delicate sorts to be compelled to take up arms, they are to learn thoroughly from the beginning of their enlistment to be wholly devoted to military service, to labour, to drill, to carry a burden and to bear sunlight and dust, living on small quantities of food and sleeping together sometimes under the heavens, sometimes in pavilions. Then and only then are they to be instructed in the use of arms; and, if the

[12] Judges 8:2–28.

campaign turns out to be lengthy, they are mainly to be occupied with servile tasks and to be kept at a distance from the enticements of cities, so that in this way both their bodies and their souls may approach strength. It is not to be denied that, after the foundation of their city, the Romans were always departing to fight wars; but then none of them would have become involved in luxuries, for their young men washed away the sweat accumulated from running and the practice field by taking a swim in the Tiber rather than immersing themselves in the public baths. The fighter and the farmer were identical; but they would merely exchange their equipment. This is true to the extent that when the ploughing Quintius Cincinnatus agreed to the offer of the dictatorship,

His anxious wife adorned him in the dictatorial regalia in front of the
    cows,
and a lictor brought home his plough.[13]

The strength of a corps is thus principally furnished from the farms. For it is asserted, 'I am not unaware that those who are less familiar with the luxuries of life fear death less.'[14]

[13] Persius, *Saturae*, 1.74–75.
[14] Vegetius Renatus, *De re militari*, 1.3.

CHAPTER 6

What ills arise from disregard by our countrymen for the selection of soldiers, and how Harold tamed the Welsh

However, the experience of military discipline falls into disuse either out of fondness for long standing peace or from the attack of effeminacy and luxury which weakens the souls of men or again because of the idleness of youth and the laziness of leaders in our times. For where do you find one who can teach energetically what he has not learned himself?

Now we endure the ills of a lengthy peace; more harsh than arms luxury dwells with us and the conquered world is avenged.[15]

[15] Juvenal, *Saturae*, 6.292–293.

Review the ancient and modern histories, and you will discover plainly that the disturbance of peoples, the collision of arms, the misfortunes of men and terrible plagues always either accompany or follow luxury. One looks no further for an example than the Britons of Snowdon, who now attack and extend their borders and, leaving their retreats and forests, occupy the flatland, and assault, take by storm, and demolish or retain for themselves the fortifications of our chief nobles before the gaze of the latter because our youth, 'who take pleasure under cover or in shade',[16] born to consume the fruits of the earth, sleeping in daylight, postponing honourable duties for whore-mongering, and pursuing pleasures the entire day, are more familiar with the cithern, the lyre, and the tambourine and the sound of the organ at the banquet than with the clarion and the trumpet of the encampment. This is why leaders have not emerged or have been erroneously selected, and why discipline has ceased or been relaxed. For, if it is necessary to join together in battle, they have too little courage in light armour, and too little mobility in heavy armour. The one so burdens them that they cannot follow the enemy; the other so terrifies them that they refuse to resist the enemy if they are exposed to wounds.

Our borders are pillaged while our youth are instructed; and, while our knights are being equipped, the enemy escapes and (as one is accustomed to saying) while the dog keeps still, the wolf enters a secure hiding place. There is no one who apprehends or chases after the departing enemy because an encumbered soldier is neither adequate nor effective against an unburdened opponent. Still, the foe does not head for the protection of a wall or a moat, but for a place which, although it is not known to all, is yet just as accessible to our troops as to theirs. In any case, he lives there securely because our troops do not trust in their own valour but in the protection of arms.

The recent history of England narrates how, after their invasion, the Britons were pillaging England. Duke Harold was sent by King Edward to vanquish them, sending a man who was conspicuous in the qualities of vigorous fighting and praiseworthy works and who could have extended his glory as far as his posterity except that, imitating the wickedness of his father, he tarnished the rewards of fame by assuming royal power. Therefore, when he perceived the mobility of

[16] *Ibid.*, 7.105.

the foreigners, he selected for the mission soldiers who fought in the same way, since he resolved that they were to engage in battle practise in light armament, assaulting in rawhide boots, chests covered by hardened straps and hides, throwing up small light shields against the missiles, and at one time hurling javelins, at another employing swords against the enemy. His troops would stick close to the enemy's fleeing footsteps in order that they might hold fast 'foot to foot and spear to spear' and might repulse shield with shield. And so he devastated everything along the way to Snowdon and, extending the expedition for two years, he captured their kings and presented their heads to the king who had sent him. And killing every male he could find, all the way to pitiful little children, he pacified the province with the edge of a sword; he established the law that from then on any Briton whomsoever, when found with a weapon beyond the boundary which was prescribed for his people, that is, Offa's Dyke, would have his hand cut off by royal officials. And thereby the strength of the Britons was so impaired by the duke that almost the entire nation seemed to die out and their women were married to Englishmen by the indulgence of the king mentioned just now.

Do you see how much the selection of leaders and the military experience of the young contribute to the republic?

CHAPTER 7

What is the formula of the oath of the soldier, and that no one is permitted to serve in the army without it

Nonetheless, no one will be given the belt of the soldier except under the terms of a sacred oath, according to the ancient law. For, just as it is read in Julius Frontinus, the first military oaths were made during the consulship of Lucius Flaccus and Gaius Varro; for previously oaths had been requested solely from tribunes, whereas afterwards soldiers took an oath, each one to the other, that they would not depart in haste and by reason of fright nor retreat from the battle line except in order to obtain a weapon or carry off an enemy or protect a fellow citizen. And this was called the military oath, which was confirmed by the authority of the most Christian emperors and by usage.

The formula of the oath, witnessed by Vegetius, is thus. The soldiers swear by God and His Christ and by the Holy Spirit and by the majesty of the prince, which according to God is to be respected and revered by the human race. For when one accepts the lawful ruler, faithful devotion is to be offered to him just as the constant vigil of devoted service is offered to the person and body of God. For God is served either by the private person or by the soldier when he who rules by the authority of God is loyally respected. They swear, I say, that they will perform with all their energy that which the prince has enjoined; they will never desert the army or refuse to die for the republic, by which they were selected as soldiers. Once they perform this oath-taking, they are given the belt and privileges of a soldier. And to this degree it obtains that selection and an oath make a soldier, since without selection no one may be enlisted or sworn in, while without an oath no one may receive the name or duties of the soldier . . .

CHAPTER 8

The armed soldier is by necessity bound to religion, in just the way that the clergy is consecrated in obedience to God; and that just as the title of soldier is one of labour, so it is one of honour

Reflect upon the words of the soldier's oath, and you will find that the armed soldier no less than the spiritual one is limited by the requirements of office to religion and the worship of God, since he must faithfully and according to God obey the prince and vigilantly serve the republic. For this reason, I have said, those who are neither selected nor sworn in, though they may be considered soldiers in name, are no more soldiers than are priests and clerics who are not called into the orders of the Church. For indeed just as the title of soldier is one of labour so it is one of honour. Truly no one may take honour upon himself, but he who is called prides himself on the honour which is collected from God.

Moses and the leaders of faithful peoples, when it was necessary for them to attack their enemies, selected strong men and those most learned in warfare. So the select are superior in these ways. He who thrusts himself into military service without selection provokes upon himself the sword which he usurps by his own rash presumption. He therefore breaks the eternal commandment that he who accepts the sword will perish by the sword. If the authority of Cicero is admitted on this matter, he is not to be called by the name of soldier, but of murderer. For in old writings those who use arms outside the decree of law are called murderers and bandits. For the arms which the law does not use must oppose the law.

The sacred history of the Christian Gospel testifies that two swords suffice for the imperial power; all others pertain to those who advance with swords and clubs in order that they may take Christ captive, desiring to eradicate His name. Therefore, of what use are soldiers who are called when they do not obey the law according to their oath but believe that the glory of their military service grows if the priesthood is humiliated, if the authority of the Church becomes worthless, if they would so expand the kingdom of man that the empire of God contracts, if they declare their own praises and flatter and extol themselves by false eulogy, imitating boastful soldiers to the ridicule of their listeners? Their courage manifests itself mainly if either their weapons or their words pierce the clergy or the unarmed soldiers.

But what is the use of the military order? To protect the Church, to attack faithlessness, to venerate the priesthood, to avert injuries to the poor, to pacify provinces, to shed blood (as the formula of their oath instructs) for their brothers, and to give up their lives if it is necessary. The exultations of God in their throats and the twin swords in their hands are for the exercise of punishment over nations, for the censure of peoples, and for the binding of enemy kings in shackles and opposing nobles in iron fetters. But to what end? In order that they may serve either rage or vanity or avarice or their own private will? By no means. Rather, they serve in order that they may execute judgments assigned to them, according to which each attends not to his own will but to the will of God, the angels and men by reason of equity and the public utility. I have said 'in order that they may execute' because just as judges prescribe judgments, so soldiers perform their duty by executing judgment. Above all, 'this is the glory of all His saints'.[17] For those who act this way are saints and those who are most

---

[17] Psalms 149:9.

devoted in their faith in God serve the prince most loyally; and those who seek their faith in God amongst the glory of things most effectively promote the glory of their own virtues.

CHAPTER 9

That faith is owed to God in preference to any man whomsoever, and man is not served unless God is served

It is of no consequence whether one serves in the army of an infidel or of a believer, so long as one serves so that faith is unharmed. We read that Diocletian and Julian and other emperors were served by the faithful, who exhibited loyalty and reverence towards them as princes defending the republic. For they assailed the enemies of the empire, but they served the commandments of God; yet if they had been ordered to violate the law, they would have preferred God to man. 'Princes sat and accused them';[18] they would have been experienced in the justification of God, constantly speaking commandments without confusion and performing His commandments with all faithfulness. One reads that David had served in the army of Achish, and had fulfilled his military duties faithfully and reverently.

In addition, this formula is to be prescribed for and fulfilled by every soldier: that he will keep unimpaired first the faith owed to God, and thereafter the loyalty owed to the prince and the republic. And the most important matters always precede the lesser ones because faith is to be kept neither with the republic nor the prince contrary to God but instead according to God, just as the legal formula of the military oath has it. For this reason, I am much amazed if some prince keeps faith with those whom he sees not observing the faith owed to God Himself, those who (to make no mention of other matters) were obligated by their military oath. I ask you, who labours under such a disease of reason that he believes that those whom he sees to be corrupt and faithless to Him to whom is owed the most will nevertheless be loyal to him? The prince is feared; certainly, if a stronger prince arrives, he will be feared the more greatly. Perhaps the prince is loved; yet if a more benign and beneficent prince appears, he will be

---

[18] Psalms 119:23.

loved the better. There is nothing to which the impious will not turn when man is preferred to God; he who makes light of his first loyalty will by no means serve his secondary one.

CHAPTER 18

The examples of recent history, and how King Henry the Second quelled the disturbances and violence under King Stephen and pacified the island

And because some will perhaps view early English history as too remote for the demonstration of the virtue of a people who are lacking not in nature but in learning, practice, skill and perhaps leadership, I approach the present and will give a condensed account of those events which are known to almost everyone.

The great virtue by which Cnut of England crushed the Daci or Danes and restrained the disturbances of the Norse is clear from the fact that, on account of the merits of the preeminent virtues of which he made mighty and obvious use, our own Kent preserves to the present day the honour of the first cohort and of the first contest with the enemy in all battles. Also the province of Severus, which is called the name of Wiltshire by modern usage and by its inhabitants, claims for itself by the same right the honour of subsidiary cohort in conjunction with Devon and Cornwall.

To descend to our own times, the King of England, who is known as Rufus – certainly an adroit fighter but not religious enough and a persecutor of saints and in particular of Saint Anselm of Canterbury – is said to have provoked against himself the invidious arrow by which he was killed. He, I say, attacked Cenomannum, captured the count, and yet was so respectful towards him as not to hand him over to the custody of a prison; and such a great work will be testified to in perpetuity by Mount Barbatus or, if you prefer to consider it by another name, it may be called Mount Barbarus or Mount Barbarorum.

I pass on to his successor, the illustrious Henry, who is called the Lion of Justice, and who, as is widely known, was feared not only by the cities but also by the castles of Gaul. But how he crushed and put to flight the King of the Franks in a heated battle I intentionally fail to mention lest the repetition of well-known events become tedious, because his victory is often mentioned and many witnesses exist in both kingdoms who were present at the battle. I believe it is superfluous to relate by what means Henry captured Robert, the Duke of the Normans – a warlike man and adroit fighter, who had returned from the liberation of Jerusalem – when he invaded the borders of a foreign kingdom under the pretext of his title, since even more junior men have seen the captive in public custody, yet maintaining respect for his dignity and descent. The Norman nobles – some captured, others imprisoned, still others disinherited to the present day – testify to this; and the tomb of the captive Duke is in our presence.

Finally, for those who seek examples not far removed, Henry's grandson, if the merits of his virtue remain in harmony until the end with the grace already given, will for all times be the best King of Britain, the most fortunate Duke of Normandy and Aquitaine, and foremost as much in the extent of his possessions as in the splendour of his virtues, his vigour, his magnificence, his prudence and the modesty by which he has lived from his infancy, if I may say so. Envy itself cannot keep silent or dissimulate, since his works are recent and manifest, and his powers extend and his titles carry on from the ends of Britain to the borders of Spain.

Obviously possession of genius and prudence
come before a beard, he understands speaking and keeping silent, . . .
and he is able to place upon vice the black stain of disgust.[19]

For indeed God, desiring to punish the malice of a dishonest people, had broken the promise which the nobility had confirmed by oath to the daughter of the Lion of Justice; new men were conceded favour to be raised to power and a foreign man [King Stephen] was allowed to rule over the kingdom in contempt for goodness and equity, one whose counsel was foolish from the outset, whose cause was founded upon iniquity and wickedness, who neglected discipline to the extent that he did not so much rule as intimidate and bring into conflict the clergy and the people, and everyone was provoked to everything; for the measure of right was force. Therefore, invading the kingdom, he disinherited and excluded the lord for whom, if there was loyalty in

---

[19] Persius, *Saturae*, 4.4–5, 13.

the man, he was sworn to die both because of the merits of predecessors in the office and by necessity of his oath. He was devoted to corrupting neighbouring nations; he contracted marriages and alliances with their princes, lest by the intercession of God the child who was still crying in his cradle might undertake the claim of his inheritance. To be sure much was plotted against the innocent but in all cases this iniquity was tricked by itself. And it may be observed that because God is truthful, the faith which he did not keep with God or his earthly lord, he in no way found among his subjects. Indeed loyalty was meted back to him in the same measure that he himself first meted it out to others, as if all had learned from Ennius: 'Neither have I given nor do I give faith to those who are unfaithful.'[20] But although he did much evil and little good, yet his worst deed was that he put his hands upon the anointed in contempt of God; still, he was not without a reputation for wickedness and betrayal which he deservedly obtained amongst everyone by his heinous works, to the extent that no one subsequently approached his court securely. Yet not only did he seize the bishops, who were the primary ones he ruined, but also he extended his traps to everyone whom he suspected of treachery. The seizure of the bishops was, however, the beginning of his evil deeds and the more recent acts of the man were always worse than the previous ones.

What more? In his days evils were multiplied in the land to the extent that if one were to review them summarily, one could exceed the history of Josephus. Notwithstanding, the virtue of the boy opposed them and, almost before the age for the obligations of military service, he so crushed the assault of the wicked ones that he is sometimes said not to be inferior (and if only he were never found inferior!) to the younger Theodosius, whom histories compare with Alexander. He did not delay; in early adolescent years the youth was already advanced in military skills and his very ferocious face and strong hands, divinely aided, shattered and subdued the hearts of his enemies. And immediately the Kings of the Franks and the English rose up against him with their collective strength and also a more savage enemy than either one of them, Eustace, the brother-in-law of the Frankish King, who, fighting in his own personal cause, was exerting himself not so much on behalf of his father but in order to

---

[20] Quoted by Cicero, *De officiis*, 3.29.104.

retain the paternal crown for himself. And not only did our Neo-
ptolomy virilely hold out against them, but he for the most part
mightily defeated them. Thereafter, the Eustace of whom I have
spoken, touched by an inward pain of the heart, did the best deed of
his life – he passed out of human existence – whereupon the good
delighted and congratulated the public fortune, since he threatened
another scourging of this country. 'Groups of female entertainers,
charlatans, beggars, mimes, clowns, all this sort'[21] mourned him. Yet
the glory of our Duke should not in any way be diminished by the
death of this man; he was alive and armed and deployed many troops
at the surrender of Crowmarsh, during which he with his father
appeared in reserve with sound troops and a more imposing number;
observing the scene, he held back his troops. Yet the Duke,
admonished beforehand by someone's counsel, was placed between
the castle which the King secured and the King's own troops, which
were numerous but by far the less practised. And so that this will not
be ascribed to men of foreign birth, Henry's army principally relied
on fellow countrymen. He who had occupied the kingdom was at last
led by the faults he committed to this: that he was constrained to
disinherit his son and to concede the royal succession to the Duke and
to bind the nobility and troops to an arrangement of loyalty.

I pass on the siege of Chinon because no one is unaware that the
English and the Normans there, who were now united by a complex
confederation, had been conspicuously outstanding and extremely
adroit in the capture of the castle. And I am silent about Nantes and
the entire county of lesser Brittany, even though it is a great province,
which would be rebelling even at the present day except that the
strength of the English nation would be terrifying. From either this
fear itself or an attraction to love or virtue (which one is unknown), the
illustrious Count of Blois and Chartres restored the castles which
were lost to the Duchy of Normandy during the time of the period of
wardship.

It would be protracted if I were to strive to enumerate the illustrious
deeds of such a great prince, which are as impossible to describe
completely as they are all necessary to be admired. And I do not claim
for myself the powers to do something which could exhaust Orosius,
Egesippus and Trogus, if the career which Henry follows is long and

---

[21] Horace, *Saturae*, 1.2.1–2.

prosperous, along the lines of its preceding portents. Certainly, the end of adolescence is mistrusted by some, and I hope that the good are fearful in vain!

CHAPTER 19

Of the honour to be exhibited by soldiers, and of the modesty to be shown; and who are the transmitters of the military arts, and of certain of their general precepts

Why do I linger in commendation of a nation which is agreed to be laudable by nature? Blessed Eugenius himself had said that England was equal to applying itself to whatever it might desire and was to be preferred before others unless frivolity hampered it. But just as Hannibal denied that the Romans could be vanquished except in their own country, so this country is invincible while roaming abroad; conversely, at its own residence it is assailed more readily. Yet perhaps the inhabitants of Britain and also Italy have this in common with other nations. If they are correctly instructed and encouraged in the practice of their lessons, however, they will advance more honourably, be treated as the defenders of their country, and glisten in the adoration which is fitting for such men; for the adoration of wantonness is not free from vice or infamy even in the female sex.

Indeed it is repeatedly discovered during wars that soldiers with wanton and splendid apparel do not so much confer victory on their fellow citizens as attract their enemies with the promise of spoils. And for this reason, Hannibal, when in exile at the court of the King of Antioch, was most genially censorious when the king displayed his troops glistening in gold and silver uniforms, exhibiting chariots with scythe-blades and elephants with high towers, and all his horsemen with jewelled bridles and gear. While the king thus took pride in the contemplation of such a great and ornate army, he had caught sight of Hannibal and said: 'Do you think all this would be enough for the Romans?' Then the Carthaginian, mocking the worthless and unwarlike soldiers with their sumptuous armour, said: 'I certainly believe it to be enough, even though the Romans are extremely avaricious.' Indeed, this was elegant, pointed and shrewd; for the king had asked about the number of the troops and their comparative value, and it is evident that he received a response about their spoils. In sum, if Ovid keeps his own art away from soldiers and directs them to be distanced from youths adorned like women,[22] who believes such men are to be admitted to valiant military service? Craftsmen of each individual art embellish those things beyond others for which they know they are honoured beyond others. For this reason, it is evident that soldiers ought to be more elegant in weapons than in clothing.

It is read that Aeneas had transferred his jewels from his fingers to his sword, Virro to his goblets. It is also generally accepted that the Maccabeans had gilded their shields and, by reason of their gleam, they demolished the courage of nations; yet it is believable that they were content with ordinary clothing. There is nothing that is less appropriate for a soldier than the cultivation of weakness and the enjoyment of exquisite clothing, unless perhaps in contempt of Mars he might like Traso devote his military service to Venus in order to assail the fortifications of Taïs. Squalor is also to be avoided, and the mean, which advances along the golden path, is constantly to be followed. I want, moreover, our countrymen to be persuaded of this: if they are practised, they have no lack of courage, which frequently falls into disuse if discipline is not maintained.

The art of military affairs is said to have been handed down by the Lacedaemonians; and for this reason, Hannibal sought a Lacedaemonian teacher of arms before attacking Italy. Whoever is desirous of peace is to prepare for war; whoever covets victory is to train his troops diligently; whoever wishes for good fortune is to fight by skill, not by chance. No one dares to provoke, no one dares to offend, those whom one knows would be superior if fought. The old annals indicate that the Athenians had commanded of their warriors one thing above all else: soldiers not yet veterans were to become accustomed to constant practise and labour. For these tend towards health in the camp and outstanding victory in battle. The same source also reports that the strength of an army consists in its infantry, and someone who does not know how to fight except on a horse is little suited to the army.

Nevertheless, neither practice nor a calling to fight is useful to him whose salary is not forthcoming. For if you omit his provisions, your

---

[22] Ovid, *Ars Amatoria*, 2.233 and *Heroides* 4.75.

soldier will refuse service or faith. For hunger, as it is customary to say, fights internally and this alone subdues that which seems most secure. A hungry rabble does not know fear; yet if provisions are forthcoming, they may be incited – alternately by fear of punishment and by hope of reward – to their duties. Above all, there are drill instructors and masters of military practise, whose services should be obtained; and you will shortly see the nation restored to that virtuous existence which flourished when the greatest of the emperors, Julius Caesar, 'exposed his back in terror after seeking the Britons'.[23] But also, hypothetical war plans are to be discussed in the camps so that the soldier experienced in strategy will know how to choose which is the best arrangement when the skill is required. Yet if the plans are for a real battle, this should be concealed from the soldiers because a military precept states: 'What happens ought to be discussed with many, yet what is to be done with the fewest and the most faithful, or better with yourself.'[24] For rarely is a secret maintained which comes to the notice of a large group. Also military precepts and examples of adroit young men are to be often recounted so that the former may instruct them in knowledge and the latter may kindle and stimulate them to valour.

But my purpose is not to teach this art of military affairs, which yet is the greatest and most indispensable of arts and without which (to use the words of Plutarch) any princely government would feel maimed. If anyone wishes to learn how to fight, he should consult Cato the Censor, and read the works of Cornelius Celsus, Julius Hyginus and Vegetius Renatus – from whom I have borrowed much because he most elegantly and diligently teaches the art of military affairs, although he only briefly touches on examples – read, I say, what prescriptions these authors have produced for posterity. Yet in all arts utility directs that precepts are by no means to be lacking practice. For, just as Cicero remarks, it is extremely easy to furnish precepts about each and every matter but the most difficult task to carry them out effectively.[25] He asserts this about the art of speaking, when writing in *Ad Herennium* on the precepts of eloquence, namely, that such precepts are ineffective and useless without the experience and practice of speaking, which I believe may be transferred to all arts

[23] Lucan, *Pharsalia*, 2.572.
[24] Vegetius Renatus, *De re militari*, 3.26.
[25] Pseudo-Cicero, *Ad Herennium*, 1.1.

inasmuch as they are neither made durable by use nor are strengthened by practice; this is true to the point that, if you dissociate usage and art, usage is more expedient devoid of art than is art which does not contain usage. For also David, who possessed the knowledge and usage of the sling and the stone, laid the Philistine low and was courageous enough to approach with a staff a man feared by all and a warrior from his adolescence; and he tossed aside the royal breastplate and armour, with which he was not practiced, supposing everything to be an impediment to battle which useful practice does not render durable. Certainly, just as art unmindful of usage is sterile, so that usage is imperfect which does not originate in art. Thus, the beginning of each thing is from nature, in opposition to which and (as it is customary to say) without the will of Minerva nothing may be properly undertaken. Development is from usage, whereas perfection is from art, at least if it is solidified by constant practice. This obtains in liberal and mechanical occupations or in those of which we have not yet heard mention: that art is barren without usage and usage is reckless without art. An army is, therefore, stagnant without art, negligent without usage. For this reason, anyone who wishes to be a soldier should learn in advance the art and make it durable through usage and practice so that, when he is selected and joined to the army by oath, he lives for the republic and its utility and is not, just as Plutarch asserts, a crippled hand. For these are the final words he uses in the 'Instruction of Trajan' when he is proceeding from the hands to the feet. We may therefore follow him and, just as he asserts himself, make something like shoes for the feet so that they are not damaged by stones or other obstacles which are in many cases thrust upon them.

CHAPTER 20

Who are the feet of the republic and regarding the care devoted to them

The feet are the name of those who exercise the humbler duties, by whose service all the members of the republic may walk along the earth. In this accounting may be included the peasants who always stick to the land, looking after their cultivated fields or plantings or pastures or flowers. Likewise, this category applies to the many types of weaving and the mechanical arts, which pertain to wood, iron, bronze and the various metals, and also the servile forms of obedience and the many ways of acquiring nourishment and the sustenance of life or enlarging the dimensions of family possessions, the management of which does not pertain to the public authorities and from which the corporate community of the republic derives benefit. And there are so many of these occupations that the number of feet in the republic surpasses not only the eight-footed crab, but even the centipede; one cannot enumerate them on account of their large quantity, yet not because they are infinitely numerous according to nature, but because there are so many varied kinds that no compiler of duties ever produced special precepts for each individual type.

Nonetheless, in order to address generally each one and all, they are not to exceed the limits, namely, law, and are to concentrate on the public utility in all matters. For inferiors must serve superiors, who on the other hand ought to provide all necessary protection to their inferiors. For this reason, Plutarch says that what is to the advantage of the humbler people, that is, the multitude, is to be followed; for the fewer always submit to the more numerous. Therefore, magistrates were instituted for the reason that injuries might be averted from subjects and the republic itself might put shoes, as it were, on its workers. For when they are exposed to injuries it is as if the republic is barefoot; there can be nothing more ignominious for those who administer the magistracies. Indeed an afflicted people is like proof and irrefutable demonstration of the prince's gout. The health of the whole republic will only be secure and splendid if the superior members devote themselves to the inferiors and if the inferiors respond likewise to the legal rights of their superiors, so that each individual may be likened to a part of the others reciprocally and each believes what is to his own advantage to be determined by that which he recognises to be most useful for others.

CHAPTER 21

The republic is arranged according to its resemblance to nature, and its arrangement is derived from the bees

Both Cicero and Plato have written about the republic, although in diverse ways, since the one had described how it ought to be, whereas the other had described how it was actually instituted by earlier generations. Yet each one prescribes this formula for both its design and its construction: that the civil life should imitate nature, which we have very often identified as the best guide to living. Otherwise, life is duly called not merely uncivil, but rather bestial and brute. Indeed, those creatures devoid of reason are themselves afforded instruction about what it is that nature decrees. The most learned poet Maro, upon whom Plutarch himself borrows as he establishes for Trajan that the civil life derives from the bees, says

Now must you marvel at the spectacle of a tiny commonwealth [of
    bees] . . .
They alone possess children in common, and share as partners
the dwellings of their city, and lead a life
under the law's majesty; they alone
know established household gods and fatherland;
and mindful of winter's coming, toil through summer,
garnering their grains into one common store.
For some are diligent to gather food
and by fixed covenants labour in the field;
some, as the first foundation of the comb,
within the house-walls spread tears of narcissus
and sticky resin from the bark of trees,
then hang therefrom the clinging wax; others
lead out the full-grown young, the nation's hope;
others pack purest honey and brim the cells
with liquid nectar. To some it falls by lot
to keep guard at the gates: in turn they watch
for showers and cloudy skies, or take their loads
from incomers, or rank themselves to drive
the drones, that lazy herd, far from the hive.
The work is aglow, and the thyme-scented honey
breathes fragrance. And as, when the Cyclopes forge
thunderbolts with quick strokes from ductile ore;

into ox-hide bellows some drink in the air
and blow it forth, others dip hissing bronze
into the trough, while Aetna groans beneath
the weight of the anvils; they with mighty force,
one now and now another, lift their arms
in rhythm, and turn the iron with gripping tongs:
So, if small things may be compared with great,
an inborn love of having is ever urging
Cecropian bees, each after its own function.
The aged have charge of the towns: 'tis they
who build the comb, fashioning the curious chambers.
But the young, late at night, wearied with labour
come home, their thighs laden with thyme-pollen:
on arbutus they pasture far and wide,
on pale green willows, cassia, and golden crocus,
or rich lime-blossom and dusky hyacinths.
For all there is one rest from toil: for all
one work-time. Through the gates at dawn they stream;
nowhere a loiterer. Again, when once
the star of evening warns them to withdraw
at length from pasturing the meadows, then
they seek their homes, then they refresh their bodies;
a humming sound is heard about the entries
and on the thresholds. Afterwards when now
they have sunk to rest within their chambers, silence
deepens with the night, and welcome slumber invades
their wearied limbs. Nor yet when rain is threatening,
far away from their homesteads do they roam,
or trust the sky when eastern gales are rising,
but close around their city walls in safety
fetch water and adventure on short flights,
and, as unsteady boats on tossing waves
take ballast, often will they lift small stones
wherewith they poise themselves through void cloudland.
Moreover you will marvel that with bees
this custom has found favour: they indulge not
in marriage, nor relax their bodies idly
in love's embrace, nor bring forth young with travail,
but alone from the leaves and scented herbage
gather their children in their mouths; alone
provide a king and tiny citizens,
and mould anew their courts and waxen palaces.

Often too, wandering among rugged rocks,
they bruise their wings, and freely yield their lives
under the load; so great their love of flowers,
so proud their glory in begetting honey.
Therefore although a narrow span of life
awaits the bees themselves (for it stretches never
beyond seven summers), yet the race abides
immortal, and the fortune of the house
stands firm through many years, while to the third
and fourth generation sires on sires are numbered.
Moreover neither Egypt nor great Lydia,
nor Parthia's tribes, nor Median Hydaspes
pay to their king such reverence. Their king safe,
all are of one mind; when he perishes,
forthwith they break their fealty, and themselves
plunder their store of honey, and destroy
their trellised combs. He is guardian of their labours;
it is him they revere; their multitudes
throng close around him in a murmurous swarm;
and often on their shoulders do they lift him,
or shield him with their bodies from the fray,
and rush through wounds to seek a glorious death.[26]

Skim through all the authorities on the republic, think over the histories of republics; nowhere is civil life presented to you more accurately and more elegantly. And cities would without doubt be happy if they prescribed this form of living for themselves.

[26] Virgil, *Georgica*, 4.3, 153–218, translated by R.C. Trevelyan (Cambridge: Cambridge University Press, 1944).

CHAPTER 22

*That without prudence and forethought no magistracy
remains intact, nor does that republic flourish
the head of which is impaired*

Moreover, venerable countries, if they follow the footprints of the bees, will progress along the path of life without difficulty and most profitably. Reflect upon Maro's account of the foundations of Carthage and you can admire the comparatively happy omens for that city. For indeed you recognise that all labour was in common and no one was unoccupied and their queen worked in order that the structure of the city might rise; and if she by no means mixed her hands with the labour of her inferiors, still she watched over the work with her eyes and her whole mind was occupied with foresight. For without prudence and foresight not only does the republic not progress, but not even the least household endures. For this reason, in his commendation of Ulysses, Homer teaches that prudence, which after poetic custom he calls by the name Minerva, had been his constant companion. Also, Homer's imitator, Maro, describing a man distinguished for arms and piety and whom he supposed so worthy that he began the dynasty of the Romans, associated him with Achates in all matters rightly conducted because prudent foresight accomplishes those actions which are most suitable. The business of a circumspect man so often succeeds in so far as the deceits of the insidious never impede him and he advances along a sort of invincible path not open to everyone towards the end of his intended destination.

Indeed, this is elegantly expressed, since neither military affairs nor the works of piety may be exercised effectively without forethought and prudence. Above all there is a drawing together of the faithful when prudence is associated with forethought because not only is an acute intelligence blunted by inactivity but also foresight is not beneficial unless it exerts itself upon the foundation of a rich inner disposition. 'Each one demands material assistance from the other and both bond together in friendship.'[27] But however well any matters whatsoever begin, they do not turn out well when Minerva retreats. You may be confronted by the Mantuan poet, who under the pretext of fiction expressed all the truths of philosophy. Heed, therefore, the diligence of the new citizens:

It was like the bees in the new summer among the rural flowers
performing their labours under the sun, when adult creatures
guide the babies, or when clear honey
and sweet nectar is squeezed from distended cells,
or when they accept burdens from newcomers, or form a battle line
which keeps a pack of idle drones from their hives;
work goes on, and the fragrant honey smells of thyme.[28]

[27] Horace, *Ars Poetica*, 410–411.   [28] Virgil, *Aeneid*, 1.445–451.

The citizens are held to their varied occupations and, inasmuch as the duties of each individual are practised so that provision is made for the corporate community, so long as justice is practised, the ends of all are imbued with the sweetness of honey.

Nevertheless, no republic is happy for long unless provision is made for the head of the corporate community. If you did not know this, you may learn from the example of Dido. For with how much frivolity was Aeneas admitted, how much favour was soon found for an unknown man, an exile, a fugitive, whose motives were unknown and whose person was suspect? With how much curiosity did the ruler receive into her ears the fabulous stories of a man avoiding his own blame, striving for his own glory, and chasing after that by which he could subvert the mind of his audience? Therefore, persuasive words paved the way for the man's entrance, the enticements of praise procured the favours of his hosts, a more elaborate banquet was planned for capturing the devotion of all, stories followed the banquet, which was accompanied by hunting and a multiplicity of frivolous luxuries. This engendered lewdness and led to the abandonment of the city to flames and to a perpetual reason for hostility. This is the end of the rulership of women and the effeminate because, although it may have a foundation in virtue, it could by no means devise a course towards subsequent prosperity. He was frivolously admitted who, however much by reason of the duty of piety he was not to be excluded from hospitality, should still more suitably have entered as a stranger, not like a ruler.

CHAPTER 24

The vices of the powerful are to be tolerated because with them rests the prospect of public safety, and because they are the dispensers of safety just as the stomach in the body of animals dispenses nourishment, and this is by the judgment of the Lord Adrian

'Go', says Solomon, 'to the ant, dull one, that you may possess foresight.'[29] Yet the philosopher sends the political man to the bees in

---

[29] Proverbs 6:6.

order that he may learn from them his duties. If the Carthaginians had acceded to them, they would never have indulged in luxury and instead would have taken pleasure in the perpetual security of their nation. But because vice took root in a female lord, the effeminate citizens were led away by the neck by men of valour. Nevertheless, even if the ruler is too loose in the virtues of his office, still he has to be honoured; and, just as the bees raise up their king upon their shoulders, so subjects, whom we have said to be the feet and members, should exhibit subservience to him in every way, so long as his vices are not pernicious. For, even if he is afflicted with the vices, he is to be endured as the one with whom rests the hopes of the provincials for their security.

> If the king is safe, everyone is of a single mind;
> if he is lost, faith ruptures.[30]

The Illyricians and Tracians, praised for the glory of their ferocity hardened through daily practice, had terrified their neighbours, the Macedonians. The latter, beaten in battle, laid their boy-king, the progeny of their dead ruler, in a cradle and positioned him at the line of the battle, resuming the fight more ardently as though they had been conquered in the previous wars because they lacked the foresight of their king, whereas in the future they would be victorious because by reason of either superstition or faith they were seized by the motivation to prevail. For they were guided by compassion for the infant king whose capture they would have realised if they were conquered. And so joined in battle, they routed the Illyricians with great carnage, showing their enemies that the Macedonians lacked a king, not virtue, during prior combat. Therefore, how important might be a king of advanced years and dignity, if these qualities had further promoted his value? Yet although one may be dealing with a somewhat hardened populace, still the authority of the rank and the usefulness of the office ought to soothe the spirits of the provincials.

I recall that I had cause to travel to Apulia to visit the pontiff, Lord Adrian IV, who had allowed me into closest friendship with him, and I remained with him at Benevento for nearly three months. And so since, as it is customary to do among friends, we frequently consulted together over many matters, and he inquired most intimately and

---

[30] Virgil, *Georgica*, 4.212–213.

diligently of me what men felt both about himself and about the Roman Church, I related openly to him the evil uses of spiritual liberty, about which I have heard in various provinces. For it was said by many that the Roman Church, which is the mother of all churches, presented itself not so much like a mother as like a stepmother of the others. Scribes and Pharisees sit within Rome, placing upon the shoulders of men insupportable burdens with which they themselves do not dirty their own fingers. They are lords over the clergy, and they do not become the models who lead the flock down the correct path of life; they accumulate valuable furnishings, they pile up gold and silver at the bank, even economising too much in their own expenses out of avarice. For the pauper is either never or rarely allowed in, the exception being him who enters not because of the glory of Christ but on account of his vain glory. They weaken the Church, inflame quarrels, bring into conflict the clergy and the people, have no compassion whatsoever for those afflicted by labours and miseries, delight in the plunder of churches and calculate all profits as piety. They deliver justice not for the sake of truth but for a price. For indeed everything done immediately comes with a price; but you will not obtain anything at some future date without a price either. They very frequently do harm and they imitate demons in this: they think they have done good at that time when they desist from doing harm – excepting a few who carry out the name and duties of the shepherd. But even the Roman pontiff himself is burdensome and almost intolerable to everyone, since all assert that, despite the ruins and rubble of churches (which were constructed by the devotion of the Fathers) and also the neglect of altars, he erects palaces and parades himself about not only in purple vestments but in gilded clothes. The palaces of priests glitter and in their hands the Church of Christ is demeaned. They pick clean the spoils of the provinces as if they wanted to recover the treasures of Croesus. But the Most High deals suitably with them, since they are themselves given over to the plunder of others and frequently to the most vile of men. And, as I believe, while they have thus gone astray from the path, the scourge of the Lord will by no means fail Him. Indeed, the mouth of the Lord has spoken that by the judgments he has judged he will be judged, and his measure meted out to him. The Ancient of the Days acknowledges no lies.

'This', I said, 'father, is said by the people, inasmuch as you desired that I should reveal to you their judgments.' 'And you', it was responded, 'what do you judge?' 'Difficulties', I said, 'exist in all directions. For I fear lest I be associated with lies and infamous for flattery if I were to contradict the people on my own; but if I act otherwise, I fear lest I be accused of high treason, just as though I had opposed my mouth against heaven, thus seeming to have merited the cross. Nevertheless, because Guido Dens, the cardinal presbyter of St Potentiana, presents the testimony of the people, I do not presume to contradict him in all regards. For he asserts that within the Roman Church exists a root of duplicity and a nourishment of avarice which is the beginning and root of all evils. And this public charge was not made by him in some quiet retreat, but at meetings of the holy brothers presided over by Eugenius, when at Florence he grew angry without provocation in opposition to my own innocence.

'Yet one thing I boldly profess with conscience as my witness is that nowhere do I see more honest clerics or clerics who despise avarice more than in the Roman Church. Who does not marvel at the continence and contempt for money of Bernard of Redon, cardinal deacon of Saints Cosmas and Damian? None is alive from whom he accepts a present. Yet what was yielded rightfully by the sincere communion of brotherhood he was occasionally persuaded to accept. Who is not amazed by the Bishop of Praeneste who, fearing the scruples of conscience, abstained even from sharing in the common goods? So great is the modesty of many, so great is their dignity, that they would not be found inferior to Fabricius, whom they excel in all ways by their knowledge of the path to salvation. Therefore, because you insist, urge and command, and since it is certain that it is not permitted to lie to the Holy Spirit, I acknowledge that what you command is to be done, even though you would not be imitated in all of your works. For whoever dissents from your teaching is either a heretic or a schismatic. But, by God's favour, there are those who do not imitate all of your works. Thus, the blemish of a few stains the pure, and the universal Church will be plunged into infamy; and in my opinion a very great number of them ought to die lest they corrupt the whole of the Church. But even the good are sometimes carried off, lest they be transformed into the wicked and because corrupt Rome is perceived to be unworthy of those in the presence of God. You, therefore, have it as your duty to search for and take in the humble, those who despise vain glory and money. But I fear lest, in so far as you proceed to inquire into what you have in mind, you hear from an imprudent friend what you do not have in mind. Why is it, father, that you discuss the lives of others and investigate into yourself so little? All applaud you, you are called Father and Lord of everyone, and upon your head is poured all the oil of the sinner. If you are father, therefore, why do you accept presents and payments from your children? If you are lord, why do you not arouse fear in your Romans and why do you not recall them to the faith, suppressing their recklessness? Yet perhaps you wish to maintain the city for the Church by means of your presents. Did Pope Sylvester acquire it by means of such presents? You are off the path, father, and not on the path. The city is to be maintained out of the same presents by which it was acquired. What is freely given is freely accepted. Justice is the queen of the virtues and is embarrassed to be exchanged for any amount of price. If justice is to be gracious, she is to be free from charge. She who cannot be seduced may by no means be prostituted for a price; she is entirely and forever pure. In so far as you oppress others, you will be oppressed by even greater burdens.'

The pontiff laughed and congratulated such great candour, commanding that, whenever anything unfavourable about him made a sound in my ears, he was to be informed of this without delay. And, when he had thoroughly responded – alternately favouring himself and opposing himself – he told me a story along the following lines. He asserted: 'It happened that all the members of the whole body conspired against the stomach, as if against that which by its voraciousness exhausted the labours of all. The eye is never filled to capacity with sights nor the ear with sounds, the hands persist in their labours, the feet put on calluses by walking, and the tongue moderates usefully between speech and silence. In short, all the members keep watch over the public advantage and, in comparison to the concern and labour of all, only the stomach remains at rest, and while all share the many things which are obtained by their labour, the stomach alone devours and consumes everything. What more? They agreed that they would abstain from their labours and destroy through painful starvation this parasite and public enemy. This was suffered on the first day; on the following day it was more annoying. On the third day it was so pernicious that nearly all showed signs of faintness. And so necessity urged that the allies should gather together again as one to act with regard to their own health and the condition of the public enemy. When all were present, the eyes were feeble, the feet would not raise the bulk of the body, the arms were stiffened, and even the tongue itself, sticking to the palate and weakened, did not presume to expound the common cause of the partners. Therefore, they all yielded to the counsel of the heart and, having deliberated thereupon, reason revealed that these evils were inflicted as a result of what had previously been denounced as a public enemy. For the tribute to it was withdrawn by them and like a public provisioner it halted nourishment to everyone. And because no one can fight without a salary, the soldiers were disabled and weakened when they did not receive a salary. But the fault cannot be traced back to the provisioner, who could hardly disburse to others what he did not receive himself. And it would be far more advisable that he should be furnished with goods for his distribution than that all the members should go hungry while getting rid of him. And so it was done; persuaded by reason, the stomach was replenished, the members were revived, and the peace of all was reestablished. And so they absolved the stomach, which, although it is voracious and covetous of unsuitable things, still asks not for itself but for others which are unable to be sustained by its emptiness.

'Such is the case, brother', he said, 'if you study the matter properly, in the republic where, although the magistrates seek after a great deal, they do not accumulate for themselves but for others. For if they are dissipated, there is nothing that they are able to bestow upon the members. For the stomach in the body and the prince in the republic are the same office, according to Quintus Serenus:

> Those who contend the stomach is the king of the whole body,
> are seen to rest upon the truth of reason.
> For its health secures the progress of all the members,
> but by contrast its affliction weakens the whole;
> indeed rather, unless one aids it carefully, it is said to infect
> the brain and to divert the senses from their completeness.[31]

Measure neither our harshness nor that of secular princes, but attend to the utility of all.'

---

[31] Quintus Serenus Sammonicus, *Liber Medicinalia*, 300–305.

CHAPTER 25

Of the coherence of the head and the members of the republic; and that the prince is a sort of image of the deity, and of the crime of high treason, and of that which is to be kept in fidelity

It is indeed satisfactory to me and I am persuaded that devoted shoulders are to support the ruler; and not only do I suffer him but I suffer him gratefully, in so far as he is subject to God and follows His decrees. Otherwise, if he resists divine commandments and wills me to be a participant in his plot against God, I respond with unstrained voice that God is to be preferred to any man. In this way, therefore, inferiors cohere with their superiors; in this way all the members are to subject themselves to the head so that religion may be preserved intact. It is read that Socrates had instituted a political system (*res politica*) and had handed down precepts which are said to emanate from that purity of wisdom which is like a sort of fount of nature. Yet these may all be condensed into the following: that the duty of the greater man in the republic is to protect most diligently those who are humbler. Reread carefully the 'Instruction of Trajan', of which mention is made above, and you will find these matters more extensively addressed. It suffices for us to have said these things about the unity of the head and members at present, to which may be added what we set out before: that a blow to the head, as we have already said, is carried back to all the members and a wound unjustly afflicted upon any member whomsoever tends to the injury of the head.

In another respect, any evil trick of malice planned against the head and members of the corporate community is a crime of the utmost seriousness and approaches sacrilege because, just as the latter assails God, so the former attacks the prince, who is agreed to be a sort of deity on earth. And as a result it is called high treason (*crimen majestatis*) because it persecutes those in the image of Him who alone, as the illustrious Count Robert of Leicester (a modest proconsul administering in the region of Britain) was in the habit of saying, preserves the truth of true and noble majesty; it reckons those who attempt anything against the security of the prince of the people, either by themselves or through another. Furthermore, in the prosecution of such a crime, everyone is on equal terms; and for the most part it happens that those with whom no one associates in life are not exonerated by benefit of death; but upon the death of the convicted party, his memory is condemned and his goods are denied to his heirs. For since he takes in hand the most vicious counsel, his mind is accordingly punished in a certain way. Once anyone has committed such a crime, it is agreed that he can neither alienate nor manumit nor can a debtor rightfully repay him.

Infamous persons, who do not have the right to accuse others, are to be admitted in these cases without hesitation, as well as soldiers, who cannot prosecute other types of cases. Indeed, those who keep watch for the peace are all the more to be heard about this accusation. Also slaves may legally accuse their lords and freemen their patrons. Yet this crime is to be regarded by judges not as an occasion for the veneration of the majesty of the prince but as a quest for truth. For one is to look at whether the person could have done it, whether he actually did it, whether he conceived of it, and whether (before he presumed this) he was of sane mind. And no slip of the tongue is to suffer by ready punishment; for although the rash are deserving of punishment, still even they are to be spared if their transgressions are not of such a kind that either they violate the letter of the law or are to be punished according to legal precedent. Even women are to be heard in interrogation about high treason; for the woman Julia exposed the conspiracy of Sergius Catiline and she aided the consul Marcus Tullius in judging him. Also, if introduced by reason of necessity or utility, those who are believed to be at fault in the matter are to be placed under tortures when they are seen to have accepted counsel and inspiration for the crime, so that the punishment earned can be put in place for all offending parties.

There is much, indeed, that makes up high treason. For example, if there is consideration of the death of a prince or magistrate, or if those who oppose the country are armed, or if one flees from a public war, deserting the prince, or if the people are solicited to struggle in revolt against the republic, or if by deceitful or evil works the enemies of the people and republic are aided with military supplies, arms, weapons, money or whatever else, or if friends of the republic become its enemies, or if by deceitful or evil works it were to occur that the pledge of a great deal of money would be given in opposition to the republic, whereby the populace of a foreign territory would be less obedient; he likewise commits high treason who releases a criminal found guilty of the act in court, on account of which he has been clamped into chains; and many other acts of this sort which it is tedious or impossible to enumerate.

But, because the formula of fidelity (or the feudal oath) should be observed above all else, from it can be most conveniently compiled a few things that are not permitted. For indeed necessity is the obverse of possibility, and what ought to be done is contradicted by what is illicit. Likewise, the formula of fidelity requires what is inserted in it as necessary to faith: it enjoins what is secure, safe, honourable, useful, easy and possible. Were we bound to someone by the constraints of fidelity, we would neither injure the security of his body nor withdraw the provisions on the basis of which he is safe nor presume to undertake anything which would diminish his honour or usefulness; and it is permitted neither to make difficult what is easy nor to make impossible what is possible. Moreover, he who possesses a benefice from someone, to whom he is faithful, owes him aid and counsel (*auxilium et concilium*) in his activities; for this reason, it is more clear than the sun how much the Lord is owed, if so much is owed to those to whom we are bound only by the constraints of fealty. But even the penalty for such crime is so great that I would not readily believe that anything more severe could be devised even by the lords of the islands who frequently engage in tyranny. And, lest it be supposed that the severity of the penalties have proceeded from the severity of tyranny, we may refer to the very words of the most moderate law itself . . .

CHAPTER 26

*That vices are to be endured or removed and are
distinguished from flagrant crimes; and certain general
matters about the office of the prince; and a brief epilogue
on how much reverence is to be displayed towards him*

I have taken care in the present little treatise to insert a few excerpts among many possible ones drawn from the pure core of the law. As a result of the inspection of these, even men ignorant of the law may withdraw themselves at great distance from high treason, and I myself will not be accused unfairly by anyone of having presumed against the authority of the prince. It is customarily said that it is not easy to remove the best parts from the cork tree without injuring one's fingers; but whoever separates the obedience of members from the head is injured far more equitably and rapidly. The excellence of the head must always flourish because the health of the whole body depends upon it.

In the satire entitled *Manipean*, which is about the duties of the institution of matrimony, Varro asserts: 'The vices of a spouse are to be either removed or endured. He who removes the vices is a preferable spouse; he who tolerates them makes himself a better person.'[32] Thus, the vices of princes and subjects are to be either endured or removed; for in fact their confederation either equals or surpasses conjugal affection. But even the words 'to endure' and 'to remove' are themselves cleverly adapted by Varro. It appears that 'removing' is meant in the sense of correction. It is beyond doubt that his actual judgment was that what cannot be removed is to be endured. Yet a faithful interpretation of this adds that what is understood by 'vice' is what honour and religion can securely endure. For vices are more insignificant than flagrant crimes; and there are a number of acts which one is not permitted to endure or which cannot faithfully be endured. A spouse may legally be separated from a spouse by reason of fornication, and he is very often a patron of turpitude who conceals the crime of his wife. Perhaps for that reason it is said: 'He who cherishes an adulteress is both silly and impious.' Moreover, this obtains equally of any sort of physical and spiritual adultery, even though the spiritual form is the worse and is to be more carefully avoided.

Similarly, even in the connection between the members, Varro's rule about enduring and removing is to be admitted. For in fact no one questions that members ought to be cured, whether the cure for their wound proceeds from the palliative of oils or from the austere wine which the Samaritan administered. That the members are likewise to be removed is clear from that which is written: 'If your eye or your foot offend you, root it out and cast it away from you.'[33] I think that this is to be observed by the prince in regard to all of the members to the extent that not only are they to be rooted out, broken off and thrown far away, if they give offence to the faith or public security, but

---

[32] Aulus Gellius, *Noctes Atticae*, 1.7.4.   [33] Matthew 18:9.

they are to be destroyed utterly so that the security of the corporate community may be procured by the extermination of the one member. Who will be spared, I say, by him who is commanded to do violence against even his own eyes? Indeed, neither the ears nor the tongue nor whatever else subsists within the body of the republic is safe if it revolts against the soul for whose sake the eyes themselves are gouged out. When God is offended by abuses of criminals or the Church is spurned, the well-being of the entire soul is in jeopardy. This is so foreign to the office of the prince that, whenever these things occur in the republic, it is to be believed that the prince either is entirely unaware or is asleep or is on a journey.

The sun shines over the whole world so that the whole world may be seen and discerned all at once; I believe the prince to be another sun. He acts rightly above all when 'he prevents the idle swarm of drones from entering the hive',[34] since they pillage the beehive and whatever honey there is they gulp down or carry off. He acts rightly when he raises the Church to the apex, when he extends the practice of religion, when he humiliates the proud and exalts the humble, when he is generous to the destitute, more frugal with the wealthy, when justice walks constantly before him and sets his course on the way of prudence and all the other virtues. Truly,

In this way does one travel to the heavens, not that Mt Ossa is set
   upon Mt Olympus
and that the summit of Mt Pelion touches the highest stars.[35]

The Book of Wisdom says: 'You are not to appear glorious in the court of the king and you are not to stand in the place of the great';[36] and this edict of the wise man pertains to the fact that whoever does not humble himself in the sight of the prince by obscuring his merits with bewilderment is deservedly stripped of the glory which he has usurped. Indeed the ruler is the distributor of honour and, so long as he administers the government correctly, the dispensation of presents is perpetually in his hands. He administers correctly when the people rejoice in his governance and the breadth of the whole land exalts in the reign of equity. 'Perpetually', I say because, as it is written, 'the king who judges the poor according to truth secures his throne in eternity'.[37] Who, therefore, detracts from the honour of him whom

---

[34] Virgil, *Georgica*, 4.168. [35] Ovid, *Fasti*, 1.307–308.
[36] Proverbs 25:6. [37] Proverbs 29:14.

one recognises to be rewarded by God with perpetual honour? Obviously, to presume anything against the immutable image of the prince at any time whatsoever is to be guilty of high treason and to be punished by a most painful death, just as the ancients decreed. Who, therefore, offends by the presumptuous impunity of malice against the image of God who is the prince? Likewise, this is the greatest counsel of wise men: 'In your thought do not detract from the king and in the privacy of your bedroom do not speak ill of the powerful because the birds of the sky will convey your voice and he who has wings will pronounce your verdict.'[38] Will anything then be permitted in deed or word when even thought itself and the secrets of the bedroom and the judgments of the heart are regulated lest anything be plotted or undertaken against the prince?

[38] Ecclesiasticus 10:20.

CHAPTER 29

That the people are moulded by the merits of the prince and the government is moulded by the merits of the people, and every creature is subdued and serves man at God's pleasure

. . . If each person laboured upon his own improvement and counted the affairs of others as outside his concerns, the circumstances of each and every person would be absolutely optimal, and virtue would flourish and reason would prevail, mutual charity reigning everywhere, so that the flesh would be subjected to the spirit and the spirit would be a servant in full devotion to God. If these events occurred, neither would the members be burdened by the arrogance of the head nor would the head languish from the abandonment or idleness of the members; for indeed these consequences are brought about by the infirmity of sin. For even the transgressions of inferiors are harmful to a good prince, and the sins of superiors are a pretext and an encouragement for subjects to transgress. For this reason, it is said: 'The entire head languishes and the entire heart laments; from the soles of the feet straight up to the top of the head there is no health in the body.'[39]

[39] Isaiah 1:5–6.

And so the prince becomes mild as a result of the innocence of the people and innocent princes restrain the passions of the people. For every gentle creature is at God's pleasure and serves man, and every creature is armed for His revenge against those undeserving of Him. The crow nourished Elias; the bear devoted his service to the prophet; the lion forgot the ferocity of his nature and ignored his hunger for food in order that Daniel might be spared; the feet of the just step on the water without becoming wet; the kindled fire did not make headway against the youths in the furnace; the air denies its rainstorms and the earth its fruits, and heaven itself pours out its fire upon the impious – all by the prayers of the faithful.

BOOK VII

Prologue

I would have turned away from the company of the frivolous, leaving the palace of the courtier, except that the authority of your precepts has detained my departure on the threshold itself. For when I revealed to you the distress of my heart and complained about the loss of time and of life, you always advised me to carry on with strong heart until God reveals Himself to others and transforms my circumstances for the better, persuading me that, in the manner of the labourer who averts or diminishes the tedium of his labours by old songs and sweet voices, I might be compensated for the waste of time and material goods. For the path seems easier and more brief for travellers if they are refreshed by a story pleasant to the senses or by the melodies of a sweet voice. So also you told me to pursue a devotion to reading or some other activity and, if nothing else is granted, to lament about my situation and the fickle forms of fortune, at least to myself and to the Muses. For in aspiring to philosophy, it is an important step to bewail the lack of virtue in oneself.

What I have responded to you about this is suggested by the comic
    poet, since
We all give good advice to the sick, when we are healthy;
yet you would experience matters differently, if you were otherwise.[1]

Thus was it demanded from captives, whose instruments were suspended in the willows, the words of songs which they were unable to sing or which they were not accustomed to singing in a foreign land. For although virtue disregards injuries within captivity, yet it cannot be deprived of its duties; extremely rare is the person whose moral character is sufficient to perform the duties of both philosopher and courtier, since these would mainly consist in the most incongruent activities.

---

[1] Terence, *Andria*, 3.9–10.

145

For this reason, you are seen to command an almost impossible thing, particularly when I am 'a man regulated under power'[2] and I have unwillingly done much in obedience to necessity. In regard to those matters which are accomplished by my own private will and impulse for wisdom, time allows me barely a small opportunity. Unavoidable and unsuitable business is transacted day and night, so that one is not permitted to apply oneself to more appropriate matters of concern; and you urge that I should write? I am also a man inexperienced in knowledge and in style of expression; and should I bequeath to others what I have not myself acquired?

> If a booted farmer asks to navigate by himself
> although untutored in the Morning Star, Melicertes proclaims that shame
> has perished from the world.[3]

And so, if you desire that I write, grant – or rather obtain from Him who is Lord of all knowledge – the knowledge on the basis of which I may write; grant free time removed from the annoyances of domestic necessities:

> for, if Virgil lacked a servant or a tolerable
> lodging, all the serpents would vanish from his hair.[4]

Besides, I fear lest, in so far as I prepare myself for devoted obedience, suffering the loss of decency, I might provoke the tongues of rivals, who readily seize upon the evil of strangers and imitate goodness with difficulty.

Yet, if not permitted anything else, you desire that I consider my fortunes and cry to the Muses, advice which is easily encouraged by my mental anguish, since (Gregory Nazianaen testifies) nothing seems more agreeable to men than talking about unsuitable matters and caring for unsuitable goals. But this seems foreign to the will of a well-arranged mind, for it is appropriate for the minds of wise men to be arranged such that every assault of fortune is opposed without complaint by the shield of reason, which is a sort of philosophical defence against fickleness. For he who quarrels with the nature of his circumstances, unless perhaps he groans over the enervated corruption of sin, does not yet walk upon the philosophical path. I can deservedly lament, of course, about myself, being so conspicuous in

---

[2] Matthew 8:9. [3] Persius, *Saturae*, 5.102–104. [4] Juvenal, *Saturae*, 7.69–70.

the misery of the weight of my faults that I would seem ready for whipping, and at night my bones are pierced with pain and those who devour me do not rest. Since my pain is, therefore, always within my purview, do you think that it can be appeased by the stridency of the pen or the sweetness of the pipes?

With the support of the Lord I will do whatsoever you exhort, however, and among the varied treasures and kinds of delights which you touch, I will consecrate to your name a barren heart and an arid tongue, regardless of how small my gifts are. For I do not presume a subtlety of judgment or a grace of expression, but I will compete with any orator whomsoever regarding the sincere devotion of my life. It is indisputable that you, a disciple of Him who preferred the two small gifts of the widow to the pompous offering of the rich man, will accept my presents ahead of the gold of wisdom and the silver of eloquence. Instead, simplicity will merit favour, and you, faithful reader, will heed not the meaning which the words at first sight designate but the origin of their meaning and the meaning for which they are created. For frivolous matters thus are intermingled with the serious and false matters with the true so that everything may concentrate upon the purpose of cultivating the supreme truth. Do not be disturbed if some of the things which are written here may be found differently elsewhere, since even historical occurrences themselves are discovered to contradict each other in different historical accounts, but they are profitable for the fruits of utility and honour. For I do not hazard to establish the truth myself; but without malice I propose to import for the utility of readers what I have read among various authorities. For even the Apostle does not assert: 'Whatever is written is true', but: 'Whatever is written is written for the sake of our learning',[5] although the entirety of those matters about which he speaks can be reduced to only those which are written in the law and the prophets, about the truth of which no one doubts except those who do not agree with the catholic faith.

Certain things which I do not find in the books of the authorities, however, I have taken from daily usage and the experience of things, as though from a sort of catalogue of behaviour. If these inquiries seem to approach more formal philosophy, the spirit of investigation would correspond to Academic practices rather than to the plan of a

---

[5] Romans 15:4.

stubborn combatant, so that in the examination of truth each person reserves to himself freedom of judgment and the authority of writers is to be considered useless whenever it is subdued by a better argument. Yet my intention is to engage in those studies from which error does not cause ruin, and not to rise up by rash presumption to an explanation of those matters one does not enter into without danger. No one should claim his own injury from anything said, since there is nothing derogatory towards particular persons but only an attack on vices that are to be avoided. In this I think indulgence is to be permitted to me to go over the bad as well as the good, in so far as in the latter is demonstrated what is to be done, and in the former, by singling out vices, people can gain advantage in order that they may be improved. But enough of this. It is yet to be explained in a brief discourse why the Academic School is preferable to others for imitation.

CHAPTER I

That the Academics are more modest than other philosophers whose rashness blinds them so that they are given to false beliefs

That the genius of the philosophers of antiquity had abounded and that study was advanced by them is now not merely opinion but a judgment of which everyone in common is persuaded. For through study and practice these geniuses prepared for themselves a path to matters which are by nature almost incomprehensible, and with their aid many discoveries were made known to posterity for which we rejoice and at which we marvel. They measured the earth, they subjected the heavens to their rules, they probed the various causes of natural phenomena, and their eyes gazed upon the Craftsman of the entire universe, if only in a sort of indirect way. Thus, as if conveyed by the might of giants and strengthened by a prowess no longer human, they puffed up and proclaimed war against the grace of God by means of the vigour of their reason and reliance upon free will, as if in Ovid's tale they were about to seize the heavens as captive by the force of those virtues which they extolled. And so they were hurled down as often as they were raised up, and by calling themselves wise they were made to be fools, and their unwise heart was darkened, so that those who became fully acquainted with almost everything were the most perniciously in error about most things. In the distraction of their various opinions they were ignorant about even the least of matters.

Yet if there are those for whom the tools of fiction are evil (although the soul of the wise man does not refuse to learn even from the enemy, since the special people of God glitter in the golden clothing and silver ornaments of all the Egyptians); if the fictions of the gentiles, I say, are evil, then a confusion of tongues was caused by God, hurling it down from on high while the impious were constructing the foundations of Babylon on the Plain of Shinar and while they were erecting the tower of exaltation and the scaffolding of opposition to God; and the withdrawal of verbal intercourse was of necessity followed by the dispersal of the population. Thus, while the genius of the philosophers erected their scaffolding on high to generate a sort of plot against God, the unity of the really immutable and unfailing truth was denied to them, and, covered up by the cloud of their ignorance, they were completely lost to the greatest knowledge of those things which are true on the basis of the one and only Truth. They were convicted by their own works of being given to false beliefs, and just as their guide (namely, the spirit of truth) vanished, so they were divided into various factions of erroneous and crazy falsehoods. And they are made the more miserable because they were by no means unaware of their own defects.

Hence it is that, in so far as the Stoic venerates his providence, he constrains everything to the necessity of law; Epicurus, on the contrary, eliminates disposition and contends that all occurrences fluctuate; in so far as he defends the freedom of material things. The supporters of each of these two views stand in diametrical opposition and they struggle over nearly each individual aspect of things. As if bound by an oath to Pallas they talk only of paradoxes and of authoritative doctrines, and they affirm these to be at all times true. But Academics, evading the precipice of falsehood, are more modest in these sorts of matters because they hardly disavow their defects and, in a position of ignorance about things, they are entirely uncertain about each one. This is by far more secure, of course, than to decide upon uncertainties rashly. The reputation of the Academic school is supported inasmuch as not only Heraclides of Pontus and our Cicero – men who in general received praise for their mental abilities – were at length converted to it, but also many others who are too numerous to mention. Are not they to be preferred to others both by their assertion of modesty and by the greatness of the advice they recommend to men?

CHAPTER 2

Of the errors of the Academics; and who among them it is permitted to imitate; and those matters which are doubtful to the wise man

Yet I do not say that all those who are included under the name of Academics have upheld the rule of modesty, since even its basic creed is in dispute and parts of it are open as much to derision as to error. For what is more foolish than to be undecided about each matter and to possess no certainty about things and yet to claim the name of philosopher? For those who are in doubt about everything are strangers to faith as well as to knowledge because they possess nothing certain. For although faith does not attain to the abridgement of knowledge, in so far as like a mirror it reflects absent truths, still it possesses a certainty that excludes the fog of ambiguity. Furthermore, if the Academic is in doubt about each thing, he is certain about nothing, unless perhaps this uncertainty which he possesses can itself be both doubtful and certain as to whether contraries exist in the same place at the same time. But he possesses uncertainty about whether he is in doubt, so long as he does not know for certain that he does not know this doubt itself.

Yet since man is superior to other animals in that he exercises reason and understanding (for in regard to the senses, which, although they are of the soul, are said to be corporal, he is readily surpassed; he is not able to equal the acute eyesight of the lynx; nor is his hearing more powerful than a pig, his sense of smell sharper than a vulture or a dog, his sense of taste more keen than a monkey, or his touch more acute than a spider); since, I say, man excels in the powers of discernment and understanding, what beast is superior to him? Or rather who believes that a man whose reason does not discern and whose understanding does not comprehend is not inferior and, if I may say so, more brutish, since even the brutes would seem to grow towards a certain measure of a kind of semblance of reason? For even a dog discerns its own loved ones, is mindful of rewards, achieves a familiarity with man on the basis of practical experience and usage and, exhibiting an almost faithful closeness to friends beyond others, it is ennobled by a sort of inborn reason and understanding. Even the camel retains a tenacious memory for injury, and the rhinoceros (which is also the unicorn) so recognises the purity of a virgin to the extent that it is generally captured in the embraces of one. Panthers pursue the scent of other animals and, what is more wondrous, fish in the sea come towards the colour of gold; and for this reason, one of the luxuries of the savage Emperor Nero, it is said, was to fish with nets of gold. What more?

> The fierce lioness hunts the wolf, the wolf itself the goat,
> the playful goat hunts the flower of the cithisum,[6]

and in this fashion most trail along after their own pleasure. This could not occur (as I believe) if even brute animals were in doubt about their feelings.

What rashness or impudence, therefore, draws those who are ignorant about each thing to the profession of the philosopher? For just as 'that which is known' is grammatically designated by the name of 'knowledge', so also 'that which is reasoned' is grammatically designated by the name 'reason', that is, certain and fixed. And indeed reason is pointless to the man who can be persuaded of nothing, but rather vacillates always and in all things upon slippery opinions. For what does philosophy confer upon him who always fluctuates in his opinions, and for whom the light of reason which reveals the path to happiness is extinguished, almost as though he plucks out the eyes of one who is showing the way in order that the traveller may advance more cautiously and correctly? Is not he who is blinded even more greatly hindered? What preferred path is to be followed by him who is pulled in so many directions? Certainly, no one reaches his home except for him who follows one path; and he who accommodates his ear to every word will never rest. Does not the idler or the fool or the madman rather than the philosopher resemble the one who, when he recalls sleep, doubts whether he has slept, and

---

[6] Virgil, *Eclogae*, 2.63–65.

who, when he is filled with food, does not know whether he is hungry, and who has knowledge of none of those things which he is doing presently or has recently done?

Such is the Academic, since he is neither able to be compared with brutish animals nor does he merit the name and honour of man, still less of philosopher; and against this sort of nonsense not only the great father and faithful teacher of the Church, Augustine, but also Cicero argued at length by means of sound reasoning and the most elegant style of expression. Nonetheless, Cicero himself witnesses that he was transformed into one of those who is in doubt about each matter regarding which wise men may pose questions; and our Augustine did not persecute them, since even he himself frequently utilised in his works the restraint of the Academics and he reported many matters to be ambiguous which others arguing with more confidence and greater rashness might not seem to regard as questionable. Still, it does not seem to me that anyone speaks with more security just because he is more circumspect with words lest he fall into falsity.

Yet there are doubtful matters about which the wise man is not convinced by the authority of either faith or his senses or manifest reason and in which contrary claims rest on the support of some evidence. Among such questions are those which are asked about providence, about the substance, quantity, strength, efficacy and origin of the soul, about fate and natural inclinations, chance and free will, about matter and motion and origins of bodies, about whether or not the progression of multiplicity and the division of magnitude have any limits at all and whether these limits are finally discovered only outside reason, about time and place, about number and language, about whether there is more friction between the same sorts of things or different sorts, about divisibility and indivisibility, about the substance and form of sound, about the status of universals, about the usage and ends and origin of virtues and vices, whether a man who has one virtue has all the virtues, whether all sins are equal and are punished equally; likewise about the causes of things and their connection and opposition, about the ebb and flow of the oceans, about the source of the Nile, about the increase and diminution of the fluids in the bodies of animals according to the motions of the moon, about the duties and kinds of cases which originate in contracts and quasi-contracts, crimes and quasi-crimes, or various other sorts of suits, about nature and its works, about truth and the earliest origins of things about which human genius falls short, whether or not angels have their own bodies at all and what sort they have, and what may piously be asked of God Himself who exceeds investigation by all rational natures and is exalted over everything which can be conceived by the mind. In this fashion, many things can be expounded about which wise men admit doubts, yet these doubts would be unnoticed by common men. And so I readily believe that Academics have doubts regarding these matters with so much modesty that I perceive them to have guarded diligently against the precipice of rashness. This is so to the extent that, when a certain number of words of uncertainty (for example, 'maybe', 'possibly', and 'perhaps') are mentioned in places among authors whose doubt is not indiscriminate, they are said to be used with Academic restraint because the Academics were more restrained than others who were known to assail all truth by the rashness of their determinations and their headlong dive into falsehood.

CHAPTER 7

That some things are demonstrated by the authority of the senses, others by reason, others by religion; and that faith in any doctrine is justified by some stable basis that need not be demonstrated; and that some things are known by the learned themselves, others by the uncultivated; and to what extent there is to be doubt; and that stubbornness most often impedes the examination of truth

There are numerous things about which the authority of the senses, reason or religion persuades us. Doubt regarding these bears the stamp of infirmity, error or crime. For to ask whether the sun shines, snow is white, or fire burns is to be lacking human sensation. Moreover, to ask whether three is greater than two and whether the whole contains its own middle-point and whether four is two doubled – these are the marks of one whose reason is dull or absent entirely. And he who places in question whether God exists, and whether this same power is wise or good, is not only irreligious but treacherous, and is deservedly instructed by the lesson of punishment.

There are in all systems of philosophy certain first and, as it is said in the words of Cratinus, original principles about which (on the same authority) one is not permitted to doubt, except for those whose labours so occupy them that they do not know anything. For just as certain things inflict themselves upon the senses of the body so that they cannot remain unknown to the sensate, and certain things are of more subtlety so that they are not sensed unless they are used regularly and are viewed and examined diligently, so there are some things so evident by their light that they cannot remain unknown to rational examination but are seen by everyone commonly, yet to a greater or lesser extent according to the capacity and power of individuals. There are certain other matters which virtually require a sort of scrutiny and, since they are consequent upon the foregoing, they cannot remain unknown to the diligent examiner. Yet both in the latter and in the former certain matters seem to be anterior which the rationality of philosophy lays down on faith as a foundation, imploring that these precepts are to be freely conceded in the hope of profiting from them. In just this way even geometricians construct first premises as a sort of foundation for their whole field of study, following which they add general rational concepts and thus proceed according to an appointed order to those things which they are demonstrating. But even the premises themselves agree to an extent with reason so that whoever does not concede them, even to an opponent, would seem to be shameless.

Yet this does not entirely apply to those matters which pertain to the practice of religion because in that instance certain premises are sought which surpass the experience of reason in order that faith may be more deserved; but although reason does not urge them, these premises are obligatory on the basis of piety itself. For in order that faith might still exercise the sacraments, wherein reason is forsaken, many services and great miracles were performed by Christ, in whom it is impious not to believe, just as it is perniciously destructive to dissent from probable conclusions. Who except a mad or destructive person would deny the fact that one can extend a straight line from one point to any other opposing point? Just as it is necessary that in buildings there be some fixed and stable foundation upon which the erected structure can be based, so in every doctrine the careful consideration of reason necessarily demands progress from a stable basis. Otherwise, whatever the builder does further falters as if he builds on shifting sands or tar or writes upon flowing waters. For that which is more certain induces faith in that which is less certain.

If, therefore, nothing follows unless something precedes it, if all motion proceeds from a state of rest, what advance in demonstration can exist for him who never rests or who accedes to nothing? Indeed him for whom all things are equally probable can prove nothing. But some matters which are evident are known by everyone, others are known by the more greatly learned according to the individual faculties of each one. For the fact that all numbers are either odd or even is so widely known that it does not escape the detection of children, the licence of whose age nonetheless allows them

> to play the game of odds and evens, to ride horseback
> upon a long pole,
> to construct toy houses, to yoke mice to toy carts.[7]

By contrast, it is only known to those who are devoted to work on numbers that the number of places from which the multiple is removed from unity equals the number of superparticulars of its own kind.[8] Indeed the more skilled mathematician knows that what is and the existence of things are different matters. And so in particular disciplines some things are known to their practitioners which are not only obscure to the masses but also to other philosophers.

Even religion has certain basic principles of its own which either common reason or piety have prompted, principles regarding the worship of God and the exercise of morals which are advantageous in the acquisition of happiness. Indeed, there is one principle of all religions which piety concedes freely and without any demonstration, namely, that God is powerful, wise, good, worthy of respect and loving. For the Epicurean denial of the existence of God, and its subjection of everything to chance, was already discredited long ago on the authority of God-made-man. Therefore, to resist principles or matters of fact known in themselves or to dispute about them is irrational or foolish or (what is worse) malicious. But it is not permitted to be in doubt about those matters which result from principles, so long as it is plain that they do logically follow; for in the

---

[7] Horace, *Saturae*, 2.3.247–248.
[8] John draws directly from the work of Boethius, *De Euclidis Geometriae Interpretatione*, 1.

meantime questionable matters are to be discussed, until their congruence with some principle or conclusion is evident. It is not useless to be in doubt about particular things; and in regard to such matters the Academics had entered into debate about probabilities, until they finally grasped the truth. Yet what does it matter or how does it make a difference if those who inquire do so constantly and about everything, always learning and yet never arriving at knowledge of the truth because they know that nothing has certainty? For this reason, therefore, Cicero prescribes regulations for Academics so that he whose intention it is to be a philosopher may inquire when things are unclear and may retire once the probable truth is evident. For he asserts: 'We who seek the probable cannot progress beyond that which appears probable and we are prepared to refute without anger and be refuted without obstinacy.'[9] For it is extremely unfavourable to the discovery of truth, if either one is roused to fury by another who states the truth or one labours obstinately in the defence of falsity. For the moralist asserts: 'Anger impedes the mind so that it cannot discern the truth.'[10] And Truth Incarnate is itself withdrawn from those who, as in the case of Chorazin and Bethsaida, obstinately resist the Holy Spirit. But obstinacy blinded even the Jews so that their eyes still watched the veil of the temple, which at the Lord's suffering was torn from the top all the way down to the bottom.

[9] Cicero, *Tusculanae Disputationes*, 2.2.5.
[10] Cato, *Disticha*, 2.4.

CHAPTER 8

That virtue is the unique path to being a philosopher and to advancing towards happiness; and of the three degrees of aspirants and of the three schools of philosophers

Nevertheless, because not everyone can do everything, and the Holy Spirit resides wherever it wishes, and it is frequently the case that those things which are discovered by the learned are understood in diverse ways by the multitude, many schools emanate from the words

of Socrates and Plato, yet all are rushing towards one goal but by
various paths. That purpose towards which all rational creatures turn
is true happiness. For in fact there is no one who does not wish to be
happy; but those who desire this do not all advance along a single
path. A single route is laid out for all but it branches into many paths
like the king's highway. This highway is virtue; for no one advances
towards happiness except by way of virtue. Perhaps one who lacks the
works of virtue and is no doubt without works at all is attracted to
happiness, but one never advances towards it except along the track of
the virtues. Virtue is, therefore, deserved of happiness; happiness
rewards virtue. And these are the greatest goods (*summa bona*): the
one of the journey, the other of the homecoming. For nothing
surpasses virtue so long as the exile is a foreigner to God; nothing is
better than happiness so long as the citizen is ruled by and rejoices
with the Lord.

These things are more outstanding than all others because virtue
includes everything to be done, while happiness includes everything
to be desired. Yet happiness excels virtue because the end is more
illustrious than the means. For no one is happy in order that he may
act rightly, but one acts rightly in order that one may live happily. For
this reason the precept of the Socratics was praised in the book of the
Saturnalia: 'Many men consequently wish to live in order that they
may eat and drink; one ought to drink and also to eat in order that one
may live.'[11] Hence, the one and unique highest good of everything is
happiness, but under it there is another good which is higher in
comparison to certain other ones and is in itself superior to certain
others because it approximates more closely that which really is the
uniquely and singularly highest of goods. Frail men improve in the
understanding of neither sort of good except under the guidance
of philosophy. For whoever seeks the path to happiness without
philosophy falls down as a result of presumption, like a blind man
travelling on a dangerous path to high ground. For this reason,
Chrysippus asserts, philosophy is master of both divine and human
affairs, and one can never praise sufficiently that which expels vice,
reveals and confers virtue, and restores a certain measure of divine
soundness to human weakness. And, in order that his meaning may
be disclosed more plainly, all who do not stay alert (which is the

---

[11] Macrobius, *Saturnalia*, 2.8.16.

essence of the matter) on the basis of philosophy or in relation to philosophy, he affirms to live like brute animals, indeed to be an astounding miracle contrary to nature, a brute human in a human body. He asserts the existence of three categories of humans who are truly human (for the others he calls brutes). For some fully enjoy the delight of wisdom, and these are the wise; others undertake study for the sake of enjoyment, and these are the philosophers; still others aspire to the undertaking, namely, those who are not yet and desire to be philosophers. For it is agreed that many exist who are not yet philosophers and emulate the life of philosophers if not in works, then at least in the strong desire to be like them.

I approve of his judgment with greater security in so far as it seems to me to receive support from the authority of the Holy Spirit; the prophet says: 'My soul yearns to desire at all times your justifications.'[12] In this, it seems to me, has been expressed the three previously revealed categories. For when Plato says that the wise man is to be a worshipper of God, how is the wise man to be regarded other than as he who attends to the justifications of the Lord and who, delighting in the cognizance of his own good works, samples and experiences by the eagerness of his whole mind in the present world the sensation of happiness? Without doubt, no one is ignorant of this who is sweetened by the knowledge of happiness, and his aspirations are filled to excess who in life tastes and sees how sweet is the Lord. Moreover, the philosopher, whose aim is to direct himself in order that he may be wise, is according to the same authority a lover of God and he applies his soul to conquering vice and becoming familiar with reality so that by this knowledge he can approach true happiness. For these things make men happy, if they both dissolve the bonds of the vices and are allowed, according to the degree of their contemplation, to look upon the clear and unfailing wellspring of goodness. For 'happy is he who can know the causes of things';[13] and, as the poet asserts (for incitements to virtue are agreeable to us, whatever their provenance):

> Happy souls were those first concerned to know this
> and to ascend to the house of the gods.
> It is credible that above both the vices and the jests
> of men they have raised their heads.

[12] Psalms 119:20.   [13] Virgil, *Georgica*, 2.240.

Venus and wine did not break their lofty hearts,
nor public duties nor military labours;
no petty ambition and no rouge soaked glory
and no avarice for the greatness of riches arouses them.
Bringing our eyes to the distant stars
and subjecting the sky to their genius.
In this way does one travel to the heavens, not that Mt Ossa is set
    upon Olympus
and that the summit of Pelius touches the highest stars.[14]

There is no military or domestic duty, however, that is not examined by philosophy, since it alone prevents vice and without it nothing can be properly transacted between human beings. Indeed, just as attending to justifications, that is, to the implementation of the commandments of God, creates the wise man (for even the prophet says: 'By your commandments I understand'[15]) so the truest philosophy makes the soul ready for their ultimate implementation. But there are those who do not yet implement them or are not yet made ready for implementing them, yet who approve of what they admire in others and desire to conform to those precepts stemming from God's authority. The most outstanding grade is, therefore, composed of those who are occupied with justifications; the middle grade, of those whose souls are unencumbered by vices so that they are occupied by matters arising from love; the lowest, of those who desire to be readied in order that they can desire God's commandments themselves; the latter are those who desire to be philosophers although they are not so. The prophet assumed their role, saying: 'My soul yearns to desire at all times your justifications.'

For indeed the beauty of this is so great that, as Plato asserts, if it could be seen with corporal eyes, men would be wondrously aroused to love wisdom, to such a great degree that it would be unavoidable for everyone to fall in love with it at first sight. Wisdom is loved and carefully sought from youth by the faithful soul whose old age consists in a dignity of character and whose period of childhood consists in ignorance and in the dangers of vices. 'Above health', it is said, 'and all beauty I have valued wisdom and I propose to have it instead of light; all good things came to me together with it.'[16] If all good things are, therefore, consequent upon wisdom, and philosophy is the study

[14] Ovid, *Fasti*, 1.297–308.   [15] Psalms 119:104.   [16] Wisdom 7:10–11.

of wisdom, then surely contempt for philosophers is the exclusion of everything good. For this reason it is deduced that however much anyone diligently pursues philosophy, to that extent does he more faithfully and correctly advance towards happiness. For philosophy assigns the virtues according to which one proceeds in particular duties. But because the ancients, although they believed for the most part in the mortality of the soul, had not yet received instruction about the eternal life which is to be after this one, they founded the greatest good upon virtue, than which there is clearly nothing better except the enjoyment of Him who is good in the highest degree and is the greatest good. For the use of virtue is the best, and it is associated with the fruits of God Himself. Therefore, since virtue alone creates happiness, those taking the opportunity of receiving instruction from the learned are struggling to ascend to their goal by means of various roads. For the Stoic, in order that his disdain for material things may be demonstrated, is to be engaged in meditation upon death; the Peripatetic, in the investigation of truth; the Epicurean is occupied with pleasure; and, although they aim at one goal, they expose their pupils to various judgments regarding the paths of happiness. Concerning these matters, one is free to doubt and inquire up to the point when truth shines forth from the comparisons of positions as a result of the collision of doctrines. But there is more extensive discussion of this in what follows. For the moment it is sufficient to have demonstrated the way in which one is permitted to imitate the uncertainties of the Academics.

CHAPTER 11

What it is to be a true philosopher; and the end towards which all writings are directed in their aim

To reject error is to be truly a philosopher, and in this is the greatest delight and the most beneficial fruit of broad reading. For indeed wisdom encompasses a knowledge of all things and the general moderation of all the actions and words of human life, and constitutes a limit upon cognition and its very boundary. Yet there is one matter for which wisdom does not know how to designate limits; there is one for which it prescribes a mean in such a fashion that it does not have a mean. Whatever wisdom does or speaks points to this: that it has no limits among good philosophers. For its very substance consists in this: that nothing whatsoever circumscribes it. For if, according to Plato, the philosopher is a lover of God, then what else is philosophy than the love of the divine? This is above all what one does not endeavour to circumscribe, lest even wisdom be restrained, which is not expedient. For what is restrained ceases to exist; and if the love of God is extinguished, the good name of philosophy vanishes.

So also the wisdom of God Incarnate, while He has prescribed the mean in many things, instructs that God be loved without moderation, in so far as charity is prescribed in such a fashion that God is to be loved by a love without limitation. For it is He who asserts: 'Love your neighbours as yourself'; and He likewise already had said: 'Love the Lord your God with all your heart, with all your soul, with all your mind and with all your strength.' Also it is added in the same vein: 'On these two dictates depend the entire law and the prophets.'[17] If, therefore, all the things which are written are at the service of the prophets and the law, if these teachings are all directed so that man is subjected to the law of God, then who disputes that everything returns to the realm of charity? He who acquires and enlarges charity on the basis of philosophy itself is pursuing the ends of the philosopher himself. And so it is the true and immutable rule of philosophers that one engages in all sorts of reading and studying, acting and refraining from action, to the end that charity may be advanced. Never is charity foolish or forsaken, but it introduces honour, modesty, sobriety, chastity and the other venerable virtues granted to men which piety consecrates like a shrine to the Lord. Whatever turns elsewhere in any kind of art or writing whatsoever is not philosophical doctrine but the foolish fables and fictions of those concerning whose impiety the anger of God is revealed in heaven. Whatever is babbled by them seems absurd, insipid and stupid to the real philosopher. Listen not to me but to the prophet speaking of such matters: 'The iniquitous have recounted to me stories but not as your law.'[18] Therefore, it is common for both philosophers and non-philosophers to express the true and the just. There are no philosophers expressing both the true and the false, teaching both the good and the evil. Even the mere futile imitator of the philosopher teaches correctly

---

[17] Matthew 22:39, 37, 40.   [18] Psalms 119:85.

sometimes; but he who correctly follows that which he teaches is the true philosopher.

CHAPTER 17

Of ambition, and that passion accompanies foolishness; and what is the origin of tyranny; and of the diverse paths of the ambitious

Some endeavour to avoid if not the stain, then still the offensive external appearance, of avarice; for they seem to abstain from what belongs to others and they are prepared to use freely their own goods when the situation demands. Yet a certain stream of vice springs from the fountain of evil which deflects their path from the route of true happiness. For just as the river of delights springs in its source from a single fountain which makes the land that God has blessed fruitful with the sweetest smells, so they dwell 'in a horrible place and an uncultivated wilderness',[19] that is, 'in the land of forgetfulness',[20] who forget themselves in that hidden world of stupidity, amusement and vanity, captivated by exhibitions, as though all the principal vices sprang from a single fountain. This is the well of passion; the authority of the Fathers themselves declares that passion is said to be the love of those things that can be lost involuntarily. Foolishness is associated with it as a companion, persuading it to love and seek what it cannot possess; and foolishness is the ignorance of those vices of which one ought to be aware.

The great Augustine describes this in his book 'On Free Will'. For if one is ignorant of that which cannot be known, it hardly falls into the category of foolishness; yet when one is ruled by his own ignorance, one is transformed into a foolish person. If one prefers goods which are patently lesser to those which are greater, one is judged foolish; if in pursuing vices one performs the meaner aspect of them, one is condemned to the curse of foolishness; if, therefore, one's error is that of inflamed passion, a labyrinthine path to the precipice lies open, since it is as a result of error that man does not know what path is to be followed and the furnace of his passion burns during his departure

---

[19] Deuteronomy 32:10.   [20] Psalms 88:12.

from the path. And also the words of the iniquitous still prevail, in so far as man, ignorant of his own proper knowledge and the obligatory yoke of subjection, affects a sort of fictitious liberty so that he can live without fear and can do with impunity that which he wills and can to a certain degree be just like God; not that he wishes to imitate the divine goodness, however, but that he wishes God to be so inclined towards his malice that freedom from punishment is granted for evil acts. Therefore, from the root of pride slowly grows ambition, namely, a passion for power and honours, so that from the one it possesses strength lest it be rooted out, while from the other it obtains reverence lest it become vilified.

There is no one who does not rejoice in liberty and who does not desire the strength through which it may be protected; there is nothing that one would not sacrifice in exchange for it, if a reason to do so was at hand. For servitude is a sort of image of death and liberty is the guarantee of life. It is out of love that riches are lavished in order to advance power; and as much as one is desirous of power, to that degree one willingly pays the price. Yet when one has obtained power, one may be raised up into tyranny and contempt for equity, and one will not be afraid to subdue those sharing one's birth and circumstances even before the gaze of God. And, although not everyone can take possession of principalities and kingdoms, still one is either never or rarely altogether immune from tyranny. It is said that the tyrant is he who oppresses the people by violent domination; yet each one can exercise his tyranny not only over the people but also over those of lesser importance. For even though one does not dominate over the people, still each one dominates to the extent that he can. No mention is intended of those who are entirely purified in their souls and who, rejoicing in continued subjection, avoid commanding anyone in life; the life of political creatures is instead under examination. Who among them will you show to me who does not wish to excel even one other person in power? Who is there who refuses to demand his own rights over someone else? Who is there who treats those subject to him just as he would wish to be treated himself if he were subject to them?

In so far as ambition becomes strong, injustice advances over oppressed equity and, attending to the origins of tyranny, pursues everything through which tyranny thrives. He who does not thus prevail by his own powers relies on the powers of others. One may see that the large numbers of power seekers, those suitors of public honours, cling to the powerful and meddle in the offices of the republic, searching for a path on one side or the other by which they can raise themselves on high, by which they can come before others or at any rate are seen to be able to do so by reason of their associates. They pour forth their patrimony, they undertake and perform immense labours; they are not afraid to press their services upon and to lure with flatteries those whom they seek to entrap. Never is an office, therefore, free of charge; no general or judge, no commander or courtly official, not even a herald or huckster, is appointed except for a price. These things are tolerable in secular affairs, however, so long as those matters which are of public concern are not corrupted; for whatever matters are of public concern ought to be consecrated to piety and faith; the remainder of these affairs are objects of ambition and seldom or never fall on someone free of charge. But in regard to this, those things which are affirmed above on the basis of the 'Instruction of Trajan' will avail to meet our needs.

I am not able without moans and tears to deplore the calamities within the House of God and the openness of its chamber of wisdom to fornicators and the conversion of the recesses of its innermost shrine into a brothel. For the house of prayer is made, God forbidding, into a house of business affairs; and the temple founded upon the rock of assistance is transformed into a den of robbers. For indeed the Church is given away as plunder, some taking possession of it publicly, others secretly. Perhaps the possession of it is permitted because its goods are conceded to no single person. And one does not, except on rare occasions, find someone who is girded with a sword upon his thigh in order to restrain the presumptions of the ambitious. Indeed, this encourages manifold schemes to the end that, defended by no one, the Church may be subdued. For some, trusting in their nobility or the strength of the powerful, violently seize upon holy places and, if perhaps they knock at the door, they are not afraid to tunnel under both the entrance-way and the wall. For they will incite sedition even against Moses and they introduce strange fire into the temple and they will contaminate the dishes of the inner sanctum.[21] Others, counting on the multitude of their riches, enter by the lead of Simon, not encountering anyone there who commands them

---

[21] Cf. Leviticus 10:1–20.

and their money to go to eternal damnation. Another man will avoid approaching Peter with presents; yet just as Jupiter slipped through the roof tiles into the lap of Danaë, so the unchaste suitor descends into the innermost parts of the Church by means of a covert shower of gold. Still others assist obediently as though ignorant of presents, as if obedient services are not equivalent in the accounting of presents; surely there is no greater present than the devotion of one man to the service of another man. By means of collusion, the generous gift to some others precedes the offer of payment; but after the contribution of his favour, the giver will be compensated more fully than Gehazi. Yet another pleads that it was not appropriate to knock at the door, but that he was summoned towards the entrance involuntarily, as though veiling the lamp of God so that he might laugh with impunity at his own fraudulence.

Once again, another dissimulates for a long time; and so he exhibits his ambitions by many signs and it is beyond doubt that he wishes to become rich, powerful and illustrious, but in another way, in another situation, with less peril or with more liberty. He has wished to be famous among the laity or with greater certainty among the clergy. On account of this, he has procured the favour of strong princes, has entered into close friendship with them, and has undertaken for them the execution of any task whatsoever. Perhaps he is in charge of the files or has undertaken the duties of the registrar or the custody of the storeroom or of the keys to the public funds or the accounting of various securities or, if he is unable to do anything else, he demands that he be put in charge of the poor-treasury – yet not because he concerns himself about the destitute or because he cherishes the care of the poor, but because he is a thief and has a purse which his avarice consumes for a while so that under the pretext of piety he fattens himself sacrilegiously and he acquires his own private riches out of the destitution and the death of the needy. For if he were motivated by the sentiment of true compassion, he would more faithfully and more usefully disperse his own goods to paupers rather than attack what is for distribution to others, as though he were a corrupt merchant.

At the moment everything is purchased openly, unless the modesty of the seller prevents it. For the profane passion of avarice threatens the holy altars to such a degree that these are all purchased in advance like some sort of property rights. Because they do not on their own come into the market place, they are purchased in a lot and bought in advance. So what? Does the praetor not approve that those things which enter into the market place may, according to ancient right, be possessed by laymen in such a fashion that they are transferred by inheritance and also title to them may be alienated as a gift or exchange? What, therefore, prohibits the right of advowson or the patronage of a church from retail sale? Inasmuch as the blessed Ambrose pronounces that such people commit the heresy of simony, they interpret this to be a provincial decree and one which ought to obtain in Italy alone and among the Lombards. With regard to the apostolic ordinance restraining those who, in so far as they solicit churches (which they more easily penetrate in secret), seek the right of advowson, and who would admit into the Church those whose advowson was procured fraudulently, they reply that this was a dictate of warning and that it was by no means to be perpetual but was to be administered according to place and time; for as blessed Cyril asserts in his letter to the Synod of Ephesus, moderation of supervision never displeased any wise man.

If you inquire about the moderation of the supervision, it is surely likely that the rigour of the canons is tempered with respect to the rich, with respect to the nobles, with respect to the powerful or courtiers. For mention of moral character is the last thing made; and the law of the canons is not in any case imposed upon them. After all, they are the children of justice and are guided by the Spirit to such an extent that they have no need of being under law. Let the law, therefore, establish what pleases the legislator; for these people, enjoying privileges of princely distinction, believe that whatever they strive for belongs to them. They place bishops under an obligation for first benefices and they are not even apprehensive about making a bargain over future succession. And so it remains only for the pact to be fulfilled by a sad event; each one of them is enlivened and aroused by the death of him whose succession he desires. And if the occupant delays passing away, they oppose, abuse and intimidate him in many ways; for actually his occupation of the office causes him to be the adversary in a sort of a civil proceeding against his rights (*actio in rem*). If some prelate, recalling his own status, will not comply with their will, he will instantly hear bitter stories because they consider it an utter indignity and outrage if their foul and dishonourable petition suffers any rejection. Thus, in the meantime they are carried off by the flapping of their own wings, they build their nests in each of the provinces, they barely know even how many nests they have, guest rooms are daily prepared for them on their travels to every region of the world, and despite the large number of available rooms, they surrender barely one little inn for a scruffy companion; and if anyone does this, it is proof of his generosity. Above all, it is a sign of prudence if someone by whatever means procures altars in such great numbers that (like the Memphitic ritual) he can offer up a sacrifice on a new altar every day. Yet they are unwilling to be burdened with priestly tasks or to serve at the altar. I will not say (as the people argue) that those who live off the altar are wanton, but they have introduced a sort of surrogate right by which some take away the profits while others take on the burdens. And although the Apostle says, 'He who does not labour does not eat',[22] he who merits the least harvests more, and the leisured or the dissolute rely upon the labours of others. Who would, therefore, say that in the purchase of this licence, one can commit simony, since it is not a sacred thing but a profane one? For as the common man is accustomed to saying, one follows along on the bridge of silver in order that one may bypass the bridge of gold upon which foul things pass.

[22] II Thessalonians 3:10.

CHAPTER 21

Of hypocrites who endeavour to conceal the disgrace of ambition under the false pretext of religion

Although the rashness of the people or the licence of the powerful can be restrained by legal precepts and divine instructions, still ambition cannot be controlled. For if it does not risk public attention, it spreads secretly and enters fraudulently. If it does not open up the gates of the Church with presents, if they are unbarred by neither its own violence nor that of another, it has recourse to the arts of deception. Everything which assails liberty, which disrupts the decretal statutes, and which is contrary to religion, it detests with the whole liberty of the Spirit. You might wonder if Sinon had returned in order that the simple and the naive might be fooled. He pretends and he dissimulates and he bears the cunning of the fox within his heart; he is more liberated than any Stoic, more restrained than Cato. He is also occasionally more sincere and more careful than Paul, the teacher of the Romans, and more fervent than Peter; and Christ is living to him and wealth is dying; and he does not pride himself on anything except the cross of Christ, which he continually bears upon his body in order that his spirit may be saved, desiring merely to be set free and to live with Christ. He, therefore, mortifies the vices and desires of the flesh and, although passing his life among men, behaves angelically and keeps company with the heavens, unlike other men. These sorts fast continually, they pray without interruption and 'yet clearly so that a visitor hears',[23] they are clothed in rough and filthy attire and they censure the people. They accuse clerics, they remonstrate about the amendment of the moral characters of princes and powerful men, acquiring evidence of their own justice when they disparage the lives of others.

In order that fraud may flourish under the appearance of honour, these men seek out the company of the praiseworthy, they submit to arduous oaths, they boast of difficult deeds and they pursue possible courses of action which are beneficial both for themselves personally and for humanity generally. They declare themselves followers of Basil, Benedict, Augustine or, if this is not enough, of the apostles and prophets; they dress in the clothes of the Carthusians, the Cistercians or the Cluniacs, and those who are deemed worthy of being canons pride themselves on their tunics of wool and lamb skin. For they come in sheep's clothing, yet inside they are predatory wolves; but, as the Lord asserts, they will be known most manifestly by their own fruits. Yet the glory of true religion is not diminished by their deceptions. For it is agreed by everyone without doubt that the causes which they profess and to which they pledge themselves are the most honourable and most faithful duties. For within these movements religious faith is so true, so excellent, that it never fears the sting of censure; indeed the Carthusians are everywhere prominent as the chief vanquishers of avarice; the Cistercians follow to precision the precepts and foot-prints of blessed Benedict, who is agreed by everyone to have been full of the spirit of the just; the Cluniacs have transmitted the plan of religion to many provinces. And it ought to suffice for the fullest praise of the canons that their rule should be imitated by all clerics.

[23] Persius, *Saturae*, 2.8.

Moreover, hermits have as the authority for their practices the Baptiser of our Saviour and the sons of the prophets. The Brothers of the Temple lay down their lives for their fellows, on the example of the Maccabeans. The Xenodochi or Hospitallers follow the footprints of the apostles and, aspiring to the height of perfection, they obey Christ most faithfully in this: they live innocently and disperse all that they have to the poor.

Yet among all of these are found both the faithful and the reprobate, and neither religion nor the profession of truth is disfigured as a result of it. For what occupation is there, or what association has there been about which we read, upon which no blemish has insinuated itself? We read of the apostate angel, of fratricide among the earliest brothers, of the reprobate prophet, and of the wicked disciples of Christ. Yet the purity of the persevering angels is not corrupted, nor is the mutual association of loving fellows less holy, nor is prophetic grace among the elect a sin, nor is apostolic authority contemptible among the faithful, nor is Christ's teaching deformed by the various errors of the heterodox. Therefore, just as the angel of Satan transfigures himself into the angel of light and the pseudo-apostles aspire to the authority rather than to the life of the apostles, so likewise hypocrites resort to the arrogance of the Pharisees, 'enlarging their phylacteries and broadening the fringes of their clothing',[24] but their fingers are unable to touch those things which are written in the law of God, inasmuch as these things may be viewed by the men from whom hypocrites expect a reward of honour or other remuneration. It is as a result of this that they display the pallor of their faces, they affect by means of practice deep sighs, they are unexpectedly flooded with artificial and compliant tears; their heads are lowered, their eyes half closed, their hair short, their heads nearly shaved, their voices lowered, their lips moving in prayer, their movements serene and their steps like a sort of well-arranged harmony. They are tattered and covered with dirt, and they commend dirty clothes and contrived tawdriness – all in order that those persons may more easily raise themselves up who seem to have cast themselves down with zeal into the lowest place and that those who voluntarily diminish themselves will be compelled to become powerful against their wishes.

[24] Matthew 23:5.

It is these hypocrites who, if some blemish has attached itself to the Church while it wanders the earth, expose it for public inspection, in order that they may be seen to be immune themselves from all blemishes. It is they who preach that the benefices which are granted to not yet holy men are to be withdrawn. It is they who persuade the powerful that churches are to be deprived of their rights on account of the vices of particular people. They carry off the titles and first fruits of churches and they accept for themselves churches from the hands of laymen without consulting the bishops. It is they who, carrying off the spoils of ancestral lands from those born to them, reduce villages and rural regions to solitude and who convert everything in the vicinity to their own uses; they destroy churches or they transfer them to secular uses. That which was a house of prayer is made into either a cattle barn or a workshop for craftsmen or woolmakers. They also perform with impunity greater evils and do not hold back from disturbing the Church, in whose lap they rest and under whose cover they are protected, with the twin, horn-like powers of Rome and court. For indeed they run away to the Roman Church, that pious mother of religion which has grown accustomed to providing for peace. They appeal for its assistance, they obtain the protection of its shield lest they might be molested by anyone's malice, and, in order that they can sustain themselves more fully and carry out the duties of charity, they are protected by apostolic privilege so that they do not pay tithes. They proceed further and, in order that they may allow themselves more with impunity, they release themselves from the jurisdiction of all churches and are made the special children of the Roman Church; thus, while they can bring legal action against a defendant anywhere, still they cannot be sued except at Rome or Jerusalem.

At the same time, they entreat the aid of secular powers and promise them divine favour. And they become mediators between God and man and they gather into their association those who need forgiveness. They receive confessions and, usurping or creeping up on the keys of Peter, they presume to bind and to loose, and they release their scythe upon harvests belonging to others which are forbidden to them by the Lord. Moreover, they too readily exonerate the powerful and the more wealthy upon receipt of favours or payment and, placing upon their shoulders the sins of others, they order them to go out in tunics and mourning garments as penance for whatever deeds they lamented that they had committed. They extend the mercy of the Lord, who wishes no one to perish, which they proclaim to be open and accessible just as much to penitents as it is closed only to those without hope. They meanwhile make allowance for those who are ardently and tenaciously involved in crimes to sin in hope; yet they are always paid something in advance for the redemption of such men and they boldly promise forgiveness, because just as water extinguishes fire, so alms extinguish sins.

In addition, while penitence is never too late if it is still genuine, these men assent to wicked morals and, contending for popular affection by means of flattery, they plug up the ears of men lest they hear the reproval of prelates. To this end, they investigate idle gossip, rejoice in disorders, search out the secrets of opposing groups and communicate them first to the friends, then to the enemies, favouring both and faithless to both. Yet they seem better suited to these activities because they are rendered less suspect by the pretext of religion. They alone are believed to have knowledge of what is expedient in the palace, in the market place, on the farm, and in the camp because those who are constantly interfering with everything are seen above others to be in charge of everything. If the elders convene at court, the citizens in the market place, the troops on campaign, in short, if council or synod is convoked, these retiring men of religion will occupy the principal section of seats. You might think that the bars on all the cloister doors were smashed, the poorhouses and hospices emptied out, and that a swarm of carousers had escaped from these venerable places – to so great an extent do these sorts of religious men insinuate themselves into the crowds and public displays. They usurp the best seats, the best beds, the highest salutations and, if you do not allot these things to them, they are most vehemently indignant.

If you reproach them, you are called an enemy of religion and an opponent of the truth. And so you endure it patiently, if your injuries and suffering have been caused by those who are seen to have obtained licence from all apostolic and royal authorities; for this is believed to be owed them by reason of their merits. Surely 'he who resists the powerful resists the ordinances of God';[25] and I do not suppose that apostolic and royal majesty is to be resisted. Speaking

[25] Romans 13:2.

with due respect to the faithful, I still wonder: how is it that they are not ashamed to usurp tithes and rights that belong to others? Perhaps they might say: 'We are religious men.' Surely it is part of religion to pay tithes, and God exacts them only of a religious people. 'But those who exact them are irreligious.' And who appointed you judge over them? Or 'Who are you that you exercise judgment over the servants of another? Every person stands or falls before his own lord. Indeed, he will stand.'[26] They say, 'We are protected by apostolic privilege, according to which we retain the benefits of physical nourishment and the tithes of our labours.' Unquestionably, the apostles are permitted all things; but everything done by the pupils of the apostles is by no means expedient. Concede that they granted this licence to you; consider whether you rightfully sought it. Unquestionably, he who desires not to do what he should do does not freely obey justice. Did not Abel have respect for the Lord in regard to his nourishment? Cain had offered his crops, and rightly so because they were owed to God, but he committed a sin in their inequitable division in so far as he subtracted some from the divided portion. Yet these presents were accepted in preference to the presents of those who divided the offspring of their animals with the Lord. And perhaps presents of animals are more rightfully bestowed because they are obtained without our cultivation and care; for there is more labour in the fruits of planting and harvesting. They respond: 'No one is forced to sacrifice from his own goods.' Yet who is to render account of the labour of others? What more may be said? By many and extended excuses they are seen to affirm that others are not prohibited from giving tithes while they themselves are immune from giving them because they are so religious that they can for their part abrogate divine statutes and by this licence they are less thankful for the grace of God, the benefits of which they experience more fully. For those things which are obtained by grace alone, such as seed and natural offspring, are not considered to be subject to religion.

While in the beginning religion rejoiced in poverty and shared fully of the depths of its own want for the needs and uses of others, the monastic orders are favoured with privileges which, ceasing to be necessary and snubbing charity, are deemed to be instruments of

[26] Romans 14:4.

avarice rather than of religion. For behold that all these privileged men occupy themselves solely with those things which are theirs and Jesus, who is commended in public, either is absent entirely or is concealed in a secret place. Thus it is that blessed Adrian observed privileges squandered for the iniquitous profit of avarice; although not wishing to revoke them entirely, he restricted their licence with this precept of moderation: that what they may appropriate from their labours is to be construed solely with regard to fallow land. For thus they can enjoy their privileges without cost to the rights of others.

Yet there is one more thing that such a great father somehow upheld; and because it evades the canons of the Fathers, it is a wonder to our eyes. For the Knights of the Temple with the pope's approval claim for themselves the administration of the churches, they occupy them through surrogates, and they whose normal occupation it is to shed human blood in a certain way presume to administer the blood of Christ. Not of course that I would call those – almost alone among men – who wage legitimate war 'men of blood', since even David was called a man of blood not because he engaged in wars which were legitimate but on account of Uriah, whose blood he criminally shed. For as is provided by the canons, none of the powers of the ecclesiastical sphere may be seen to be ascribed to laymen, even if they are religious men. Above all, it would be a sign of true religion if they refrained from the administration of those things which by God's prohibition it is not permitted for them to touch. And I do not believe that hospitality is to be carried out from the spoils of plunder (I mean neither that of churches nor that of any of the faithful whomsoever) because God hates the bread of sacrilege and he spurns sacrifices which are offered out of blood; and as often as He is called upon by such means, He closes His ears so that He is not open to their supplications.

It was by no means intended to speak at present about these deeds, which are committed by such men in injury to the justice of God. Still it is entirely wicked that, enticed by the love of money, they open churches which were closed by bishops. Those suspended from office celebrate the sacraments, they bury the dead whom the Church refuses, and they act once a year so that during the rest of the year the erring people are deaf to the voice of the Church; and he who cannot be coerced seems to be corrected. Therefore, they travel around to the churches, they praise the merits of their own orders, they bring absolution for crimes, and sometimes they preach a new gospel, falsifying the word of God because they preach living not by grace but by a price, by pleasure and not by truth. And in the end, when they convene in their lairs late at night, 'after speaking of virtue by day they shake their hips in nocturnal folly and exertion'.[27] If one moves in this fashion towards Christ, then the doctrine of the Fathers which teaches that the narrow and steep path heads towards the true life of man is false and vain.

Indeed when these men disdain the Church, none are so disturbed with utter propriety as those truly religious men upon whom all of these injuries will back up. The people are roused to anger, but the religious orders are more justly stirred up against the disgrace of these hypocrites. For this blemish is said to have been caused not by the hypocrite but by the Cistercians or the Cluniacs or others in whose apparel these jugglers and ventriloquists dress and whose lives they falsify. The cloistered who are clearly religious men, in so far as they keep their vows, are exempted from this malice. No life is more faithful, none more simple, none happier than the life of those who live humbly in a cloister, rejoicing in their submission, obeying their prelates in all matters of subjection and reverence, neither desiring mastery under the pretext of obedience nor the licence to be deceptive or to roam or to be idle, possessing their vessels with holiness and honour, waiting in silence and patience to pay respects to God, unfamiliar with grumbling and defamation, receiving in tranquillity from the mouth of the Lord the words which can save their souls, participating in courteous discourse with God; like terrestrial angels, they are totally ignorant of all earthly troubles. If there is something that seems to sadden them, this is to be traced back to their fraternal charity, since even the angels in heaven feel pity in a certain measure for our errors and they rejoice together over even one sinner moved to repentance.

Although it is difficult to imitate the philosophers in our own times (when virtue is dissipated and it is agreed that Astrea, abandoning men, has returned to the heavens), the life of the cloistered excels incomparably the virtue of the philosophers or, what I would rather believe, it is to be a philosopher in the most correct and secure manner. Truly those who step out of the cloister humbly in order to

[27] Juvenal, *Saturae*, 2.20–21.

satisfy the needs of their brothers and who are faithfully engaged in their labours are occupied with more useful, even though not more secure, lives and are deemed worthy of great praise and reverence; by no means do they resemble the faction of Epicureans or hypocrites. For you will correctly group hypocrites together with Epicureans, who teach philosophy and who serve their own private wills. When they foment disputes, abuse privileges, are slaves to passion, never exercise the duties of charity and seek their own private glory, do they not proceed according to the flesh although they style themselves as spirituals? Deservedly anticipating the annihilation of the flesh, will they not be partners in Hell with him who is a spirit and who was cast down and thrown headlong into the lake of eternal damnation because, swelling up with vain glory, he wished to be equal to and preferred before the Most High? Doubtless those who move along this path are foolish and more miserable than all the gentiles, since they are deprived both of a good life in the present world and of eternal life – the more so since He who had suffered sin to be done for the sake of sinners and who had shown Himself an intimate of tax-collectors and prostitutes, had not been able to maintain peace with hypocrites who were not in need of His justice. This much is clear to those who attend diligently to the debates He carried out with the Pharisees. Yet they strive to possess the chief offices, on the example of the Pharisees.

CHAPTER 25

Of the love and acclaim of liberty; and of those
ancestors who endured patiently free speaking of the
mind; and of the difference between
an offence and a taunt

Liberty, therefore, judges in accordance with the free will of the individual, and it is not afraid to censure that which seems to oppose sound moral character. Indeed, nothing except virtue is more glorious than liberty, if however liberty is ever properly separated from virtue. For it is evident to everyone of sound wisdom that true liberty does not arise elsewhere. For this reason, because virtue is agreed to be the greatest good in life and that which alone banishes the heavy and hateful yoke of servility, philosophers strongly advise that, if assailed by necessity, one is to die for virtue, which is the sole reason for living. Yet this does not arise in its perfection without liberty, and the loss of liberty demonstrates irrefutably that virtue is not present. And, therefore, anyone is free according to the virtue of their dispositions (*habitus*) and to the extent that one is free the virtues are effective. By contrast the vices only bring about servitude and they subject men to persons and things in undue servitude; and although servitude to people sometimes appears more pitiable, servitude to the vices is always far more miserable. And so what is more attractive than liberty? What is more favourable to him who has some reverence for the virtues? We read that it has spurred on all outstanding princes; and none has ever trampled on liberty except for the manifest enemies of virtue. The legal experts know that laws were introduced in support of liberty and the testimony of historians is continually mentioning what great deeds were done for love of it.

Cato drank poison, stabbed himself with a sword and, lest some delay prolong an ignoble life, he enlarged the wound by laying his hand on it and distinguished blood poured out – all so that he would not see the rulership of Caesar. Brutus aroused civil strife in order that the city might be freed from servitude; and the seat of an empire preferred to be afflicted always with lamentable wars rather than to sustain a lord (*dominus*), even a very gentle one. I pass over to the weaker sex. The wives of the Teutons, out of love of chastity, begged Marius after his victory that they might be sent as a gift to the Vestal Virgins, promising that always in the future they would abstain from sexual intercourse. When they were not heeded at all, they set free their spirits the very next night by hanging themselves by the throat lest they might become enslaved or be subject to the loss of their chastity. If I attempted to relate all such instances, time would run out before the examples.

And so practice of liberty is excellent, and it displeases only those who live in the manner of slaves. Those things which are said and done freely are devoid of rashness just as of timidity and, so long as the correct path is advanced, they are entitled to praise and esteem. Yet when under the pretext of liberty rashness has released the vigorous force of its own spirit, it runs into censure; yet it is more favourable to the ears of the vulgar than acceptable to the mind of whomever is most wise, inasmuch as it frequently takes refuge in the favour of others rather than in its own prudence. The best and the wisest man is moderate with the reins of liberty and patiently takes note of whatever is said to him. And he does not oppose himself to the works of liberty, so long as damage to virtue does not occur. For when virtue shines everywhere from its own source, the reputation of patience becomes evident with more glorious renown.

A certain resident of Privernum, when he was questioned about how well peace would be kept by the captives of Privernum, given their exemption from punishment, responded to the Roman consul: 'If you would grant good terms, perpetually; if bad terms, not very long.' Through this voice of liberty the residents of Privernum not only obtained pardon for their rebellion but further the privilege of Roman citizenship because this was ventured to be spoken in the Senate by a man of Privernum. A certain consul named Philip once exercised his liberty against the senatorial order and, reproaching their inaction in front of the rostrum, he said that another Senate was necessary. And yet the dignity of the Senators could not be disturbed, just as the prudence of the consul Philip could not be agitated when the accused, whom he commanded the lictors to seize into their hands, was reported as saying to him: 'You are not Philip, my consul, to me because I am not a Senator to you' . . .

When Pisistratus, the tyrant of Athens, was exhorted by his wife to inflict capital punishment upon a youth who, inflamed with love for their daughter, was encountered kissing her in a public street, he responded: 'If we destroy those who love us, then what will we do to those whom we hate?' Such a saying is more worthy of a citizen rather than a tyrant, since it bears commendably the injury to his daughter and more commendably the injury to himself. The same tyrant, verbally attacked at a banquet with endless abuse from his friend Thrasippus, held back both his mind and his voice from anger and, although Thrasippus in his inebriated passion had splashed his spit on the tyrant's face, still he restrained his sons and family from vengeance; and when on the following day Thrasippus voluntarily pleaded for and demanded death for his insults, Pisistratus welcomed him back into his former position of friendship with a gift of trust.

Servio Sulpicius, a man of humility but of free spirit, heard that the province of Spain would be delegated by the Senate to two citizens who were both of the greatest nobility yet of differing fortunes. When, therefore, the people had manifested their assent to the Senate,

Sulpicius said: 'It does not please me that either one be sent, since the one has nothing and the other is satisfied with nothing', judging poverty and avarice to be equally bad teachers of arbitrary power. Also, the Roman consul Brutus, commander of Lusitania, could have been upset by the harsh words of the ambassador of the Cinnii, who had taken up arms against the Roman Empire, except that Brutus was a Roman, since the Romans, beyond all other peoples, were always a friend of moderation. For when the Cinnii were invited to buy up their liberty, the ambassador responded that they were bequeathed iron by their ancestors by which the city might be defended, not gold by which they might buy it from an avaricious commander. Junius Paschelius, a man of great liberty and much learning and famous both at home and abroad, but devoted only to philosophy, was asked about what gave him such great licence that he said whatever he wished. 'Two things which men loathe', he responded, 'old age and destitution. For what would a destitute old man fear?' Pyrrhus inquired of those who at a banquet had spoken of him with little respect whether what he had heard was true. In regard to this, one of them said to him: 'If our wine had not run out the things related to you would have been child's play and a joke in comparison with what we might have said.' So witty an excuse of intoxication and so simplistically truthful a confession transformed the tyrant's anger into laughter.

A woman of barbarian blood included herself within the virile spirit of freedom when, mourning the disturbances created by King Philip, she said: 'I must appeal against my condemnation, but to a sober Philip.' By this she thus shook Philip out of his intoxicated yawning and, taking charge of his drunken mind, he compelled himself to turn his attention to her case and by diligent inspection to offer a more just sentence. A certain woman of Syracuse, praying all alone to the gods every morning for her wishes, most devoutly pleaded for the safety of the extremely harsh and cruel tyrant Dionysius. He discovered that this was the case and, wondering about such benevolence which was not owed to him, he questioned her at his summons about why or for what kindness of his she did this. She said to him: 'There is a definite reason for my prayers. For as a girl, when we had to endure a harsh tyrant, I had desired to be rid of him. Once he was killed, a considerably more foul man occupied the ruling office; I also valued highly the ending of his domination. We have undertaken you for our third ruler, who have been more cruel than your predecessors. And so fearing lest, if you were taken away, you might be succeeded by someone still worse, I sacrifice my own head for your safety.' Dionysius, even though the most foul man, still was ashamed to punish such witty audacity.

For what will be secure if even the virtues, among which liberty holds nearly the principal place, are punished? Therefore, just as the Romans stood out as more excellent than others so also they were more patient than others with censure, to such an extent that, while criticism should be avoided at banquets and in situations lacking sobriety, still whoever loathes and evades it when fairly expressed seems to be ignorant of restraint. For, even if it conveys obvious or secret insult, patience with censure is among wise men far more glorious than its punishment.

To be given to offences and taunts against men of great power is to exercise licence more than is permitted. An offence, as Eustachius [Macrobius] teaches in his book *Saturnalia*, is that which contains direct reproach and abuse. A taunt is a figurative attack because it is concealed either by deceit or urbanity so that it says one thing and means another; and yet it does not always advance to bitterness, but sometimes it is even sweet to those against whom it is thrust. The wise or other urbane people chiefly employ the latter sort, especially among dinner guests and at drinking parties, where it is easy to provoke anger. For just as even a light touch pushes over someone standing on a precipice, so with someone drunk and polluted with wine, even the smallest animosity develops into fury. Therefore, caution must be taken at banquets to abstain from taunts that have injuries hidden within them. For such sayings cling with so much more visibility than direct offences, just as curved hooks affix themselves more tenaciously than a straightened sword point, especially because such sayings move those present to laughter, by which the injury is confirmed just as surely as if assent were produced. For example, an offence is of this kind: 'Have you not forgotten the fact that you once sold pickled fish?' A taunt, which is spoken in order for the abuse to be hidden, is of the following sort: 'We remember when you used to wipe your nose with your forearm.' For, although each one is saying the same thing, still the offence is the one in which reproach and censure are open, whereas the taunt is the one in which they are figurative. Taunts are of a lesser sort of severity which may be compared to the bites of a toothless beast. For instance, Tullius says of the consul who had only carried out the consulship for one day: 'We are accustomed to the existence of cult-priests for the day; but now we have consuls for the day'; and of the same event: 'A most vigilant consul is our Caninus who was not seen to be asleep throughout his entire consulship.' And when the same Caninus complained that Cicero had not visited him during his consulship, he answered: 'I would have visited him but night fell.'

There is further discussion of offences or taunts and civility in what follows; for the present it suffices to have made known that it is permitted to censure that which is to be equitably corrected. I may add on to the above one example of the taunts of Alexander, as a footnote to this book. King Darius, having tested Alexander's prowess in one battle and then another, offered him the part of his kingdom as far as Mount Taurus and his daughter in marriage, along with one million talents. When Parmenion, a great man among the followers of Alexander, had said to him that, if he were him, he would accept these conditions, the king responded: 'And I, if I were Parmenion, would accept the same conditions.' Tacitly censuring the timidity of his counsellor, he had given a response with the voice of two victories and of one who merited a third, just as soon happened.

Therefore, man is to be free and it is always permitted to a free man to speak to persons about restraining their vices. Thus, there is even a legal right according to which it is permitted to express the truth in speech, and this December liberty indulges even slaves in opposition to their lords so long as they speak the truth. Thus, at that time, without obtaining permission, since it is due to them as their right, they exercise their tongues and they disapprove with impunity of whatever irritated them during the whole year, even exposing crimes publicly, yet provided that in discharging the Saturnalian rites they do not hasten beyond their leave by the indictment of their lord or patron. I use this December liberty, therefore, and obeying your instructions that with the support of common law I faithfully censure what irritates you and me, it is not necessary to obtain confirmed permission for such remarks which serve the public utility and which are acceptable to your will.

BOOK VIII

Prologue

Those who sail upon the sea are in the habit of feeling grateful and of conveying their thanks to those by whose help hazards have been avoided. Fires are lit, cries are sent out, and signals are erected by which the swirling Scylla, the whirling Charybdis, concealed rocks, and the pulling and gripping of Syrtes can be safely avoided by sailors. So also thanks are most properly owed to those who by their service warn of threats which endanger human salvation; and he who does not repay his debts is deservedly to suffer the loss of his salvation for his ingratitude towards kindness. Moreover, there is no one who does not know that salvation is impeded by the vices and it is important that out of love the vices of our neighbours are publicly singled out for avoidance. Indeed human life is more turbulent than any sea you please, and its dangers cannot be evaded unless their signs are made known. To this work, however, I am driven by the stimulus of the public utility and your commands, although I am aware of nothing within me that might rouse the attention of readers, being in any case a defenceless and weak man whose life is adequate as an example neither of moral sense nor of learned knowledge nor of good works. For this reason it is complained against me by many that I should keep still; it is said that nothing, even the praise of virtue, is splendid in the mouths of sinners.

The only ones who say this are those to whom vice is agreeable, rushing headlong into death persuaded by no one, or those who are saved against their will. For those to whom goodness is agreeable do not heed the speaker but rather what is said and, weighing words according to the circumstances in which they are spoken, they feel grateful for anything regardless of origin that advances the procurement of the virtues. Therefore the reader should heed diligently not who I am but what and out of what circumstances I have written and, where he finds evil words, as a sincere judge and not one aroused by motives of jealousy or hatred or some other emotion, he may present evidence of my evil; and where I have spoken well, let him not attack me. Yet it is of little concern to me if my innocence is freely disparaged by the corrupt whom I have wanted to correct, so long as the favour of your benevolence still supports me. Whatever I might suffer from contemporaries, I hope that, with the authority of God and the charity by which I am urged to write as the warrant for my confidence, the gratitude of posterity will not be denied to my labours. For indeed the judgments of the present times, whether motivated by hate or love, will for the most part disintegrate. In any case, nothing is introduced into the present work by design that is not supported by the authority of reason or the precedents of scripture. Yet in regard to these matters it is left to the free will of the reader to choose what path is to be followed, so that vice and the infamy of deceit have been performed at a distance from my name. But so much for this issue. Now we may cross over to the camp of the Epicureans, and reveal in public what may be established about them for certain. For those who in all matters serve their own personal will are indubitably known to tend towards the Epicurean sect.

CHAPTER 12

That some long to be modelled after beasts and insensate creatures; and how much humanity is to be afforded to slaves; and of the pleasures of three senses

None are more properly modelled after the genera of the animal kingdom than those who designate the pleasures (I would even say extravagance) of tasting and touching as the greatest good in life. Certainly this does not excuse the extravagance of the other senses, since human dignity is manifestly thrown away if man devotes himself to being on the same level with, if not goats and pigs, then lions and panthers, leopards and satyrs, peacocks, nightingales and parrots, or any beasts or insensate creatures whatsoever. For indeed one who is honoured by the creation of human birth should more properly aspire to the purity of the angels, so that in the fulfilment of true and eternal happiness he can be likened to angelic perfection. Even the indestructible authority of the Fathers has decreed that God alone is of more dignity than the nature of the human mind and that all those things at which man mistakenly marvels were made by Him in order that they might serve man; God created man in order that he might act as a participant in His eternity and happiness. Therefore, who does not deprecate the directing will of God if he esteems the vile and base condition of the slave? Yet I would not say that slaves are to be treated with contempt, unless they live according to servile vices. Just as the true and unparalleled liberty is to serve the virtues and to perform their duties, so the true and unparalleled servitude is to be subjected to the vices. Whoever supposes that either condition befalls one in some other way is clearly wrong; for indeed the whole race of men upon the earth arose from the same origin, consists of and is sustained by the same elements, draws the same breath from the same source, delights in the same heavens, lives the same, and dies the same . . .

Nothing is proper that has not proceeded from virtue, and shamelessness and vice mutually trap themselves in a vicious circle. Whoever falls into vice is impelled solely by this: that he abases himself and is devoted servilely to that which he was born to rule. Those who flock to spectacles or produce for themselves dishonourable spectacles or wish themselves to be esteemed by the foolish for their frivolous spectacles – since these enticements of vanity cannot please the truly wise – are lured by the enticements of the eye and, although they are crushed gently, still they sink from the dignity of their circumstances and they fall into that servility which they disavow. Therefore, what else is done by mimes, actors, parasites and this sort of human monster except to cultivate the foolish servility of the prosperous? And those who are lured by singing (although hearing is the purest and most refined sense) are also slaves, yet they are restrained by a gentler yoke, if no vices prevail elsewhere. Likewise, hardly anyone at all is lured by smell, except perhaps those who live like Lotus Eaters.

In any case, I do not contrive anything against singers or musicians, since (as witnessed by Quintilian, Valerius, Flavianus and many others) even Socrates devoted himself to music, believing that he would deny himself the pinnacle of wisdom if he were to disregard music. Yet to be occupied too greatly with this is to step outside of philosophical seriousness. Would any such thing be suitable for a man of wisdom, especially that which does not escape the mark of shame even among members of the female sex? Sallust censured Sempronia not simply because she knew how to dance and to sing but because she knew too well. He asserts: 'She dances and sings more exquisitely than is necessary for decency.'[1] Yet to sing very well, if it can be achieved without frivolity, is plainly desirable. For in all things which are desired honestly, those which are more directed towards the qualities of goodness are the more desirable ones. But some things can be suspected on the basis of their context. Lucius Sulla, a man of fame, was reported to have sung very well; but the marks of lustfulness and cruelty had detracted from his talent. It was also Cato's view that to sing well was not to be a serious man. For this reason, to be sure, he called Marcus Cecilius, a not ignoble senator, a street-walker and a smooth-talker, and accused him in these words of performing slow dances: 'He dismounted from a horse, thereafter presenting slow dances and uttering jokes'; and elsewhere: 'Besides he sang whenever it pleased him, he sometimes acted out Greek verses, he told jokes, he debased his voice, and he performed slow dances.'[2] Nonetheless, the pleasure of the ear is acceptable to the honourable, who are the companions of virtue, or at least it is not an accomplice of shamefulness . . .

There is also that pleasure conspicuous in men of dignity as a result of their luxury, which is thought to consist in the ornamentation or colour or shape or novel use of their expensive clothes. For as the moralist asserts:

> Maltinus walks along in his low-slung tunic; it is he who
> is finely dressed right down to his low-slung filthy genitals.[3]

Another one removes the clothes of the wintertime chill and, while everything stiffens with the fetters of frost, he perspires in thin garments, and even silk clothes irritate his skin or constrict his frolics. Yet another one, with more layers than an onion, covered in furs and hidden in a jersey, pulls a topcoat over himself and, like a balled-up circle, is much better suited to rolling than to walking forward. Then again, someone else avails himself of a topcoat, on the one hand, and a wrestler's loincloth, on the other; his only motive is that he may be regarded as different from others. Still another affects such exquisite

---

[1] Macrobius, *Saturnalia*, 3.14.3.
[2] *Ibid.*, 3.14.9–10.
[3] Horace, *Saturae*, 1.2.25–26.

ornamentation in appearance that he is seen to approach the vulgar in the excessively splendid cultivation of his extravagance. For whatever is indecent and in a certain measure defiles or, more correctly, rejects honour is shameful and partakes of shameful things.

Yet what necessity introduces is not to be censured, since everyone cannot do everything, and there exist some whose natures demand what is oppressive or what cannot be borne by others. The observance of philosophy enjoins this: that everyone is to avoid notoriety in all affairs, each imposing upon himself rectitude of action lest he be reviled, caution in speech lest he be despised, and modesty in apparel lest he stand out; for notoriety demonstrates intemperance. To the present day the outrageous behaviour of Hortensius is censured; it was him after whom those who are powdered white call themselves 'Hortensians', not because he was the first to do so but because he was the most prominent, so that he was suffused with the notoriety of his own generation; he was above all soft spoken by design, maintaining elegance in all his own dress. For he would be dressed carefully to the point of impurity and, so that he would go out in the right style, he would examine his appearance in the mirror. Gazing upon himself there, he would so arrange the toga on his body that the folds fell not by chance but were bound tight by a knot arranged with the skill of an artist, and the curves, flowing by these adjustments, would move around him in harmony with his flanks. One day, while he was marching around elaborately in full public view, he filed a report concerning an injury by a companion to the effect that the structure of his toga had been destroyed when the man bumped against him accidentally during an encounter on a narrow street; and he had considered it a capital crime that the folds arranged upon his shoulders had been disturbed. Such behaviour is never suitable for a wise or virtuous man; indeed even honourable matrons and virgins yet to be married blush at such great concern about their wardrobe, even though this would be more acceptable and more wholesome among those of delightful beauty. And so it is astonishing that, according to the shamelessness of the times, our fellow

> men wear a style of clothing
> scarcely desirable for young women.[4]

What leads soldiers to this? What leads clerics to this? Indeed all of

[4]Lucan, *Pharsalia*, 1.164–165.

these things are modelled after the crafty deceits and mischiefs of prostitutes. What, therefore, does a man need with a mirror, except for the reason that Flavian reported that Plato had carried one: in order that in it he might see by the evidence of his face, which bears most faithful witness to good and evil, how its natural appearance had changed with the amount of travel, the exertion of emotion, the ravages of time, and the advance of age? Surely he did this so that he might preserve or alleviate nature, lest it be corrupted by labour or unfamiliar experiences.

In order that we may pass over to other matters, who of those who affect the endowments of beasts deem it proper for themselves actually to be a beast? Or who of them would not consider himself to be better if the reason of animals was compared with that conferred upon them? Do admirers of physical strength wish to be lions or panthers? Physiologists say that other animals follow the scent of the lynx or the leopard; yet I do not imagine that those who are pleased and stimulated by musk or some other type of exotic smell would wish (if they could) to be transformed into a leopard or a lynx. Nor would I believe that he who dresses up as a satyr wishes to be a satyr; and neither can those who decorate themselves transform the embellishments of the peacock on to themselves. They may sing harmoniously and perform all their musical melodies in full voice; yet none of them will equal the nightingale or the parrot. Is it not, therefore, indecent and an insult to man's eminence if, disregarding his own gifts in which he prevails, he aspires to the endowment of others in which he is surpassed? If moderation is displayed, however, I do not judge it disgraceful for a wise man to dwell occasionally upon these pleasures of the senses; as is oftentimes said, nothing is proper without the mean. It is appropriate for even the wise man to enjoy leisure occasionally, yet not in order that the practice of virtue may be diminished, but rather that he may be to some extent reinvigorated and revived.

For now Laelius and Scipio, illustrious for their mutual affection, would read together constantly and, on the most certain authority of Scaevola's testimony about their recreation, would play a game of ball when fatigued by civil business. Also, the same Scaevola is reported to have occupied some of his time with dice games and checkers, after he had attended carefully and at length to the rights of citizens and the ceremonies of the gods. For just as Scaevola would spend time on serious matters, so he would spend time with the amusements of men, whom nature does not permit to be inflicted with continual labours. And Socrates, who is said to have been ignorant of no aspect of wisdom, perceived this; and so he was not ashamed by the time when, interrupted while playing with his children on the legs of their hobbyhorse, he was mocked by Alcibiades. Moreover, when the poet of heavenly talent, Homer, portrayed a melodious harp in the most violent hands of Achilles, he thought of nothing else except that he might relax their military toughness with a mild peacetime endeavour.

In summary, it is frivolous and disgraceful to occupy oneself with actors, dancers and these sorts of seducers. And to be amused by them leads to laziness on some occasions and to disgrace on others. If done moderately for recreation, it may be excused under the licence of enjoying leisure; if done for the wanton pleasures of the passions, then it becomes criminal. The above-mentioned discretion of place, time, manner, person and cause most readily separates out these differences; there might perhaps be excessive repetition of this by means of overly effusive speech, but one cannot excessively repeat and keep in mind this warning. For this is the fount and origin of all moderation, without which nothing is correctly executed in one's duties. On this basis one thing is established to be proper or another to be improper.

For what is shameful for the good Seius and Titus would be
    suitable for
Crispinus.[5]

It is, therefore, clearly a misleading basis for fame and glory to consume one's life with those things which are either slothful occupations or shameful dealings. Moreover, he who offers wantonness to people is a participant in such transgressions, and he is seen to be the author of the extravagance of others who prefers presenting them with luxuries or favours rather than punishing them by the use of censures and the refusal of luxuries. For indeed it is on the authority of Ambrose that he who gives anything to such men commits a great sin; this encourages in them those things which are most evil.

[5] Juvenal, *Saturae*, 4.13–14.

CHAPTER 16

Of the four rivers which spring for Epicureans
from the fount of lustfulness and which create
a deluge by which the world is nearly submerged;
and of the opposite waters and the garments of Esau

All rivers flow together into one so that it is disclosed that a calm condition in both public and private affairs cannot arise except from the fount of wisdom, whatever Epicurus supposes. This was said to be the origin of the most fertile delights, from which the four rivers of the cardinal virtues spring. By contrast, the fount of the Epicureans has as its source lust, which brings forth rivers that irrigate a whole valley with tears and misery, into which is hurled the exile who prefers what is pleasing rather than what it is lawful to do. And one sort of river is the love of possession, by which an abundance of things is sought for the sake of sufficiency, and in which avarice labours to possess or to know more than is permitted. Another river pours out the enticements of luxury and flows down into various pleasures, while it aspires to the aim of the delights of tranquillity and pleasure. The third river acquires the strength by which it can guard natural liberty and repel the injury of any troubles whatsoever, and when it has reached full strength, it bursts forth into the hateful stream of tyranny. The fourth river swells up deceptively from the desire for renown and respect, in so far as it seeks eminence. These are the four rivers which pour into and submerge the world, and the perversions of the will flow out from this fount which has its source in the lowest depths and draws its origins from the mire of vanity.

When they have enlarged in size, these rivers generate diverse streams and, like the swelling waters of a flood, they inundate the world, annihilate living creatures, and so eradicate everything that the earth might appear to be reduced to solitude, except that the house of the Lord, the ark, preserved a few (that is, eight) souls, namely, the children of the resurrection. These are above all those whom God selected out of all carnal creatures. 'Nonetheless, those who are in the deluge of many waters will not draw themselves near to Him.'[6] And also the love of personal advantage, about which it was spoken

[6] Psalms 32:6.

188

previously, pours into these waters as if it were a second sea. As evil grows strong, the Lord, as though opening the flood gates of heaven, rains down an enlargement of the flood by various opportunities for transgression, permitting by the removal of grace that he who exists in shame becomes the more shameful, and he who undertakes his own private will He slaughters as if wreaking vengeance. I would not say that the desire for personal advantage, if it is temperate, is to be blamed, nor would I regard an abundant supply of material goods or the delights of the mind or love of natural liberty or the reward of eminence to be criminal. But these do not yield what they promise; by the manner in which they are sought, they work rather to the contrary effect. Yet all these things are good if the children of God – instructed by grace, struggling against flesh and blood, and blessed by the Father of joy and exultation – use them properly and dress in them as in blooming, fertile and agreeable garments. However, if the brother of flesh and blood, disdaining intimacy with motherly grace, usurps all these clothes of moral character, they neither smell good nor are suitable nor restore nourishment. And perhaps this is why it is written that the garment of Esau had pleased Jacob, and it is not written that Esau used them or that he had given off the odour of sweetness to his father. For, so long as he abused good intentions, he could not be healed by grace. Therefore, the deceptive appearance of goodness neither satisfies nor enriches nor liberates nor exalts.

Furthermore, the arguments against luxury, avarice and gluttony are discussed above; striving for power has in certain measure remained untouched up to this point. Yet even though it may seem to contribute to the approval of liberty and eminence, it destructively diverts the wanderer from the truth of both of these. For power-seeking introduces the most destructive pestilence and, advancing the origins of tyranny, it endeavours to extinguish the framework of calm and peace, than which nothing is more advantageous. Indeed this river extinguishes charity towards those whose way of life is rejected. The Tantalus of fable labours within this river and the words of the prophet censure the thirst of degenerates for its water. The prophet, therefore, invites those who thirst to the opposite waters, which flow out of the Spirit, freely receiving wine and milk therein without charge by means of grace. 'Why', he asks, 'do you pay out your money for what is not bread and your labour for what does not satisfy? Listeners, heed me and eat well, and your soul will delight in its fullness.'[7] This pertains not to those delights in which not the soul but the flesh partakes – to those in which 'the favourite would be disobedient, grow fat, become heavy, be covered with fatness'[8] – but in which the children of God are blessed, so that in the surpassing dewdrops of grace and the fatness of a free will one may reasonably understand God, satisfy Him effectively and obey Him patiently. And so these waters are fattening and sweet, and they temper all others because the wood of the cross has absorbed their saltiness and has sweetened them, and the infusion of heavenly wisdom renders them drinkable for the salvation and fulfilment of souls. These waters also liberate men and obstruct or curb or avenge all assaults of tyranny. It is not false power, therefore, but truth consisting in equity that liberates; and although liberation is falsely promised there are no truly free men except those who have been liberated by the Son. Distinguish the liberties of grace, glory and nature and you will find none of them to be connected with falsehood, nor will any more servile condition than tyranny present itself to you. For 'wherever is the Spirit of the Lord, there also will be liberty';[9] indeed he is weighed down by a most miserable servitude who stirs the spirit of evil.

[7] Isaiah 55:2.   [8] Deuteronomy 32:15.   [9] II Corinthians 3:17.

CHAPTER 17

In what way the tyrant differs from the prince;
and of the tyranny of priests; and in what way
a shepherd, a thief and an employee
differ from one another

The way in which a prince differs from a tyrant, in so far as it is reviewed in the 'Instruction of Trajan' of Plutarch, was discussed above and the duties which belong to the prince and the members of the republic were diligently expounded. For this reason, one can more easily and in fewer words come to know those directly contrasting traits which are ascribed to the tyrant. As the philosophers have portrayed him, the tyrant is, therefore, one who oppresses the people by violent domination, just as the prince is one who rules by the laws.

Furthermore, the law is a gift of God, the likeness of equity, the norm of justice, the image of the divine will, the custodian of security, the unity and confirmation of a people, the standard of duties, the excluder and exterminator of vices, and the punishment of violence and all injuries. It is attacked either by violence or by deceit and, one might say, it is either ravaged by the savagery of the lion or overthrown by the snares of the serpent. In whatever manner this happens, the grace of God is plainly being assailed and God is in a certain fashion being challenged to a battle. The prince fights for the laws and liberty of the people; the tyrant supposes that nothing is done unless the laws are cancelled and the people are brought into servitude. The prince is a sort of image of divinity and the tyrant is an image of the strength of the Adversary and the depravity of Lucifer, for indeed he is imitated who desired to establish his throne to the north and to be like the Most High, yet with His goodness removed. For if he had wished to be like Him in goodness, he would never have endeavoured to snatch away the glory of His power and wisdom. Yet perhaps he aspired to be rewarded by being raised to the same level.

As the image of the deity, the prince is to be loved, venerated and respected; the tyrant, as the image of depravity, is for the most part even to be killed. The origin of tyranny is iniquity and it sprouts forth from the poisonous and pernicious root of evil and its tree is to be cut down by an axe anywhere it grows. For unless iniquity and injustice had advanced tyranny through the extermination of charity, secure peace and perpetual calm would have dwelled among the people throughout eternity, and no one would think of advancing his borders. As the great father Augustine has testified, kingdoms would be as calm and friendly in their enjoyment of peace as are different families in orderly cities or different persons in the same family. Or perhaps it is more believable that there would be absolutely no kingdoms, for as is evident from the ancient historians, these were iniquitous in themselves; they either encroached upon or were extorted from God. And of course not only kings practise tyranny; many private men are tyrants, in so far as the powers which they possess promote prohibited goals. One is not to be troubled that I am appearing to have associated kings with tyranny, since, although it is said that 'king' (*rex*) is derived from the 'right' (*recte*) which is fitting for princes, still this name incorrectly refers to tyrants. Here is one example:

> Whatever a free people would extend to one man,
> I have achieved, and I have lacked nothing over them except
> royal power.[10]

And elsewhere: 'My hope of peace will be to have influenced the right hand of the tyrant.'[11]

And if it is permitted still to call what is against duty and the standard of living rightly a duty, then a single statement reveals all the duties, or on the contrary vices, of tyrants. This is in the mouth of Photinus (from whom tyrants could not undeservedly name themselves Photinians), the first in the monstrous house of Pelleas – that is, one among the other horrors of Egypt – distinguished by his filthiness and cruelty, who, daring to condemn Pompey to death or rather expressing the moral qualities of tyrants with his usual self-confidence, asserts:

> Rights and divine law cause many, Tholomee, to be harmed.
> Praiseworthy faith receives the penalty, when it sustains (it is said)
> those whom fortune humbles; assent to fate and the gods,
> and protect the fortunate, avoid the wretched. As stars and earth,
> as fire and water, differ, so do rectitude and utility.
> The power of the sceptre is completely lost if it begins to weight
> matters of justice, and battle undermines respect for honour.
> The liberty of the criminal is what protects the hateful power of
>   kings,
> as well as the exalted measure of the sword. Doing everything harshly
> is not allowed to go unpunished, except when you actually do them.
>   Let him exit from court
> who wishes to be pious; virtue and great power
> do not go together; he is always afraid who would be ashamed of
>   harsh deeds.[12]

Therefore respect for the honourable and the just rarely or never exists in the sight of tyrants; and, whether they are ecclesiastical or earthly, they wish to have power over everything, disdaining what precedes and follows this power.

Yet I wish that both sorts of tyrants might be persuaded that the divine judgment which was imposed upon the first humans and

[10] Lucan, *Pharsalia*, 2.562–563.
[11] Virgil, *Aeneid*, 7.266.
[12] Lucan, *Pharsalia*, 8.484–495.

their children has not yet expired. It was decreed that, because they had not been willing to comply with justice when they were able, they would no longer be able to conform to justice even when they wished to do so. One is also accustomed to saying the proverb: 'Because of him who does not wish to act when he can, he is not able to act when he wishes.' The great Basil was the author of similar words. For it was requested of him by a common woman that he might intercede with her prince and, approving her petition, he wrote to the prince thus: 'This poor woman has approached me, asking me to prevail upon you; if I have influence, please show it.' And he gave the petition to the woman who, departing, gave her letter to the prince; and reading it, the prince wrote this back to him: 'On your account, O holy father, I would will to show pity upon this common woman, but I could not on account of the fact that she is subject to the tributes.' The holy man wrote back to him: 'If indeed you could not have done what you willed, then fine, no matter how the case turns out; if you could have done what you did not will, then Christ will lead you to the chorus of the needy so that whatever you will you cannot do.' And the Truth, which is always present to the elect, by no means disregarded its instrument. For in a short time the same prince, inciting the indignation of the emperor, was led bound into captivity, hence giving satisfaction to those unjustly oppressed by his own punishment. Yet after six days of prayer by Basil he was liberated from captivity, abandoning his imperial display just as the holy man had demanded.

And so the king is sometimes called by the name of tyrant and conversely the tyrant is sometimes called by the name of prince, according to the maxim: 'Your princes are faithless, associates of thieves.'[13] And elsewhere: 'The princes of the priesthood made counsel so that they might detain Jesus by deceit and kill Him',[14] who by the just judgment of the law ought to have been freed. For even among the priesthood many may be found who are driven by all their ambition and all their talents so that they can be tyrants under the pretext of exercising their duties. For the republic of the impious has both its head and members, and it endeavours to be fashioned like the civil institutions of the legitimate republic. Its tyrannical head, therefore, is the image of the devil; its soul is formed of heretical, schismatic and sacrilegious priests and, to use the words of Plutarch,

[13] Isaiah 1:23.   [14] Matthew 26:4.

prefects of religion, assailing the laws of the Lord; the heart of impious counsellors is like a senate of iniquity; its eyes, ears, tongue and unarmed hand are unjust officials, judges and laws; its armed hand is violent soldiers, whom Cicero labels mercenaries; its feet are those among the more humble occupations who oppose the precepts of the Lord and legitimate institutions. Of course all of these can be readily controlled by their superiors.

Priests should not be indignant with me, however, if I acknowledge that even among them one can find tyrants. Otherwise, why is it that the prophet says: 'Son of man, prophesy about the shepherds of Israel, prophesy and say to them: "This the Lord God says: Woe to the shepherds of Israel who would themselves graze. Are not the flocks to be led to graze by the shepherds? You have consumed the milk, you have covered yourselves in the wool, and you have killed those that were fattened, yet you have not led my flocks to pasture. You did not strengthen what was weak, and you did not cure what was sick; what was bruised you did not bandage, what was thrown away you did not recover, what was lost you did not search for but you commanded them with severity and might; and my sheep were dispersed because there was no shepherd and they were made into easy prey for the beasts of the field and were dispersed." '[15] What else is demonstrated by this condemnation and censure by Ezekiel to have been of concern to him except that the shepherds were lacking the things which ought to have been present and had present the things which they ought to have lacked? Accordingly the Lord said this: 'Behold that I myself am above the shepherds and I will search for my flocks in their hands and I will cause them to desist so that they do not lead my flocks to graze any further nor do the shepherds nourish themselves anymore, and I will free my flocks from their mouths and they will not feed any further.'[16] Does this not seem to express the manifest tyranny of priests and to depict the lives of those who in all matters seek those things which are their own and who render the things which belong to Jesus Christ last of all? For indeed, this is said not by me but by another and absolutely incorruptible source, the oracle of Truth in which is described by an intimate of the Most High the manifest difference between an employee, a shepherd and a thief; for 'the good shepherd lays down his life for the sheep'.[17]

[15] Ezekiel 34:2–5.   [16] Ezekiel 34:10.   [17] John 10:14–15.

If you inquire about these duties, you will find them in the words of the prophet: 'Behold I will search for my sheep and will visit them, just as the shepherd visits his flocks in their midst on days when some of his sheep are scattered. I will guide them out of the clouds, I will gather them together out of the fog, I will lead them to their lands and I will take them to graze in the mountains of Israel among the rivers and all the abodes of the land; their pastures will be in the most fertile grazing lands and the highest mountains, they will find relief among green vegetation and they will graze upon dense pastures up in the mountains of Israel. I will nourish them and make them to lie down; I will search for what is lost and I will recover what was thrown away, I will bandage what was bruised, and I will cure what was sick, and I will guard over even what is fat and strong.'[18] For this is the diligence with which shepherds ought to watch over their flocks. To this the prophet appends: 'And I will nourish them in judgment and justice;'[19] this responds to what he said before: 'But you commanded them with severity and might.' For it is written that 'different weights and different measures, both are abominable to the Lord'.[20] Among men who are employed in business dealings it would seem to be a matter of great but still illicit prudence, since it is cunning and fraudulent, if they sell according to their own weights and measures and buy according to the weights or measures of someone else. Yet for a prelate the calculation of equity demands that he is to pronounce on himself the burden that he imposes on others and that he is devoted to performing the works that he wishes to teach. This is to nourish in judgment and justice and not to command with severity and might.

Such commanding is done above all by those who fasten upon the shoulders of men heavy and unsupportable burdens, and yet who refuse to touch them with their own fingers. For this reason it follows: 'And when you drank of the purest water, you muddied the remainder with your feet, and my sheep were nourished with those things which were trampled under your feet, and they drank from those waters which were muddied by your feet. Behold, consequently, that I myself judge between the fattened and the lean cattle for the reason that you have kicked their flanks and their shoulders and you have stirred up all the weak cattle with your trumpets until finally they were dispersed

---

[18] Ezekiel 34:11–16.   [19] Ezekiel 34:16.   [20] Proverbs 20:10.

in all directions.'[21] Or for the sake of appearances, an employee leads the sheep to graze; but because he does everything for a price, he abandons the sheep and he flees if he sees a wolf attacking. He who is not a shepherd but an employee has no concern for the sheep but only for money – he is like a sort of mute dog, being unable to bark so that the approaching wolf might be frightened off by the clamour and commotion. Indeed the employee fears him who plunders his temporal riches and he does not consider Him who will torment his soul in hell. For he is blind to great matters and becomes terrified about matters which are of no importance. About these sorts it is said: 'Woe to the foolish prophets who follow their own minds and see nothing; like foxes in the desert they are your prophets, Israel. You have not approached the enemy nor have you erected a wall against them for the house of Israel so that you might stand firm in battle upon the Lord's appointed day.'[22] There is no liberty in them in order that they might condemn the powers of this world, no virtue that they might protect truth from danger; they seek payment in all things, and none or few seek the salvation of souls. As long as they keep hold of their possessions, as long as they move towards their ambitious and avaricious desires, they will disdain the loss of the things which pertain to Jesus Christ. Let peace be made in their times, let their sheep be abundant, let their cows be fattened, let their storerooms be full, let the food and vessels loaded upon their tables gleam in the admiration of observers, let them cherish various and precious furnishings of costly extravagance, let them be honoured and esteemed by the multitude, let them be rich, let them be visited by subjects with presents, in short, let them be free with impunity and let them without stigma order the performance of any whim whatsoever. To each they say: 'Bravo! Well done!' so that, according to the condemnation of the prophet, they would seem to have applied mortar without straw to the hardened wall of sin, which by the declaration of the Lord was to be excavated so that it might collapse and the worst abominations be removed from the house of the Lord. These are the men who sew up pillows, slipping them under the head of an entire generation of necks, and who consume the milk and who are covered in the wool of sheep whom they have guided into a sort of sleep by negligence or audacity.

---

[21] Ezekiel 34:18–21.   [22] Ezekiel 13:3–5.

A thief is convicted by his deeds because 'he does not come except that he may rob and kill and destroy and corrupt'.[23] The most pernicious and obvious enemy is the one who has neither the trappings nor the appearance of a shepherd, and does not nourish for money but counts his money after he kills the sheep. And so love is owed to the shepherd because he loves; patience is due to the employee because he is seen to be imitating love; the Church owes nothing to the thief, however, except punishment. 'If the head of the household knew the hour at which the thief would come, he would keep watch and would not permit his house to be broken into.'[24] The sheep hear the voices of shepherds and they follow; they occasionally hear the voices of employees, but they disdain following him because he does not advance towards life; the voices of thieves they despise, loathe and flee because in criminal hands they see and in criminal mouths they hear the works of death. Indeed he is not only a thief and a bandit but a rapacious wolf, following in the footsteps of the lion which roars around seeking that which it devours. Who, therefore, would not resist, or at any rate flee from, him who enters into the fold of sheep in order that he may destroy and kill? 'If anyone desires the episcopacy', the Apostle says, 'he desires good works.'[25] But I do not know in what way the situation was turned to its opposite, so that while nearly everyone desires the episcopacy, when they have attained what they desired, they are enfeebled by leisure; or, what is more disgraceful, they are occupied by works of vanity.

The extent to which ambition hastens them ever forward I have proposed above, but as the matter stands, I could not explain fully; and indeed I could only with difficulty relate how uselessly many men busy themselves with the position desired by them. Yet I do know one thing, that they do not hasten eagerly forward in order that they may lay down their lives for others. They even refuse to spend upon brothers in need the gifts of fortune or, what is more correctly said, the temporal gifts of the grace of God, bestowed upon them to be used in order that they might prove worthy of eternal life. Yet this has already been shown to be the model of pastoral duties as much by the examples as by the words of the Prince of Shepherds. Therefore, such men moved by ambition hurry forward to become employees and thieves. Still, those sheep, which are entrusted to the

---

[23] John 10:10.   [24] Luke 12:39.   [25] 1 Timothy 3:1.

custody of someone who feeds them, even for a price, are better off. For even among employees themselves there are grades and differences. Of course, they all extend nets towards prey; but some fish for the capture of both souls and material things, others for material things alone, in disregard of dangers to the soul; and they frequently disturb everything to the end that a more fertile opportunity might come forth for fishing to their satisfaction. You may marvel at the various furnishings, and as it is said, Croesian riches among those who preach the poverty of Christ. Because they are not constrained to perform military service in their own person, they proclaim the Gospel in order that they may squander and abuse the duties of the evangelist . . .

I leave untouched the Roman Church, which on the authority of God is the parent and nurse of faith and moral character and, protected by heavenly privilege, cannot be judged and censured by men. It is not believable that members of the Roman curia presume or think it suitable to commit acts which are agreed to be illicit according to the laws of the gentiles regarding the governors and proconsuls of provinces, that is, the legates of Caesar. With what impudence indeed would a disciple of the Crucified One, a vicar of Peter, a shepherd of souls, dare to attempt those things which the imperial vicar, the rector of the body politic under the office of the consul, did not dare to encroach upon even when the doctrines of the pagans were flourishing? The penalty for extortion is evident from the preceding pages, and it is known by our generation as much by the principles of law as by the examples of the history books. Except in the cases of food and drink, judges are not permitted to accept anything from the provincials, and even then nothing accepted may have been granted in the manner of a present. Who, therefore, believes that the fathers of the Church, the judges of the earth and, if I may say so, the brightest lights of the world would esteem presents, chase after payments, intimidate provincials to the extent that they are frightened, exhaust the wallets of others in order to make their own more dense, preach the words of poverty and rush towards riches in criminal ways, condemn commerce in spiritual goods as though it were permitted to them alone to make deals for such things, act so that they are dreaded by all and are loved by none, teach peace in order that they may cause quarrels, proclaim and pretend humility so that they may advertise their pride, repulse the avarice of others and support their own, prescribe generosity and pursue stinginess? And, so that all the detailed aspects of the problem may be unfolded in a few words, would they place themselves on the side of all wicked and shameful men or claim their crimes together so that they would be seen as a council of vanity, a synagogue of evil-doers, a church of the malignant, in whose hands are iniquities and whose right hand is filled with presents? God forbid that anyone would dare to suspect this, lest someone fall into such great wickedness that he would direct his mouth against heaven and disclose the nakedness of the fathers which is not to be seen. All their possessions are spotless and beautiful, there is nothing among them which may be available to be devoured by the hounds or, as the satirist asserts, about which they may fear mocking behind their backs.

If anyone might suppose otherwise, however, he may be answered by one extremely valid argument which all of our adversaries would not dare to resist or contradict. What is this argument, you inquire? The works which they themselves do, I would say, furnish testimony about them. If you inquire about the reason, study the effect which is consistent with the cause of honesty; for that from which a good work derives is also itself good. If you inquire about the authority, it is He who asserts: 'By their fruits you will know them . . . For an evil tree cannot yield good fruits nor conversely can a good tree yield evil fruits.'[26] More could be proposed on behalf of this position if there is still anyone who supposes that it is to be disparaged; but this one point may suffice in defence. For it is agreed that one ought to revere the footsteps of the apostles and that those who occupy their position and imitate their lives are to be honoured like fathers and revered like lords. This page instead turns attention towards those who are transported on beating wings, who dispute about fasting with full stomachs and who knock down with their works what they build up with their words; the eunuchs of the Queen of the Ethiopians are set in chariots and they speak the Scriptures aloud with their eyes covered, and Him who is led like a sheep to the slaughter and does not open His mouth before His shearer they refuse or are unable to observe; they disdain to collect together the interpretations of the disciples of the truth, up to the time when they descend into the waters in which the works of the dead are cleansed. Above all,

[26] Matthew 7:16–17.

although they sit upon the chariots of the Scriptures and are carried along by the propulsion of winged animals, their tongue, when it argues about higher matters, licks up the ground. They do not understand the Scriptures because their heart does not open to the Lord of knowledge who, as it is written in the Acts of the Apostles, opened the heart of Lydia the purple-dye merchant so that she might hear those words which were said by Paul, words through which the commandments of faith, humility and obedience might become better known to those fearful of God than through verbose disputations.

A thief is someone who is to be restrained in a twofold respect. For he who ascends from earthly habitation by means of pride up the ladder of ambition and through the levels of the vices supported by contempt for the sheep of Christ – that is, neglecting the right path, he tunnels straight under the twisting curves in the road to the entrance or he breaks through the joinery of the walls or he enters through the tiles on the roof – is a thief or a robber. Yet also he who walks through the door opened by Christ, that is, one who is called to the Church, and who thereafter is made into a persecutor under the pretext of a shepherd, that is, plunders, destroys, kills and corrupts, is indubitably a thief. You must consider into which category would seem to be placed those for whom the licence of divine right to shear and devour the flock does not suffice but who also appeal to the aid of secular laws and who, making themselves officials of princes, are not afraid to commit deeds which would readily embarrass any other tax collector. Meanwhile, they serve their own pleasures or avarice, and they pillage and oppress those who selected or admitted them into custody over themselves, and they desire the death of those whom they ought to have supported in flesh and spirit. Surely they recall the statement of the prophet: 'Behold I have empowered you over peoples and kingdoms so that you may eradicate and destroy and disperse and build and plant.'[27] Therefore, what they have found planted they strive to pull up, so that they may build the house of the Lord themselves by means of the presents offered from the hand or the tongue or obedience; or they substitute the uprooted plants for those which they select out of carnal affection, that is, either their offspring or the offspring of the flesh of someone other than them-

---

[27] Jeremiah 1:10.

selves. This opens up an immense task and extends the route for my pen; but I pause, refraining from the articulation of matters which have already been brought into public view. If anyone falsely accuses me of saying anything too callous, he will readily bestow his forgiveness upon me if he reads those things which were said by the Fathers. For if in human and divine law the tyrant is to be slain, who supposes that the tyrant within the priesthood is to be loved and esteemed? If this seems bitter, I call in my defence upon one who would not speak anything except true and sweet words: blessed Gregory, who persecuted these crimes more bitterly still. And, so that I might otherwise keep still, everyone is familiar with his remark to the effect that the prelates ought to know that, when they themselves transgress, they are deserving of as many deaths as there are the examples of perdition they transmit to their subjects.

CHAPTER 18

Tyrants are the ministers of God; and what a tyrant is; and of the moral characters of Gaius Caligula and his nephew Nero and each of their ends

Yet I do not deny that tyrants are ministers of God, who by His just judgment has willed them to be pre-eminent over both soul and body. By means of tyrants, the evil are punished and the good are corrected and trained. For both the sins of the people cause hypocrites to reign and, as the history of kings witnesses, the defects of priests introduced tyrants into the people of God. The first fathers and the patriarchs were in obedience to nature, the best guide to living. They were succeeded by leaders following the laws of Moses and by judges who ruled the people according to the authority of the law; and we read that these were priests. Finally, against the wrath of God, they were given kings, some good, yet others bad. For Samuel had become old and, when his sons did not walk in his path but pursued avarice and impurity, the people, who perhaps had deserved that such priests should preside over them, had extorted a king for themselves from God, whose will was disregarded. Therefore, Saul was selected according to the aforementioned rights of the king, that is, one who would take away their sons in order that they might be made into charioteers, and their daughters in order that they might become bakers and cooks, and their lands and estates in order that they might be distributed to his servants according to his will, and who would oppress all people with the yoke of servitude. Yet the same man was called the anointed of the Lord and, exercising tyranny, he did not lose the honour of kingship. For God had aroused fear in everyone, so that they venerated Saul like a minister of God, whose image he would in a certain measure display.

I might also add more: even the tyrants of the gentiles, condemned to death from eternity, are the ministers of God and are called the anointed of the Lord. For this reason the prophet says: 'Leaders will enter the gates' of Babylon, namely, Cyrus and Darius; 'for I have commanded my sanctified and summoned my strong in my anger and those exultant in my glory.'[28] Behold that He called the Medes and the Persians 'sanctified', not because they were holy men but because they carried out the will of the Lord against Babylon. Elsewhere it is also said: 'Behold that I will bring to you Nebuchadnezzar my servant and because he has served me well at Tyre, I shall give him Egypt.'[29] All power is good since it exists only from Him from whom everything good and only good exists. Yet occasionally power is not good, but bad, for the person who uses it or suffers under it, although it is good in general, created by Him who uses our wickedness for goodness. For just as in a painting a dark or blackened or some other colour is considered unattractive in itself and yet is appropriate within the whole painting, so certain things are viewed as shameful or evil in themselves, yet they appear excellent and good when related to the broader perspective, since all things are adapted by Him whose works are absolutely good. Therefore, even the power of tyrants is in a certain sense good, yet nothing is worse than tyranny. For tyranny is an abuse of the power conceded to man by God. Yet this evil is used for many and great goods. It is therefore evident that tyranny exists not among princes alone, but that everyone is a tyrant who abuses any power over those subject to him which has been conceded from above. Furthermore, if power is assumed by the wise man, who knows and has experience of all things, it is agreeable to all good men and to the utility of all. Yet if power falls to the foolish man, even though it cannot be an evil for the good man, to whom everything works jointly

[28] Isaiah 13:2–3.   [29] Ezekiel 29:18–19.

for the good, still it is injurious for a short period of time. It is clear that power falls to the lot of both sorts, although (driven by the wickedness of our contemporaries who have constantly roused the anger of God against us) it is more frequently conceded to bad, that is, foolish, men.

For what in human affairs can be recorded by any memory to be more powerful than the Roman Empire? If you reflect upon the sequence of reigns from the foundation of the city, you will discover that bad men have frequently governed it. For who was more foul or more savage than Gaius Caligula, third successor of Augustus, apart from Nero, who surpassed all predecessors and successors with the vileness of his life and the shamelessness of his outrages? . . . Caligula was so ferocious, as may be briefly stated, that he is reported to have exclaimed: 'If only the Roman people had more than one neck!' And because he lacked an enemy, a great and extraordinary mission was prepared to seek an enemy and, his forces travelling at leisure through Germany and Gaul, he halted by the ocean coast within sight of Britain. Then he turned back to Rome, the cause of warfare abandoned and no business completed except that he accepted the surrender of Belinus, son of the King of the Britons, who had been expelled by his father, and a few followers. He was conspicuous for his extreme hostility towards the Jews and he commanded that the sacred places of Jerusalem should be profaned and filled with idols and that they should venerate him as God. He imposed upon Pilate, governor of Judaea, such great anguish that the latter had sought a short cut out of his misfortunes by swift death, by piercing himself with his own hands. He condemned his sisters, whom he first wantonly violated, to exile and he later commanded all of the same exiles to be killed. He himself was slain by his own bodyguards. Among his effects were found two books, containing the names of the most influential citizens whose deaths he had planned; and one was titled 'By the sword', the other, 'By the dagger'. In addition, there was discovered an enormous strongbox with many sorts of poisons, which, when submerged on the order of Claudius Caesar, were reported to have affected a great number of fish in the sea itself, a public demonstration of their destructive power.

Caligula was succeeded by his nephew, Nero (yet with Claudius in between); and he followed, indeed excelled, his uncle in material possessions and vices, and he exercised lewdness, lustfulness, extravagance, avarice and cruelty to any extremity of wickedness. And on the evidence of Orosius,[30] Caligula was aroused to lewdness, passing through almost all the theatres of Italy and Greece, and he was often seen to have surpassed horn players, lutenists, tragedians and charioteers, dishonouring himself by the assumption of their various garments. He was also incited by such great lustfulness that, it is told, he would not abstain from his mother or his sister or anyone else out of reverence for blood relations; he took a man in wedlock and was accepted by the man as his wife. His extravagance was so unbridled that he fished with golden nets and purple string; he would wash himself in hot and cold perfumes; he never wore a garment twice, and it is reported that he would never undertake a journey with fewer than one thousand carriages. In the end, he made a bonfire out of the city of Rome as an exhibition for his pleasure; for six days and seven nights the burning city trembled before the gaze of its ruler. The storehouses constructed of stone and the great islands of the ancients, which the rushing flames could not enter, were destroyed with the great machines previously prepared for foreign enemies and were also set on fire; the unhappy masses were driven into different sacred dwellings and tombs. Looking down on all this from the highest tower of Mercenas and rejoicing (as he would assert) in the beauty of the flames, he recited the ode of Heleifeles in the garb of the tragedian, and he sang repeatedly the hymns of the city in which the splendour of the sun is worshipped. His avarice was so conspicuous in its cruelty that after this burning of the city, which Augustus once bragged had been transformed by him from brick into marble, he permitted no one to approach the remnants of their material possessions. Everything that survived the flames in any manner whatsoever he carted off for himself; he ordered ten million sesterces to be conferred upon him annually by the Senate; he deprived most Senators of their goods for no apparent reason; on a single day he completely removed from all businessmen all their possessions by the application of certain tortures. His cruelty was so insanely unbridled that the larger part of the Senate was killed and the equestrian order was nearly decimated. But he did not even refrain from the murder of close relations: he destroyed mother, father, sister, wife and all other kin and relatives without hesitation.

This massive structure of criminality was enlarged by the rashness

---

[30] John's presentation of the story of Caligula is heavily dependent upon Orosius, *Historiae adversus paganos*, 7.7.1–12.

of his impiety against God. For he first inflicted torture and death upon the Christians at Rome and he also ordered them to be tormented with the same persecution throughout all the provinces. And in the attempt to eradicate the name of Christianity itself, he killed the most blessed apostles of Christ: Peter on the cross, Paul by the sword. Soon thereafter the most bitter calamities sprang forth from everywhere to oppress the wretched city. For the following autumn such a great plague had fallen on the city that thirty thousand corpses had entered into the reckoning of Libitina. Quickly afterwards a calamity struck Britain in which the two principal towns were plundered with great injury to and slaughter of citizens and confederates. Moreover, in the east the great provinces of Armenia were lost, the Roman legions yielded under the yoke of the Parthians, and Syria was preserved only with difficulty. In Asia three cities – Laodicea, Jerapolis and Colossae – were devastated by an earthquake. This is approximately what Orosius reports; his words and sentences I use the more freely because I know that as a Christian and a disciple of the great Augustine he would have provided the truth diligently on account of our religious faith. All of this can also be found spread throughout other historians, who wrote more fully about the atrocities of tyrants and their miserable ends. If anyone wishes to examine this matter more diligently, he may read those things which Trogus Pompeius, Josephus, Egesippus, Suetonius, Quintus Curtius, Cornelius Tacitus, Titus Livy, Serenus, Tranquillus and other historians, who are too extensive to enumerate, recounted in their histories.

From all of these sources it will be readily evident that it has always been permitted to flatter tyrants, it has been permitted to deceive them and it has been honourable to kill them if they could not be otherwise restrained. Clearly this is not to discuss private tyrants but rather those who oppress the republic. For the private sort is readily restrained by public laws, which bind all lives; yet among priests, even if one of them is engaged in tyranny, it is not permitted to exercise the material sword on account of reverence for the sacraments, unless perhaps he extends a bloodstained hand against the Church of God after he has been defrocked; indeed, it always obtains that one is not to withstand two punishments on account of the same case. It does not seem beside the point if we were to append some further examples to those things which have been stated already.

CHAPTER 20

That by the authority of the divine book it is lawful and glorious to kill public tyrants, so long as the murderer is not obligated to the tyrant by fealty nor otherwise lets justice or honour slip

It would be tedious if I wished to trace down to our own times the sequence of gentile tyrants; but this litany is beyond narration during the life span of a single man, for it escapes the mind and defeats the tongue. Yet in a book which is entitled 'Of the Ends of Tyrants' one can discover more fully what I have observed about tyrants, even though I have abridged its contents with diligence so that neither the tedium of wordiness nor the obscurity of brevity are generated. But lest the authority of Roman history be impugned, since it was for the most part written by infidels and about infidels, it may be verified by the examples of divine and faithful history. For it is everywhere evident that, as Valerius asserts, the only secure power is one which imposes limits on its own strength. And surely nothing is so distinguished and so magnificent that it does not require tempering by moderation.

The first tyrant thus presented to us in the divine book is Nimrod the valiant hunter confronting the Lord (whom several histories testify is also called Ninus, even though it does not agree with the calculation of the time), and he was said above to have been damned. For indeed he wished to be king and not from God, and during his rule there was an attempt to erect a tower into the heavens by a blind, scattered and bewildered human race. We may progress to him who was given command over the people by divine selection and who forfeited that gift to damnation for dominating them according to his will and not reigning royally; and Saul was so crushed that he was compelled by the burdensome distress of his afflictions to inflict death upon himself. For the correct ascension of the king is seldom or never advantageous if his following life is inconsistent with it, and the origins of a case do not concern judges, whose sentence is determined by the outcome. There is a famous history in the Books of Kings and Chronicles in which, on the authority of Jerome, it is taught that Israel had laboured under tyrants from the beginning and it is demonstrated that all the kings of Judah are to be considered damned except for David, Josiah and Hezekiah. Yet I would readily believe that Solomon and perhaps some others in Judah would have flourished once the Lord summoned them back. And I will be easily persuaded that tyrants instead of princes would have been deserved by a people of stiff neck and wild heart and a people who always resisted the Holy Spirit and who had provoked not only Moses, the servant of the law, but God Himself, the Lord of the law, to anger by their gentile abominations. For penitence annihilates, drives out and kills those tyrants whom sins obtain, introduce and encourage. And even before the time of their kings, just as the history of Judges narrates, the children of Israel were repeatedly enslaved under tyrants. They were afflicted at many and various times according to divine dispensation, and they were often freed by crying out loud to the Lord. And after the termination of the period of divine supervision, the death of their tyrants permitted them to remove the yokes from their necks. Not a single one of those by whose virtues a penitent and humble people was liberated is to be censured, but the memory of posterity is to recall them favourably as ministers of God . . .

It is also accepted by another history that it is just for public tyrants to be killed and the people to be liberated for obedience to God. Priests of the Lord themselves count their slaying as an act of piety and, if anything appears to contain an element of deceit, they call it a mystery of religion consecrated to the Lord. Thus Holofernes was laid in his grave by a woman with a sword not on account of the valour of his enemy but by his own vice, and he who was a source of terror for men was vanquished by luxury and drunkenness and was slain by a woman. And the woman would not have been accorded access to the tyrant unless she had concealed her hostile purpose in a pious deception. For that which maintains the faith and serves charity is not deceitful. And indeed it is through faith that she reproved the priests who had prescribed the time period of divine compassion on the basis of an agreement to surrender themselves and the city unless the Lord had rescued them within five days. Moreover, it was through charity that she never became afraid of the dangers as long as she might liberate her brethren and the people of God from their enemies. For these aims are also demonstrated by her departing prayer for her safety: 'Lord, bring it to pass', she said, 'that by his own sword his pride may be cut off and that he may be captured in his own net with his eyes upon me, and you will strike him by means of the charity of my lips. Grant to me a constancy in my soul so that I will despise him and strength so that I will destroy him. For it will be a monument to your name when the hand of a woman kills him off . . .' Thus she called her maid and, going down to her house, she removed her hair shirt from herself and she stripped off the garments of her widowhood, and she bathed her body, and anointed herself with the best myrrh, and arranged the hair on her head, and placed a headband on her head, and put on her most pleasing garments, binding sandals upon her feet, and she obtained bracelets and lilies and earrings and finger rings and she adorned herself with all her ornaments. And the Lord conferred splendour upon her since all these arrangements were determined not by lust but by virtue. And so the Lord increased her beauty in order that she might appear incomparably elegant to everyone's eyes.'[31] Arising and captivating the public enemy, therefore, Judith said this to Holofernes: 'Receive the words of your slave girl, since, if you follow them, God will cause things to be perfect for you. For Nebuchadnezzar, the king of the earth, lives and also alive is your strength which exists within you for the correction of all erring souls, since not only men but also the beasts in the field serve him and obey him through you. For the strength and industry of your mind is proclaimed among all peoples and it is declared to our entire generation that you alone are powerful and good among all in his kingdom and your learning is preached to all peoples.'[32] And additionally she asserted: 'Come, I will proclaim everything to you, so that I may lead you through the middle of Jerusalem and you will possess the entire people of Israel like sheep for which there is no shepherd; and not even a single dog will bark against you, since these events were related to you by the providence of God.'[33] I ask you, could anything more insidious be devised, could anything more captivating be said, than this dispensing of mystical counsel? And so Holofernes said: 'There is nowhere else upon the earth such a woman in appearance and beauty and in the discretion of her speech.'[34] For his aroused heart burned with his desire. And he said: 'Drink now, and recline in pleasure, since you are finding favour in my heart.'[35] She who did not come to be extravagant was skilled in a false extravagance as the instrument of her faith and courage. And once he was stupefied with pleasures, she destroyed his cruelty with the weapons of charity for the liberation of her people. Therefore, she struck Holofernes on

[31] Judith 9:12–15 and 10:2–4. [32] Judith 11:4–6.
[33] Judith 11:15–19. [34] Judith 11:19. [35] Judith 12:17.

the neck and chopped off his head and she handed it to her maid so that it might be put in a bag to be brought back to the city whose safety was achieved by the hand of a woman.

The histories teach that we are to take care, however, lest anyone cause the death of a tyrant who is bound to him by the obligation of fealty or a sacred oath. For it is read that even Zedekiah was taken captive as a result of his neglect of sacred fealty; and, in another instance, a king of Judah (I do not recall who) had his eyes plucked out because, lapsing into faithlessness, he did not keep his promise before the sight of God, to whom he swore an oath, since even the tyrant is justly to be given surety in lawsuits. And I do not read that poison was licensed by the indulgence of any legal right at any time, although I have seen that it was sometimes made use of by infidels. Not that I do not believe that tyrants are to be removed from the community, but that they are to be removed without loss to religion and honour. For even David, the best of the kings about whom I have read and one who (except for his plot against Uriah the Hittite) advanced blamelessly in all his affairs, endured the most grievous of tyrants. Although he enjoyed frequent opportunities to destroy the tyrant, David still preferred to spare him, trusting in the compassion of God who could free him without sin. He therefore decided to wait patiently to the end that the tyrant might be visited by God with a return to chastity or might fall in battle or might otherwise be extinguished by the just judgment of God. For indeed his patience can be distinguished in the fact that, at the time when David had cut off his cloak in the cave and on the other occasion when, entering into camp by night, he found fault with the negligence of the guards, the king himself was compelled to admit that David acted upon the more just cause. And this method of eradicating tyrants is the most useful and the safest: those who are oppressed should humbly resort to the protection of God's clemency and, raising up pure hands to the Lord in devoted prayer, the scourge with which they are afflicted will be removed. For in fact the sins of transgressors are the strength of tyrants. For this reason, Achior, the leader of all the children of Ammon, gave this most beneficial counsel to Holofernes. 'My Lord', he said, 'examine if there is any iniquity of the people in the sight of their God, and we may surpass them, since their betraying God will deliver them to you and they will be subjugated under the yoke of your power. Yet if there is no such offence of the people before their God, we cannot withstand them, since their God will defend them and we will be in disgrace throughout the entire earth.'[36]

[36] Judith 5:24–25.

CHAPTER 21

All tyrants reach a miserable end; and that God exercises punishment against them if the human hand refrains, and this is evident from Julian the Apostate and many examples in sacred scripture

The end of tyrants is confusion: either they are destroyed if they persist in wickedness or they are forgiven if they turn back to God. A fire is prepared for the scourge itself after it has been used by the Father for the correction of his children. And it is said: 'Ahab is restored to my sight; I will not introduce this evil into his days.'[37] Yet Jezebel, persevering in a harshness which wholly merited a cruel end, offered up her blood to be lapped up by dogs in the place where the dogs lapped up the blood of the innocent Naboth. But if the blood of the innocent Naboth was thus sought out, will not the blood of so many other innocent people be demanded? She impiously desired the vineyard of a just man and in exchange she lost the rights to her entire kingdom. Wickedness is always punished by the Lord; but sometimes He uses His own sword, and sometimes He uses a sort of human sword in the punishment of the impious.

Pharaoh harassed the people of God and he was scourged by Him with the most severe plagues, as is read in Exodus. In order that these plagues may be consciously mastered more reliably, I have taken the trouble to insert the list in verse:

First a red flood, and second a plague of frogs.
Then the foul gnats, afterwards the fly more noxious than that.
Fifth the cattle were destroyed, sixth the boils were produced.
Hail proceeded after, followed by the unspeakable teeth of the
    locusts.
Ninth the sun was hidden, finally the first child was slain.

[37] I Kings 21:29.

I do not care who created this verse; I am instead concerned only with the fact that it contains an adequate abridgment of the plagues of Egypt under Pharaoh. Yet in all of this, his anger was not diverted from the people of God, but chasing after the departed Israelites, he was drowned in the sea along with his chariots and mounted soldiers. Therefore, the Lord used the waters like a wall for the defence of the people and like a weapon for the destruction of the tyrant.

Moreover, during the reign of Hezekiah, Salmanasar oppressed the people of God and, abiding in prayer, Hezekiah held the shield of divine protection against the threats of the tyrant. For this reason the Lord comforted him through the prophet, saying: 'He is not to enter into this city nor is he to release an arrow into it nor will he occupy it with his shield nor will he surround it with a trench. He is to return by the path along which he came, and he is not to enter into this city, the Lord says. And I will protect this city and I will save it on account of myself and on account of my servant David.'[38] And it was thus done on that night. The angel of the Lord came and struck down 185,000 souls in the Assyrian camp; and when he got out of bed at dawn, the king saw all the bodies of the dead and, withdrawing, he vanished. And Sennacherib, the king of the Assyrians, was turned back and he remained in Nineveh. And when he worshipped at the temple of his god Nisroch, his sons Adramelech and Sharezer struck him down with a sword and they were driven into the land of the Armenians; and his son Eseradon ruled following him. And let it not disturb anyone if one or the other name is declared in different histories, since according to Hebrew tradition the same king was known by five names, as Jerome has discovered. For he was called Salmanasar, Sennacherib, Phul, Teglad Phalasar and Sargon. For unless he had many names, the authority of the histories would be untrustworthy whenever different texts disagreed. In this case, therefore, the Lord was first using the sword of the angel against his army, and then the hands of his sons against the impious king himself. Nature itself is sometimes confounded by the vengeance of the Most High and its laws acquiesce miraculously when the Creator is provoked by the wickedness of men. So it was that Nebuchadnezzar, rising up against the Lord, was driven to pass seven years as a beast and, repenting, was restored once again to manhood, and his material possessions and

[38] II Kings 19:32–34.

kingdom were returned, although afterwards he earned a miserable end by plundering them.

I pass over to Christian times, since among all nations and peoples the harmfulness of tyrants and the evidence of their punishment is manifested. The Emperor Julian, a vile and base apostate, persecuted Christians by deceit rather than by force, and yet he did not prohibit force entirely. For under him there began the most grievous persecution of Christians, in so far as he had endeavoured by his impious efforts to extinguish the name of the Galilean, which He was called. Inasmuch as he led an unfortunate expedition against the Parthians and upon his return devoted himself to the massacre of the Christians as a sacrifice to the idols, God was merciful towards the prayers of the great Basil and the other saints. God selected the martyr Mercurius, who stabbed the tyrant in his camp with a lance on the command of the Blessed Virgin and compelled the impious emperor on his deathbed to confess that the Galilean (namely, Christ) whom he had persecuted was the victor and had triumphed over him . . .

In addition, among the nation of the Britons the hand of the most glorious martyr and king Edmund was employed for the suppression and punishment of the savagery of tyranny, as is witnessed by certain of our histories. For when the island of Britain was for the most part occupied, pillaged and ravaged by Swain, who was assailing the members of Christ with many persecutions, he burdened the province with the imposition of a tax, which in the language of the English was called the Danegeld, and he ordered the tax to apply to the possessions of the just-mentioned martyr. There was a public supplication to Swain; he spurned these requests. The brother of a religious order was dispatched by the martyr in order that the tyrant might be restrained by means of intimidation lest he oppress the Church of Christ, the house of the martyr and his free family with undue servitude. But in his impiety, he paid no attention to these demands, he got angry at the prohibition, he was hardened by the threats and, inflicting abuse and injury upon the humble messenger, he hurried along vengeance at the hand of God, provoked a scourging and ran with blind rashness into death by his contempt for the patience of God. And there was no delay. While walking alone among his soldiers in camp, as was admitted by them, he saw beside him the blessed Edmund with a sword; the martyr censured him most harshly and then hacked him to death. The tyrant died in his footsteps. And from that day, although the island has endured grievous tyrants, the Church of the blessed Edmund has remained immune from the imposition of the foregoing tax. For none of them was bold enough to provoke the martyr or to cause peril by the oppression of his Church.

Yet in our own times Eustace, the son of Stephen, was resolved to rage against the Church of God. When all things were plundered by his might, he saw the wealth of the lands of the blessed Edmund, which all raiders had kept safe, and he saw that they were not his. Consuming the treasure of the kingdom, from which the payments for his soldiers proceeded time and again (for gifts of largesse were in short supply by now), Eustace plundered the spoils of this already mentioned Church. He had not yet digested the food, however, which he had acquired from the riches of the place, and on the day before he was to retire to his home nearby, he was touched by the hand of the martyr and, struck down with a fatal illness, his life and affairs ceased on about the eighth day. Why do I concentrate upon a few examples? In order that I might speak of familiar events, where are Geoffrey, Miles, Ranulf, Alan, Simon, Gilbert – not so much counts of the kingdom as public enemies? Where is William of Salisbury? Where is Marmion who, pushed by the Blessed Virgin, fell into the pit which he had prepared for others? Where are the others whose mere names would consume a book? Their wickedness is notorious, their infamy is renowned, their ends are unhappy and of them the present generation cannot be ignorant. Therefore, if anyone is unfamiliar with ancient histories, if one is ignorant of how Cyrus, who caused the flight of kings, was destroyed by Tamiris the Queen of the Scythians, if one does not recall the calamities and ruinations of preceding tyrants, one may study those events which are thrust before one's unwilling eyes, and one will observe more clearly than day that all tyrants are miserable.

CHAPTER 22

Of Gideon, the model for rulers, and Antiochus

And so I do not see what those who would endeavour to oppress the republic, that is, the people of God, with the yoke of undue servitude wish for themselves, unless perhaps they aspire to power for the reason that they may suffer more powerfully the torments of the wretched. If they aspired only to reign and not to dominate, calculating the burden of their duties, they would by no means pursue power with such eagerness. For the will of the ruler is determined by the law of God and does not injure liberty. By contrast, the will of the tyrant is a slave to desires and, opposing law which supports liberty, it ventures to impose the yoke of servitude upon fellow slaves. Scripture, which one is not permitted to oppose, teaches this: 'All the men of Israel said to Gideon: "Dominate us, you and your sons and your sons' sons because you have liberated us from the hands of the Midianites." He asserted to them: "I will not dominate you, nor will my sons dominate you, but the Lord will dominate you." And he said to them: "I ask one request of you, that the earrings from your booty be given to me." '[39] I myself seem to observe within this passage the elements of what I had previously said. For Gideon, who is interpreted as avoiding the harmful or iniquitous temptation of the Israelites, appears to proclaim by his words the responsibilities and duties of the prince. It pertains to him to avoid harmful matters and either to eradicate them or to restore them to fruitfulness and to exclude from his borders whatever wickedness he discerns, so that he might advance to victory against his enemies. He is offered the honour of lordship (*dominium*) and he declines; yet he subjects to the law those whom he released from the yoke of servitude. The honour of succeeding their father is offered to his sons; yet he chooses instead that God is to be honoured by them.

Who will properly compare this man to those who confuse good and evil, and who are engaged in labours and hardships in order that their sons can have an inheritance not so much of honour as of plunder and iniquity? For who is there who would prefer his children to the law of God and His justice which consists solely in charity? 'Whoever loves', He says, 'his father or his mother or his children more than me is not worthy of me.'[40] And certainly those who place transitory things before Christ pass away more rapidly than transitory things; and the glory of them is not perpetuated by those to whom, in relation to other things, Christ remains inglorious. Therefore that prince who, moved by love of children or the flesh, diminishes divine honour by forgetting charity may fear his own destruction. There is no one who admits to rising up against God; yet many rise up, and at

[39] Judges 8:22–24. [40] Matthew 10:37.

present they perform such acts openly. Antiochus entered holy places with pride; and many others also do this. Uzziah, whom the irrefutable book reports to have been just in many ways, usurped the offices of the priesthood not so much with piety as with presumptuousness after the death of Zechariah, whose surname was 'understanding'; and he disdained to listen to the cries of the Levites: 'Are you Uzziah the king, and not Uzziah the priest?' And immediately leprosy invaded that part of his body which the priests by law had to conceal with a golden helmet, so that according to the prophetic curse his face was filled with his disgrace. This king was thus singled out from contemporary kings and he was also distinguished above all because in the year of his death was born Romulus, from whom was descended the Roman people. Uzziah is imitated by many in encroaching upon priestly powers, but very few are shamed by his leprosy. Still many people follow Antiochus who entered the holy place not with devotion so that he might sacrifice in the manner of a priest, but so that he might destroy if there was anything in the holy temple of the Lord. For after Antiochus had fashioned an idol to desolation and abomination, he tore apart and destroyed with fire the books of the laws of God; and whoever was found with books of testimony to the Lord, and whoever observed the laws of God, was to be brutally killed according to the edict of King Antiochus.

I have seen during my time numerous men meddling with sacred offices and rashly setting them upon their shoulders, so that the ark is snatched away from the shoulders of the Levites, forgetful of the place which even in the present day is called 'the striking of Uzziah'. I have seen others who consign the books of the laws to the flames and are not afraid to tear them apart if the laws or canons fall into their hands. During the time of King Stephen the Roman laws were ordered from the kingdom, although they had been admitted into Britain through the household of the venerable father Theobald, primate of the Britons. It was prohibited by royal edict for anyone to retain the books and silence was imposed upon our Vacarius. But by the appointment of God, the law was rendered all the stronger in its virtue by those who in their impiety endeavoured to impair it more fully. Who among so many thousands desiring to rule wishes to be like Gideon? Or who wishes the law to be dominant over himself and the people? Yet all ought to be satisfied with that which Gideon sought for his people, that is, if he acquires for himself only the earrings from the booty. For if he took care to order those things which the law declared, the people would acquiesce in obeying him so that there would not be iniquity and dispute in the community; and the governor ought certainly to satisfy the people over whom he governs.

CHAPTER 23

The counsel of Brutus is to be used against those who not only fight but battle schismatically for the supreme pontificate; and that nothing is calm for tyrants

But should you concede that it is permitted for those who are of the flesh to struggle for preeminence, I think that this is at all times to be forbidden to men of the Church. Yet following the example of men of the flesh, impiety creeps in under the pretext of religion and at present there is not only struggle for priestly power but actual battle for it. Formerly, the men of old would be seized unwillingly and thrust into martyrdom, but they would avoid the chief offices as worse than prison and the cross. These days priests openly declare the opposite and call proverbs insignificant. 'We refuse to be martyrs', they say, 'but we will not surrender our seats of glory to another.' This is a miserable and lamentable speech in the mouth of one who acknowledges Christ in such fashion that he may openly confess that he does not follow Him. Can it be doubted whether one dies a true confessor who does not await persecution if it is necessary? For Cyprian asserts: 'If a bishop is afraid, salvation is driven from him.'[41] But although he may be afraid, it is still forbidden for him to tarry in case of necessity. Deserting is harmful and disgraceful.

Yet there is one way in which the constancy of the martyrs would seem to be imitated, namely, if they must fight for their offices. It is reported by certain people and it is true that there is sometimes, indeed often, dispute by ambitious men over the Roman pontificate and that the pontiff does not enter the Holy of Holies without the blood of brothers. On occasion there are conflicts of greater magnitude than civil wars, and the battles of priests absolve all those

---

[41] Cyprian, *Epistolae*, 59 in Migne, *PL*, 3.823.

impious deeds of Caesar and Pompey and whatsoever was encroached upon at Philippi, Leucas, Mutina, in Egypt or Spain. Do Christians arrange the shedding of blood so that they before others may be permitted to lay down their lives for the flock, which is the pastoral office? Do they destroy the Church and profane the holy place in order that it might be necessary to rebuild and resanctify what exists? Perhaps they intimidate peoples, torment kingdoms, and steal the riches of the Church so that they might fashion for themselves the materials of merit, so that they might set everything straight, so that they might snatch away from other contenders the goods necessary for showing mercy to and providing for the poor. For if they commit these acts so that they may allow themselves greater impunity, so that they may collect money, so that they may support, extend and corrupt their flesh and blood, so that they may ennoble their family, in sum, so that they may procure their own glory among the clergy by dominating their flocks and not providing to them a model of honesty, then they approximate tyrants more readily than princes, although they might by their lips and functions assume a semblance of the pastoral office.

The philosophers say (and I believe truly) that nothing in human affairs is more useful than man himself, and that among men none is more useful than an ecclesiastical or earthly prince. Conversely, nothing is more harmful to man than man, and among them there is none more harmful than a secular or ecclesiastical tyrant. But surely of the two sorts of tyrants, the ecclesiastical excels the secular. For salt deprived of its taste is good for nothing at all except to the extent that it is thrown out of doors and trampled on by men. Furthermore,

> fear of the sword and of death is alone
> unknown to love of gold; there is never a risk in the destruction
> of lost laws; but wealth, you who are the most vile part of things,
> you arouse conflict.[42]

Therefore, unity is divided, wholeness is broken up, honesty is corrupted, even sanctity is defiled, a new judgment of the world is solemnised, and its prince, who was ejected by the passion of Christ, returns to spread temptations so that he is blessed who is not captured in these snares:

---

[42] Lucan, *Pharsalia*, 3.118–121.

How great are the new
crimes produced by those two who strive that they may command
the world?
There is barely enough civil war to ensure
that neither one commands.[43]

The most proper path to excellence was taught by Christ, who did not
wish His disciples to be modelled after those kings of the gentiles who
dominate over their subjects and those who exercise power under the
pretence of benefaction. Rather, he who is greater is to diminish
himself voluntarily and is to claim for himself the duties of ministry in
preference to others solely according to the law of peace, disassoci-
ated from power and conflict. Yet these men have preferred another
path, ascending through opposition to their brothers, and they aspire
to dominate even ahead of the gentile kings, rejecting the humility of
ministry. No doubt they arrange themselves and their thrones
towards the north, their charity being frozen or, indeed, extinct; for
the promotion of peers is abhorred by them.

If only those who reflected upon these events had been following
the counsel of Brutus, who by the influence of Cato turned away from
the imminent civil war. For he resolved to hold back his hand from the
civil strife, since to the extent that one willingly and forcefully
becomes enmeshed in such conflict, one is in that measure the more
iniquitous and the more savage. Therefore he asserts:

Neither in Pompey nor in Caesar will Brutus
have an enemy after victory in the war.[44]

Therefore if those for whose lordship (*dominium*) the schismatics
dispute were wise, they would permit the contending parties to fight
on their own, and they would fear to offer assistance to either side,
given their uncertainty regarding the likely victor and their certainty
about the extent of the painful destruction which threatens the
conquered. 'The hands of none are judged pure by the other side.'[45]
And also 'the cause of the victor pleased God but the vanquished
pleased Cato'.[46] The world may of course rejoice when one by himself
defeats the other, but it exults with more willing joy if neither or both
are defeated. Therefore, if it pleases, let them meet on the island of
Licaonia or anywhere else if it is still some location which is suited to a

[43] *Ibid.*, 2.60–63.   [44] *Ibid.*, 2.283–284.
[45] *Ibid.*, 7.263.   [46] *Ibid.*, 1.128.

war or duel; for Quintilian testifies that those events to which we apply the name of 'duels' the ancients called 'wars'.[47] Without peril to the world or the city, one of the duellists may be defeated by the other, namely, him whom God has approved or permitted to be the victor. If it pleases the victor, the vanquished is also to be drowned in the Tiber or, if called upon to treat him more gently, he may be pushed away into the Monastery of the Cave. When the abbot has opened the cloister, indeed the prison, he is to testify that it has been provided not for one who is condemned, but for one who is defeated; for indeed 'no one loyal ever chooses misery for his friends'.[48] Yet he who is victorious, that is, he who is more violent, is to be deported as a perpetual exile to Lipare or another island and sentenced to cutting rock in a quarry or mine. The crime of the schismatic equalises those who are rendered unequal, except that generally the one who is stronger, or indeed more ferocious, is also the one who is more wicked.

What is more destructive or more unpleasant than civil war? Certainly nothing besides the frenzy of schismatics or the plague of the heretics. However I would not readily say which of them is the most destructive if there is even a quantitative way that one may be separated from the other. Plainly civil wars will cease if presumptuous rashness is lacking an assistant. And there is none who can urge fellow citizens to madness unless their own insanity to some extent entices them. Above all, the need for fighting is either insignificant or for the most part imaginary. This leaves open very many and great dangers, of which no one may adequately avoid the results unless one watches out for the powerful. This was intimated by the most dignified poet, or if you would favour an orator to state the matter more properly, I do not object to Quintilian. Both agree that precautions can exist against those things resulting in peril and that the corporate community cannot be coerced by any one person so that it yields to wickedness unwillingly. For the poet says:

This soldier although not stained by blood
fears that which he could have done. Why beat your chest?
Why do you moan insanely? Why do you cry pointless tears?
Do you not confess to yielding to the crime by your own free will?

---

[47] Quintilian, *Institutio Oratoria*, 1.4.15.
[48] Lucan, *Pharsalia*, 8.535.

Do you so fear him who you made to be afraid?
Let him give the signal for war; you may disregard the ominous
    sound:
Let him bear the standards; remain still: then does civil frenzy
abate and the private citizen Caesar will love his son-in-law.[49]

Thus if the Church were to be built upon the liberty of the Spirit, if
it were to refuse to suffer the service of wickedness, either schisms
would be settled entirely or, the framework of unity enduring, the
schismatics would fight only amongst themselves. Meanwhile the
Church may hold back its hands because the sword of Peter, who
thirsted for blood with fleshly desire, is at present protected in its
scabbard by God's command, and the disciples rushing to uproot the
undesirable weeds are ordered to await reaping angels. May the
Church pray for the wholeness of unity so that the uncut stone upon
which the Church itself is founded, of which schismatics disapprove
and which makes the two sides one, may bring together the dissenting
parties, even as He had preferred His garment to pass complete to
one of the faithful in a lottery rather than to be divided. May it pray, I
say, that faith does not die out and that, in aspiring to the sieve of
Satan, the wheat is not trampled underfoot and destroyed. May it pray
for peace, seek after peace, and pursue peace even as it flees. The
Church is to recall Him who, although He could bring forth over a
dozen legions of angels, obtained everything praiseworthy upon the
cross; for His own destruction so deserved to be praised that every
knee is to bend to His glory.

Priestly wars are undertaken by harmful schismatics but they also
do harm to just men who consent to them. Therefore they ought to
remain quiet, standing at a distance with Peter until they see the end.
They may recollect the words of the moralist:

If anger has given weapons to the denizens of heaven,
    or if terrestrial giants assailed the stars,
still human piety is not to dare by either its weapons
    or its worship to make itself useful to Jove.[50]

This seems to be heeded in those affairs where 'it is sinful to know
who more justly bore arms'.[51] If the heretic or schismatic fights
against orthodoxy, then it is pious to assist the truth and for the

---

[49] *Ibid.*, 4.181–188.   [50] *Ibid.*, 3.315–318.   [51] *Ibid.*, 1.126–127.

Roman pontiff to be served most devotedly. This is surely so when the matter is clear-cut; yet the schismatic frequently pretends to be orthodox. Who may presume to judge the supreme pontiff, whose case is reserved for the examination of God alone? Above all, whoever might attempt this can labour but by no means profit. And I do not limit the name of 'pontiff' to the anointed; whoever has ascended by canonical election is to be treated as the pontiff. In order that a shipwreck might be avoided, Jonah caused himself to be shipwrecked and preferred to perish alone rather than to involve others in his perils; yet he had not accepted responsibility for ruling the ship. Maternal affection was irrefutably proven to Solomon by this: that one woman preferred to yield her child to the deceit of a prostitute rather than have it divided. Yet schismatics prefer for the Church to be endangered and torn apart rather than not usurping honour and not making false accusations against innocent Mother Church. 'This woman', said Solomon, 'is its mother',[52] since on the basis of love she refused its division. By contrast, the schismatic is a stepson who 'examines the entrails of his mother with steel'.

How many and how great were the upheavals, confusions and shocks when the son of Peter Leon struggled to rise up from the north against Innocent of happy memory, the fifth predecessor of the Lord Adrian, whose life and happiness the Lord ought to prolong? Did not his destruction pull down with him even a part of the stars? Who is ignorant of Aegidius of Tusculum? Who is ignorant of Peter of Pisa, like whom there was none or hardly any other in the curia? Who may survey those bishops within almost the whole of Italy who were destroyed? Surely in so far as their destruction occurred within the memory of our generation, it is incredible for anyone to be so wretchedly ambitious that he is not afraid to tear apart the Church. I believe that no one is so stupid as to be one who does not prefer his own annihilation to the creation of such great disorder for his own sake. If, demanded by our own sins, any such tormentor might ascend to the seat of Peter and undertake the government of His ship in resentment against the Lord, he will clearly create a not unearned shipwreck, since even Peter (who was called by the Lord) began to be afraid of drowning in a strong wind and the ship which contained the Lord as its passenger despaired of its safety until prayers roused the

[52] I Kings 3:27.

sleeping Christ. Above all, he who ascends wrongly is tossed about in misery and cast down most wretchedly; and those affairs which commence in bad beginnings do not have happy endings. Discord is the most certain indication of iniquity and failure; for indeed

> discord disturbs the smallest matters;
> the greatest matters are kept in peace.[53]

The Phaëthon of fable, in so far as he desired his father's chariot, set fire to the world and at last, by the mercy of God and his own anger, he fell headfirst in ruins, his chariot broken apart. Then 'it is said that there was a day without sun';[54] and, while the Church burns with the anger of schism, Christ seems to be absent. Moreover, Icarus, in so far as he was borne into the heavens by the elation of youthful frivolity, was drowned in the waves of the sea. For he was cast down while he was elevated; for indeed the carrying up of the impious is preparation for their more severe destruction.

Who is more iniquitous than he who casts the ministry of the peace and the duties of sacrifice into quarrels and torments? What is the point of such great savagery? Does it lead to life? But their end is destruction. Does it lead to glory? But their glory is in confusion. Does it lead to pleasure? Therefore their god is their stomach. Does it lead to the end that they may be ennobled in flesh and blood? But flesh and blood will not possess the kingdom of God. It is not I but the Apostle who cries out with his trumpet against carnal men in these or more serious words: 'Whose end is destruction, whose stomach is God and whose glory is in confusion because they savour earthly things';[55] if they are dominating others, which is tyrannical, then nothing less happens to them. For indeed there is no security or peace for the tyrant. Question Damocles and he will confess to having learned this from the tyrant of Sicily, when he was threatened with destruction from all sides by burning coals and was assailed at the pleasure of the ruler by a sword, hanging like an executioner over his neck on virtually a woven thread in the midst of other royal amusements. The same precept was ascribed by Claudian to Theodosius:

> He who terrorises is more afraid himself; this destiny of tyrants
> is settled; they envy the famous and butcher the brave.

[53] Lucan, *Pharsalia*, 2.272–273.
[54] Ovid, *Metamorphoses*, 2.331.
[55] Philippians 3:19.

They live protected by swords and walled off from poisons;
they endure the restrictions of uncertainty and are threatened by
  disturbances,
conduct yourself as a citizen or a father, take advice from everyone.
And do not guide yourself according to your own wishes, but the
  public will.[56]

'Be ashamed, Sidon, for the sea speaks',[57] because here a man of the
flesh declares that which a man of the spirit cannot hear. For if priests
heard this voice, they would by no means run a weapon through their
enemies in order that they might occupy the chief offices.

But although everyone defers to the loftiest peak of the pontificate,
I think that this office is to be avoided rather than undertaken by the
wise man to the extent that the safety of religion permits. For so that I
may speak the truth according to my awareness of it, it seems to be the
most difficult and most miserable position, to the extent that it tends
towards the general condition of the present age. If the pope is a slave
to avarice, it is death to him; if not, however, he does not escape the
hands and cries of the Romans. For unless he possesses some means
by which he might obstruct their mouths and restrain their hands, he
is to inure his ears, eyes and soul to bear abuse, outrage and sacrilege.
Indeed, there are three things which beyond others subvert entirely
the judgment of even the prudent man: love of presents, esteem for
persons and a trusting disposition. No one can be influenced by all
these things and dispense justice. Therefore it is necessary for the
Roman pontiffs to be immune from these things, since it is they who
ought to limit all excesses. If the pope hates gifts, who would confer
gifts upon him against his will? What is there to be bestowed by him
who accepts nothing? Or how will he please the Romans if he does not
bestow anything? If the personages of Rome do not receive anything,
then how does he maintain his position before their sight? For he
could hardly deliberate on a priestly case in conclave in such a way
that he is not compelled to admit all of them into counsel. What about
the fact that he is compelled to condemn simony, presents and
payments? If he pursues these activities, does he not condemn himself
with his own voice? If in supreme power there is the least licence, then
surely he who directs the laws, while he is subject to none of them, is
more strictly prohibited from illegal acts. And therefore, the Roman

[56] Claudian, *Panegyricus de iv consulatu Honorii*, 290–295.
[57] Isaiah 23:4.

pontiff is allowed the least licence as a result of the fact that he is allowed the most power.

What is more burdensome than the care of all churches? The privileges of the apostles pass down to their successors, and a part of the privileges is that matter of which the Apostle speaks to the Corinthians: 'Who is weak', he asks, 'and I am not weak? Who is led astray and I do not burn with anger?'[58] If you do not want to review the entire matter, still, should he who contends for primacy ever truly vindicate himself, I think that he will quickly achieve the position. Moreover, he who is Roman pontiff is necessarily to be a 'servant of servants' as a result of the circumstances in which the Church now exists; he is 'servant of servants' not just in name for the sake of glory, as some believe, but in substance, namely, as one who serves the servants of God, even involuntarily. For all persons subject to God are servants and dispensers of His mercy and justice. The angel is a servant, man is a servant, the good are servants, the bad are servants and the devil himself, the prince of the world, is a servant. Therefore even the Romans are servants of God, and it is necessary for the pontiff to serve these Roman tyrants. This is so to the extent that, unless he is their servant, it is necessary for him to be no longer pontiff or no longer Roman.

Who therefore doubts him to be 'servant of servants'? I call upon Lord Adrian, whose times may God render happy, as witness for the fact that since there is no one more miserable than the Roman pontiff, there is no condition more deplorable. And, even if there is no other trouble, it is necessary that he will be most rapidly weakened merely by the labour itself. For Adrian admits that he has encountered such a great number of miseries upon his throne that, in the comparison of the present with the past, all preceding sorrow in life was delightful and extremely happy. He says that the seat of the Roman pontiff is full of thorns, that his garments are always woven with the most pointed prickles and are of such great bulk that they would weigh down, wear out and crush even the strongest shoulders, and that his crown and mitre deservedly appear to shine since they are on fire. But he says that he would have preferred to have never departed from his native land of England and to have remained perpetually in the cloister of the blessed Rufus rather than to have entered into such

----

[58] II Corinthians 11:29.

great anguish, except that he did not dare to resist divine dispensation. While he is still alive, question him and trust his experience. Furthermore, Adrian most wisely repeated this fact to me: as he ascended step by step from a cloistered cleric through all the offices to the highest pontificate, nothing was at any time added by his ascension to the happiness and tranquil calm of his previous life. And, in order that I might use his own words (for when I am present, his courtesy wishes that nothing about him is to be hidden from my eyes), he said: 'The Lord has always strengthened me with his anvil and hammer; but now, if He pleases, may He support with His right hand the burden which He has imposed upon my weakness, since it is insupportable by me.' Therefore, is not misery most deserved by him who fights for such misery? No doubt, should it be the richest who is elected, on the following day he will be poor and will be bound by obligations to an almost infinite number of creditors. What, therefore, will happen to him who is not called by election but who forces his way into office by ambition which is blind and stained by the blood of brothers, in opposition to the members of Christ? This is, of course, to succeed Romulus among fratricides, not Peter in the stewardship of the sheep entrusted to him.

CHAPTER 25

What is the most faithful path to be followed towards what the Epicureans desire and promise

Yet I do not heap slander upon that judgment which defines happiness to be the always joyful and calm condition of a tranquil life. Instead, I believe it is defamed by evil interpretation and vicious application to such a degree that, although there are many Epicureans, that is, adherents to futile pleasures, few profess this name. For they are embarrassed to be called what they are and they endeavour to conceal their own private wickedness with another name, in so far as they desire to seem rather than to be good. Yet if the definition is given a faithful interpretation and its meaning is adjusted for use by one who puts his hand to his mouth (that is, who does what he says), then there is nothing truer and more correct within the Stoic and Peripatetic schools. You will prove this beyond doubt when teaching those whom I have led to you by the delightful shortcut to the grand path.

Yet lest you suppose that any path to happiness inclines towards the definition of the Epicureans, I will attempt to prove otherwise to you in the end of this book, as though it were the end of a path. The path is steep and narrow, yet it is level and straight for lovers of God, by whose leadership, instruction and support their feet do not stumble on stones. For indeed the stumbling stone and the rock of temptation Himself encourages and strengthens those walking towards Him whom He receives, so that, humbled in themselves and exulting in Him, they may freely and boldly announce that we can do all things in Him who greatly strengthens us. Indeed, His is the path of virtue, set between and confined to two boundaries, namely, the knowledge and practice of goodness. For to know the good and not to do it is not the path to happiness but is deserving of damnation. For this reason you say: how may I who am without a path and not on the path advance along this path? Among a great variety of paths, how may I, a foreigner and a stranger whose eyes are enfeebled on account of deprivation and are at present almost extinguished, discern the signposts so that the tranquillity and joy you promised may be reached? I answer

There is an elevated path manifested when the heavens are fair;
it has the name of the Milky Way.[59]

Your fair heavens will not be unsettled before the eyes of your soul on account of indignation and you will easily recognise this milky path. Return to yourself, look towards the chronicles of the Fathers, and then consider diligently where you diverted your steps from the path and where you fell into error.

I recall to our minds the place where, having first gone astray, man was pushed and subverted so that he fell by deviation from the commandment when, persuaded by the devil, he extended his rash and reckless hand towards the forbidden tree of knowledge. From then on 'sin, accepting the opportunity of the commandment, seduced me and through the commandment killed me'.[60] The commandment itself stimulated all desire in me because always 'we strive for the forbidden'; and 'what is not allowed irritates more keenly'.[61] Man

---

[59] Ovid, *Metamorphoses*, 1.168.
[60] Romans 7:11.
[61] Ovid, *Ars Amatoria*, 3.4.17, 2.19.3.

extends his hand towards the tree of knowledge, satisfies his gluttony, and contrary to the promise of the deceitful enemy and in accordance with the injunction of the truthful God, he is plunged into darkness and thrown to the ground in hunger, making a compact with death and creating a covenant with hell. Knowledge of good and evil is achieved through experience, and he made a place in himself for many miseries. Therefore, while prohibited, he nevertheless climbed and fell from the tree of knowledge and strayed from truth, virtue and life, and he does not come back to life unless he returns to the tree of knowledge, and procures from it truth in learning, virtue in works and life in joy. And so he is to exercise the subtlety of his reason so that he may distinguish between good and evil and recognise whether good or evil is preponderate in each thing. Then he is to look out with constant attention so that he does not act like an inferior sort of person but instead is devoted to preferable kinds of conduct through the exertion of his whole mind and body. Moreover, his labour may be sweetened and all the bitterness of the present world may be tempered (as the blessed Gregory asserts) by the hope of things to come. For even the prophet is fed day and night with tears in anticipation of his God; and to those who grieve, Truth, which neither deceives nor is deceived, promises true happiness in return. And one is not to be afraid to extend a hand towards the tree of knowledge of good and evil on account of the example of the first prohibition because He who teaches men knowledge and who, according to the promises of the prophets, discloses to the ignorant what is good, invites exiles and wanderers to it. Therefore, in the tree of knowledge is found a certain branch of virtue, through which the whole life of man as he progresses is consecrated. No one except for him who extends the branch of virtue cut from the tree of knowledge may return by other means to the Creator of life, namely, God . . .

Clearly, he who tears off the branch of good works from the tree of knowledge alone knows what sorrow is concealed on the earth or what can be obtained from it. And when it is removed another is not lacking, since the more knowledge and virtue are practised, the more they are renewed and progressed. Yet I do not follow the steps of Virgil or the gentiles to such a degree that I believe that anyone may attain to knowledge or virtue by the strength of his own will. I acknowledge that grace is operative in both the will and the accomplishments of the elect; I revere it as the way – indeed, the only true way – which leads to life and renders satisfaction to each one's good wishes. This is the milky way manifested by the splendour of innocence, and its devotion to nutrition fulfils the duties of the wet nurse and alone prepares for progress; for without it no one progresses. This message is announced to transgressors with the sound of a trumpet, so that they may return to the heart. It is promised to them that 'the revolving and flaming sword' will be removed from the tree of knowledge so that they may be led and enter into their native country.[62] I might say more. The tree of knowledge and the wood of life, in which all the treasures of wisdom and knowledge are concealed and in which dwells corporally the fullness of divinity, is pulled up (yet with its substance uncut) and is taken out to the land of our wandering and is planted in the midst of our Church, so that from it there might be illumination through knowledge, strength through virtue and exultation through mercy; and the joy of the Church is to be complete, joy from God and in God, joy that no one may detract from it.

Therefore he who, distracted by desire, transgresses against the tree is to approach the tree, guided by grace, since our salvation is procured from grace in the wood of the cross because in the past death has proceeded from the tree. But it is to be approached by a different route, since it is expedient that different sorts of things are to be treated in different ways. And because man would not have been hurled down by the tempter unless passion had taken precedence in his mind, he for this reason understands by means of fear that one who desires to be exalted on the day of the visitation is to be humbled before the power of the hand of God. Let him who has already tasted illicit fruits abstain from unlawful things, and let him pacify burning desire by well-disposed charity. He is to delight in these things; he may see even now that the tree is beautiful in appearance and sweet to eat, and that it will give in its own time the fruit of true happiness and the condition of an ever joyful life of tranquillity. Moreover, pleasant fear, which becomes love for the revered, does not know how to be idle or to be in violation of those laws prescribed for it, but it throws out of doors the sting of fear and it does good out of love, adhering by its own free will to justice. He who had rushed towards his death through disobedience stemming from the frivolity of the will struggles

---

[62] Genesis 3:24.

forcefully with grace to obtain life, as though obedience had strengthened him.

Fear gives birth to innocence, obedience to commandments advances the justice of good conduct, and the just man is led by the right trail to true happiness. He is the one whom the Lord has led along the right paths, giving him the knowledge of saints, honouring him with labours and satisfying him with happiness in all the things for which he labours faithfully and profitably. I could say that the entirety of law and all the prophets and canons of Scripture strive for this end because they aim towards the Son. For there is no doubt about this, since even the doctrines of the infidels have no utility unless they contribute in some way to happiness. But omitting or rather dispatching in advance this fact, I say that these are the only paths which can alone create and protect the happy man, since the one branch of justice provides that there is to be no injury to anyone, while the other provides that one is to do whatever is good for oneself and for others. Do you wish to be certain about what I say to you? Do you not wish to be happy? Then 'happy is the man who fears the Lord'.[63] Do you not desire power? Not only himself 'but even his seed will be powerful upon the earth'.[64] Or do you pursue the favour and praise of men? 'The generation of the righteous is blessed.'[65] Or do you extend yourself out to fame and open up your wallet to riches? 'Glory and riches are in his house.'[66] Or do you seek the eternal persistence of your works? 'Just men will be in memory forever.'[67] Do you not wish to be secure? 'He will not fear the voice of evil' but 'is to despise all his enemies'.[68] Do you not desire elegant speech? The lips of the just drip with grace. Likewise, 'Just men are remembered with praises; the name of the impious rots.'[69] Do you wish to come to know your future? 'The expectation of the just is joy.'[70] Do you wish your enjoyment to be extended into eternity? Just men live in perpetuity and they are in peace, although they appear to the foolish to be dead.

Behold that you possess the truest and most faithful path and have achieved the state which is desired by Epicurus; and if you keep to it, 'You are blessed and things will be well with you.'[71] This path alone can suffice for good and happy living, to such a great degree that the external world adds either little or nothing to perfection. And I do not

---

[63] Psalms 112:1.   [64] Psalms 112:2.   [65] Psalms 112:2.
[66] Psalms 112:3.   [67] Psalms 112:6.   [68] Psalms 112:7–8.
[69] Proverbs 10:7.   [70] Proverbs 10:28.   [71] Psalms 128:2.

prohibit you from wrapping yourself in a variety of glittering garments overlaid with gold, nor from feasting splendidly every day, nor again from occupying the foremost public offices, and – so that I may express much in a few words – from yielding to the times and even perverse morals (even though you are yourself righteous in all moral matters), and from laughing with a world which is amused by its own enticements. For you are so great that you ought not and cannot be captured by these traps (although many have already been taken prisoner by them).

The illustrious king of the English, Henry the Second, the greatest king of Britain if the result of his deeds were to match their beginning, is thundering near the Garonne River and (so it is reported) you guide him with your counsel; and besieging Toulouse with a successful blockade, he terrorises not only Provençal all the way to the Rhone and the Alps but he has aroused fear in the princes of the Spanish and the French (as though he were presently threatening the whole world) by destroying fortifications and subjecting peoples. In the midst of such tumultuous events, I implore you to defend innocence and see and speak and preach equity; do not stray from the correct path through either love or hate, hope or fear. For the just will inherit the earth and, as is generally accepted on the authority of the Most High, the seed of the impious will perish. If you do not have the time during such great upheavals to read this, which I have taken care to write to you with such sincere devotion, or if it does not please you because its ideas are insipid and its words are uncultivated, still may you not be displeased by the devotion itself, which has been zealous to serve your honour. If you should approve of my efforts, you will be patron of the work; if not, it is condemned as you wish. How is it that some judge the servant of another? This book stands or falls according to you, its lord, just as does every book.

I do not fear the judgments of the ignorant multitude, yet I beg that they spare my little work, even though some of them are courtiers, because I have at no time detracted from their books in any way. If they are unwilling to listen to my prayer, they will be restrained by the verdict of dangerous wickedness because, as Martial asserts, 'He acts wrongly who is ingenious with the book of another.'[72] Those things which are said about the frivolities of courtiers have never been

---

[72] Martial, *Epigrammata*, I.

detected in such men but only perhaps in me and those like me; and clearly I am restrained by too narrow a law if it is not allowed for me to correct and chastise myself and my friends. Surely he who would wrinkle his nose at this, who lets his brow contract or his face be adorned in red or his pallor be clouded over, whose lips are pulled together or quiver, whose tongue is poisoned, whose knees tremble, whose hands are bold – such a man proves beyond doubt the dangers of our frivolities. In this regard, it was always the intention to pass from frivolities to the serious concerns of goodness and to what is fitting or is advantageous for arranging one's life. Yet he who has seen just reason for blame may make use of it freely by reason of charity, and through his correction of me he may acquire and possess the prize of life for himself. For I know that in a multitude of words sin is not lacking. But I invite and exhort my reader in order that, mindful of the charity of God, he will implore in his prayers that the Son of the living God and the God made man through the immaculate Virgin manifest Himself, and make public the path along which there is movement for us in His gracious purpose, and direct our steps upon it.

Index of proper names

Index

Index of subjects

238

CAMBRIDGE TEXTS IN THE
HISTORY OF POLITICAL THOUGHT

Titles published in the series thus far